C0-ALY-743

Analogue and Iterative Methods

in Computation, Simulation, and Control

MODERN ELECTRICAL STUDIES

A Series edited by
Professor **G. D.** Sims
Head of Department of Electronics
University of Southampton

Analogue and Iterative Methods

in Computation, Simulation, and Control

B. R. WILKINS

B.Sc.(Eng.),C.Eng.,M.I.E.E.
*Senior Lecturer in Electronics
at the University of Southampton*

CHAPMAN AND HALL LTD
11 NEW FETTER LANE EC4

First published 1970
© *B. R. Wilkins* 1970
Printed in Great Britain by
Willmer Brothers Limited, Birkenhead
SBN 412 09960 8

Distributed in the U.S.A.
by Barnes & Noble, Inc.

621.3919
W684a

Preface

This book arises out of lecture notes developed over several years of teaching analogue computing techniques to Electronic Engineering students in postgraduate and final year undergraduate courses. When trying to find a book that could be recommended to the students, and perhaps used as a course text, it soon became apparent that there was in existence no book that fulfilled the requirements that I had in mind. It seems to me that any analogue computation course being put on now should be strongly influenced by four critical considerations:

(a) Pure computation, in the sense of obtaining solutions to mathematical problems, is not now of widespread interest as an analogue computer problem, because such problems can generally be solved by the use of a digital computer. Such interest as still exists is likely to decline over the next few years as digital computers become even more widely available.

(b) Analogue techniques have always been potentially useful for data processing and for providing elements in instrumentation and control systems, but they have for a long time been ruled out by the high cost of implementation. Microelectronics has changed this, and has made a systems approach to many circuit problems essential.

(c) The combination of analogue components with high speed switching circuits (also conveniently and cheaply available in microcircuit form) has made possible a greatly extended range of computational ability, including the use of iterative techniques.

(d) The use of analogue computers in hybrid systems, or more simply as peripherals to digital computers, is likely to remain important, particularly in real-time simulation problems. This

v

must retain interest in the performance of analogue computers, particularly with respect to iterative facilities and automatic mode selection.

The first of these considerations suggests that a course dealing only with pure analogue computation is hardly worth doing except as a preliminary to a more complete treatment. The other considerations suggest that a useful course would be one in which the emphasis is on iterative methods and on non-computational uses of analogue techniques. It is this shift of emphasis away from the established form of analogue computation course that has created the need for a new text book; a need that this volume is intended to satisfy.

The first chapter discusses at greater length the general philosophy behind the book; the basic ways of using simple analogue elements are discussed in chapter 2. Chapter 3 describes in some detail scaling methods for simple analogue circuits, and chapter 4 gives a brief discussion of the methods available for putting problems into a computer and getting results out. Although these matters are rather mundane, the rest of the machinery is useless without them!

Chapter 5 deals with the crucial subject of the control of a computer. Starting (as it must) with the basic control modes applicable to any analogue computer, it goes on to describe in detail the possibilities opened up by asynchronous control methods and in particular the ways in which iterative procedures can be implemented.

Chapter 6 is devoted to computational errors arising out of the ways in which computing components depart from the ideal. This is a subject that is glossed over or even entirely omitted from many books (and, presumably, courses) but which seems to me to be of considerable importance, particularly when contemplating the use, in instrumentation and control applications, of analogue computing elements that are far from ideal.

Chapters 7–10 are devoted to non-linear operations, starting with a general discussion of the classification and description of systems, leading up to State Space methods and the Normal Form of sets of system equations. Besides being fundamental to modern control theory, this method of system description is particularly suited to an analogue computer simulation, and can be used as a synthesis procedure in designing analogue systems. Particular emphasis is laid in chapter 8 on the all-important piecewise linear techniques that nowadays dominate non-linear function generation devices; the aims in this chapter have been

    (*a*)   to describe methods by which diode circuits can be analysed;

    (*b*)   to explain how different kinds of segment are produced, and to suggest how they can be put together to give prescribed composite characteristics;

    (*c*)   to include, among the examples given, enough of the commonly required non-linearities to allow the chapter to be used as a convenient recipe book.

Special purpose function generating devices (servo-multipliers, cathode ray tubes and so on) are mentioned briefly in chapter 9 but not discussed at great length; their usefulness is now restricted to a very few special purpose applications, so that a very detailed treatment does not seem worthwhile. A chapter on forcing function generation completes the non-linear section of the book.

In the final chapter I have attempted to draw together the various themes of the book and to look ahead to what the future might hold for analogue methods in general.

In considering how the applications of analogue techniques could best be presented, it did not seem to me to be worth while to offer the solutions to a range of relatively simple mathematical problems, since such solutions are readily available in many existing analogue computer textbooks. Instead, I have taken one particular practical problem and discussed in detail a way in which it can be formulated and manipulated mathematically into a form suitable for solution on an analogue computer. The particular example chosen has the merit that it utilizes many of the techniques described elsewhere in the book and puts them together into a single system.

The book finishes with a brief description of some areas of application of analogue concepts and techniques which seem to me to be likely to prove of continuing importance. Digital simulation languages are bound to become more widely used, and may make the analogue computer obsolete. This has not happened yet, however, and the main obstacle that still remains is the difficulty of real time working: the DDA is possibly a way round this. Finally, I return to stress my own conviction that the use of the operational amplifier as a circuit component in its own right is going to spread a good deal further than it has done so far, and will make substantial differences to the way that circuits are designed in the future.

At the end of each chapter is a section entitled 'Notes and

References', which is intended to provide a guide to some of the other books and sources of reference material. This makes no pretence at being an exhaustive bibliography, but has been confined to those works that provide additional material that is useful to the student.

Throughout the book, explanations have been particularly concentrated on those features of analogue circuits that seem to cause most difficulty to students and to be least adequately explained in other books.

Having now come to the end of a book on which I embarked several years ago, it only remains for me to offer my sincere thanks to all those who have helped in all sorts of ways to make this book possible. A tremendous number of errors and faults of expression have been removed thanks to the many colleagues and students at the University of Southampton and elsewhere who have read various parts of the manuscript. Mrs J. Y. Wright-Green has patiently typed the whole thing, and my wife has accepted my excuses that I was too busy to dig the garden/wash up/ paint the house. Finally, Chapman and Hall have shown remarkable restraint even when the manuscript is long overdue.

Contents

ix

1 Introduction

1.1 Model building

The characteristic of men that most clearly distinguishes them from lower animals is their ability to communicate knowledge and ideas to each other. Perhaps the most remarkable feature of this ability is that it is ever able to work at all, because the principal medium of communication – language – is a complex code, the secrets of which are imparted to each individual by means of the code itself. At first sight it would seem to be impossible that this completely recursive process could ever succeed; the inherent difficulties in the arrangement are illustrated by the frustrating experience that must at one time or another have been the lot of every reader who has ever consulted a dictionary. This clearly is a process that in the last analysis should fail, since each word in the dictionary is defined in terms of other words in the dictionary, so that eventually all definitions must be circular. Language, in fact, becomes understandable by an individual only because he makes irrational guesses at the meanings of words, subsequently modifying the guesses if this should prove to be necessary in the light of experience.

Expressed in this way, the initial learning of language can be seen as a prototype of the scientific method of advancing knowledge about the natural world: a working hypothesis is formed by making a guess about the way things work, taking into account as far as possible the known facts; this hypothesis is then subjected to tests, and if the results of the tests are inconsistent with the hypothesis, it has to be modified and the cycle repeated. This process of iteration, surprisingly enough, often seems to lead ultimately to useful results.

Another way of looking at a scientific theory is to regard it as a model of the system it is trying to describe. In this, it again has some similarities with a dictionary definition of a word, which attempts to

1

describe the meaning and use of one word by means of a sentence composed of other words that are, in the opinion of the compiler (if not always of the user), simpler or more generally understood. Similarly, a model attempts to describe an unfamiliar system in terms of other systems or subsystems which are in some sense easier to understand or perhaps easier to manipulate. The ease of manipulation is of particular importance when we are constructing a model for the purpose of system design. The requirement of the model in this case is that it should be able to predict the performance of a particular design in a particular environment; if this performance is not satisfactory it is then necessary to change part of the design. It is therefore important that modifications to the model should be easy to introduce and that the effects of these modifications should then be easily assessible.

The classical type of model that has been used with considerable success is a mathematical model, in which the operation of each component of a system is described by some form of input–output characteristic expressed either explicitly as a transfer function or implicitly by sets of equations or graphical relationships. Having constructed a mathematical model, whether it is of an existing device or only of a paper design, the response of the system to any given input, starting from any given state, can be determined by solving the equations using the appropriate forcing function and subject to the appropriate boundary conditions. The overall performance of the system can then be evaluated by repeatedly solving the equations for different inputs and for different settings of the various parameters. Even when a system has been fully described by an equation, however, its analysis can still present difficulties, because the solution of even a very simple equation can require a very large amount of computational effort, particularly when either the equation or the forcing function is non-linear. Consider for example a simple second order linear differential equation

$$\frac{d^2y}{dt^2} + a\frac{dy}{dt} + by = x \tag{1.1}$$

and suppose that we wish to solve this equation (that is, to obtain a graph of the variation of y with time) when the input, x, is a square wave. The result would have to be evaluated in a piecewise linear manner, calculating afresh over each interval during which the input remains constant. If, as would be very probable in a practical problem, results are required over a range of frequencies of x, and when using a number of different settings of the coefficient a, each graph would have to be separately obtained in the same way. The labour involved in performing these calculations is considerable, even for this very simple case; if the system equation 1.1 had itself contained a non-linear element (as practical systems commonly do) a manual solution would become impracticable, while a more realistic system described by a set of simultaneous non-linear differential equations makes manual solutions impracticable whatever the form of the input. It is therefore necessary, when attempting to solve the kinds of equation that arise with practical systems, to make use of some kind of computational aid whose purpose is to obtain these solutions automatically, to give the results in some convenient form, and above all to do the job quickly, and without the requirement of any extensive intervention on the part of a human operator.

This purely mathematical requirement for computing devices – the need for a machine that will solve equations – represents one area in which the methods to be described in this book are of use, but nowadays it is by no means the most important one. Of far more significance is the possibility of using computing devices and computing methods for various non-computational purposes.

Perhaps the most important non-computational use of computers is that of simulation, which has already been briefly mentioned. There are several reasons why simulation might be desirable, of which the most common is probably as a design aid. It is clearly advantageous if projected designs can be assessed by a theoretical study before being converted into hardware: the only practicable way of conducting a theoretical study for most practical systems is by the use of a computer, not only because of the number of equations involved but more importantly because of the inevitable non-linearities in the system. Another important application of simulation for design is where the design relates not to the system being simulated but to a separate sub-system whose function is to control the simulated system. There are many cases in which a prototype control system cannot be tested directly with the plant it is intended to control because the cost of failure would be unacceptable. An incorrectly operating controller, for example, could cause an explosion in a chemical plant or a nuclear power station, so that in such cases preliminary trials with a simulated plant may form a necessary part of the design process.

Simulated systems can also be very valuable for the purpose of training operators to control the system. The best known example of this use of simulation techniques is the flight simulator, which nowadays takes the form of a very complex and realistic model of an aircraft cockpit where all the controls and the instruments are coupled to a computer. In the most sophisticated of these machines the pilot even receives an appropriate view from the cockpit, by having television projectors controlled by the computer. The performance of this system from the pilot's point of view is almost indistinguishable from that of the real aircraft, but for instructional purposes it has several major advantages:

(a) The cost of running the simulator is several orders of magnitude less than that of running an actual airliner.

(b) The pilot can make mistakes – and can even crash – without incurring any cost in either life or materials.

(c) The instructor can inject emergencies (such as engine failures) in order to test the pilot's reactions. Again there is no penalty for poor performance.

Similar advantages are obtainable by using simulators in other situations where the actual systems are very expensive in both capital and running costs. Such situations commonly occur in military training programmes, where tactical training simulators are sometimes used, although not perhaps as much as they should be. The particular value of these simulators is due to the fact that a major part of the expense of tactical exercises is accounted for by the cost of transporting men and equipment from their normal depots to the 'battle' area and back again. A substantial amount of time is also taken in grouping or regrouping, whereas a simulation can be stopped at any time by the instructor in charge, and all forces can be returned almost instantaneously either to the same or to a different starting position.

Simulation also plays a part in the analysis of complex and ill-understood systems such as biological or economic systems. The complete range of data that would enable such systems to be fully analysed in the usual way (with or without the aid of a computer) is often not available, and one method that has proved fruitful in these areas is to set up a model representing an intelligent guess at the structure, and to use this model and its performance to predict the behaviour of the original system under particular prescribed conditions. Differences in the behaviour of the two systems can then be used to modify the model so that eventually the operation of the system may be better understood. Computer models are particularly necessary for this kind of task, since mathematically tractable equations very rarely seem to be adequate to describe the workings of real systems, particularly in the fields of biology and economics.

There are several other areas in which the use of simulators can be of great value in obtaining an understanding of a system, and can also effect considerable savings both in cost and in time, but enough has probably already been said to indicate that model-building, far from being a recreational activity, forms a serious and important part of the processes of analysis and design.

1.2 Simulation methods

In everything that has been said so far, the word 'computer' has been used without qualification. Computers can be divided into two types, depending on the way in which they encode information. On the one hand a quantity can be represented by a sequence of pulses where every pulse is identical and quantitative information is conveyed by the presence or absence of pulses at specified instants of time. This method forms the basis of the digital computer, so called because it deals with discrete numbers; all operations on these numbers are performed essentially by a process of counting pulses; more complicated mathematical operations are achieved by using approximations that also amount to addition. In the other type of computer, a quantity is represented by a variable that can take any value within a continuous range, and the amplitude of this variable at any instant is proportional to the quantity being represented at that instant. In this case a particular variable behaves in a manner analogous to that of some quantity in the system being simulated, so that this kind of computer is called an analogue computer. Data manipulation in this case depends on the existence of units that give continuous outputs in response to continuous inputs, the output at any instant being a particular function of the input or inputs. The differences between the two kinds of computer may be summarised as follows.

(a) The digital computer is much more accurate. The resolution can be made indefinitely small by using more digits, whereas an analogue computer is limited by the accuracy of electronic circuits to (at best) about 0.01 to 0.1%.

(b) The digital computer tends to be more expensive. Comparisons of costs are very difficult to draw because of the completely different natures of the two devices, but the evidence suggests that analogue systems are somewhat cheaper in both capital and running costs.

(c) Analogue computers are much faster. This is because computations are carried out in parallel, the only delays being those of electronic propagation, whereas digital computers operate essentially in series.

(d) Analogue computers allow greater man/machine interaction. This is often felt to be a major advantage in analysis or design, but is becoming much less of an issue between the two types of computer since digital computers are now having better input/output facilities incorporated.

The choice of computing method is often suggested by the particular application, analogue methods being ideally suited to the study of dynamic systems while digital methods are appropriate for book-keeping problems. With simulation studies, however, the issue is often not clear-cut, and both analogue and digital methods have been used with success. Although this book is devoted basically to analogue methods, it will soon become apparent that the distinctions between the analogue and digital approach have recently become thoroughly confused by the use of hybrid methods incorporating some features of both. It is not within the scope of this book to consider full hybrid systems, in which a complete analogue computer and a complete digital computer are operated together, with data fully interchangeable between the two. Although the importance of such facilities should not be underestimated, they are necessarily confined to large and very expensive computer installations: the equipment for converting information from analogue to digital form and back again is a complex piece of equipment which by itself can cost as much as a small computer, so that such facilities are rarely found with small installations. Of considerable interest, however, is the use of some digital facilities fitted to an essentially analogue machine. The power of an analogue computer is thereby enormously increased, and the implications of these 'iterative' computers will be considered in some detail.

1.3 Instrumentation and control

A particularly important development in the use of analogue techniques has been brought about by the growth of microelectronics.

The implications of this growth as far as analogue techniques are concerned are two-fold:

(*a*) With the fabrication of complex circuits as single units, it has become possible to build very elaborate systems using these units as basic building bricks. This is in contrast to earlier methods, where the basic bricks were individual active and passive circuit components. This has led to a great interest in the study of the behaviour of systems with elaborate information processing capabilities; such studies need computers, and analogue computers are often the most suitable.

(*b*) The availability of these complex circuit blocks, and in particular the dramatically reduced cost compared with that of the corresponding circuits built of discrete components, has made the use of analogue computer techniques economically feasible in non-computational applications. The two main areas in which this applies are those of instrumentation and control. In each case there exists the same need – to perform mathematical operations on continuous signals – and analogue computer methods which are designed for exactly this purpose are obviously suitable, but have until recently been too expensive to use.

Microelectronics is perhaps more generally associated with digital circuits than analogue ones, and this too is not without significance for the theme of this book, since iterative methods, which have already been mentioned as being an important recent extension of analogue techniques, depend for their operation on digital circuits. The existence of both types of microelectronic unit, analogue and digital, means that the full range of these operations is available for use not only in computation and simulation, but also in instrumentation and control.

1.4 Notes and references

The importance of models in the analysis and synthesis of engineering systems and in the investigation of theories of operation of natural systems has been stressed by very many writers. James, Smith and Wolford discuss some methods by which models can be established in various areas of mechanical engineering, including such diverse problems as the effect of earthquake tremors on buildings and the operation of a mousetrap. Systems of this kind present great difficulties to experimental investigation, and the value of the model lies particularly in the ease with which it can be subjected to tests. The design of microwave components, however, presents a different problem in that the performance depends critically on mechanical size and shape; the merit of models in this case, as described by Norris, is that the effects of changes in mechanical layout can be rapidly and easily assessed. In the chemical industry, models are particularly valuable for two reasons: the real processes have very long time constants so that experiments would take a long time to complete, and the cost of an unsuccessful experiment could be disastrously expensive. These features are well brought out by Womack: the same features are present in economic systems, which are also better studied by simulation rather than by direct experiment, (although politicians usually seem to prefer the second, more exciting, method).

Yet another different kind of problem appears in all investigations involving biological systems, because the internal structure can usually not be determined (particularly since the nervous system invariably forms an essential part of the system). The model here becomes essentially a means of testing hypothetical structures. Fogel discusses some attempts to describe a human operator by means of a transfer function (necessary for designing control systems such as autopilots that have got to operate with humans), while Milsum describes at greater length some of the difficulties associated with the development of mathematical models generally in the context of the systems controlling biological functions. The value of models in this field was discussed very well by Licklider, talking about psychological models in particular, when he concluded that the main values were as 'an organizer that . . . pulls a variety of facts together into a compact diagram, and . . . consolidates the experience thus far obtained', and '. . . that it will be useful in formulating experiments and in leading to new observations'.

The historical developments of the analogue computer are described in many of the older books on the subject, and a brief account is given by Levine. Detailed comparisons between analogue and digital approaches to simulation and computation are discussed by Ashley and by Hersee. Ashley takes a specific problem and derives programmes to solve it by both methods, drawing particular attention to the approximations and simplifications that are necessary in each case. Hersee discusses the relative merits of the two approaches by examining the implementation of the basic computing elements. The importance of analogue methods in instrumentation can hardly be over-emphasised. Microelectronics has brought about a need for a reapprasial of the ways in which electronics as a subject is studied so that, as Walker rather neatly put it, we can see that 'electronics is essentially about what can be done when amplification is available'. This leads logically to the emphasis on systems studies, taking an amplifier as a basic unit, and this approach is being adopted by a number of electronic engineering and applied physics departments in Universities (as described, for example, by Gosling). These trends will certainly continue.

REFERENCES

ASHLEY, J. R. (1963). *Introduction to Analog Computing*, Wiley, New York.
FOGEL, L. J. (1963). *Biotechnology: Concepts and Applications*, Prentice-Hall, New York. Extracts reprinted under the title "Human Information Processing" (1967). Prentice-Hall, New York.
GOSLING, W. (1967). Microcircuit Teaching at Swansea, in *Education for the Microcircuit Era*, University of Southampton.
HERSEE, E. H. W. (1966). *A Simple Approach to Electronic Computers*, Blackie, London.
JAMES, M. L., SMITH, G. M. and WOLFORD, J. C. (1966). *Analog Computer Simulation of Engineering Systems*, The International Textbook Company, Scranton, Pennsylvania.
LEVINE, L. (1964). *Methods for Solving Engineering Problems Using Analog Computers*, McGraw-Hill, New York.
LICKLIDER, J. C. R. (1961). On Psychophysiological Models, in *Sensory Communication*, ed. W. A. ROSENBLITH, M.I.T. Press and Wiley, New York.
MILSUM, J. H. (1966). *Biological Control Systems Analysis*, McGraw-Hill, New York.
NORRIS, A. (1968). The Analog Method in Electronics, in *Simulation: the Modelling of Ideas and Systems with Computers*, ed. J. MCLEOD, McGraw-Hill, New York.
WALKER, B. S. (1967). The Future of Electrical Engineering Education in the Microcircuit Era, in *Education for the Microcircuit Era*, University of Southampton.
WOMACK, J. W. (1967). Chemical Engineering Applications, in *Analogue Computer Applications*, ed. A. MCKENZIE, Pitman, London.

2 Basic Analogue Computation

2.1 Analogous systems

The principle of studying a system indirectly by reference to an analogous system may be applied in a number of different ways. The relation between a system and its analogue is basically a mathematical one in which the set of equations that describes the interactions between various system variables is identical to the set of equations describing the interaction between corresponding variables in the analogue. The earliest analogue computing devices were based on mechanical systems, in which the analogue variables were the positions of shafts. The movements of these shafts could be amplified or reduced (multiplied by a constant) by the use of simple fixed gearing; two variables could be added or subtracted by means of differential gears; integration was achieved by a ball and wheel assembly. Different problems were solved by adjusting the mechanical layout of the analogue system so as to satisfy the appropriate set of equations – a rather time-consuming process if the computer was required as a general-purpose device, but perhaps acceptable for a special purpose model of a particular system.

It is also possible to build an analogue computation system based on hydraulic or pneumatic principles, and for some applications special purpose analogue models of these kinds have proved to be useful. For general purpose computers, however, where the requirement is for a device that can be set up to solve any one of a large range of problems, there can be no rival to an electrical system. This can achieve a flexibility, compactness, accuracy, and speed of operation far beyond anything possible with mechanical components. In the remainder of this book the term 'analogue computer' used without qualification will be taken to imply an electrical system. Modern analogue computers are often entirely electronic in operation, although electromechanical equipment is frequently met with as an output device (see section 4.2) and can also appear within the computer (see sections 5.8 and 9.1). The use of such equipment, however, is often avoided in modern general purpose computers, mainly because of the speed limitations that it imposes on the system. The significance of these limitations will appear later (see section 4.2 and chapter 3).

The dynamic analysis of a physical system gives rise in all but the most trivial examples to a differential equation or to sets of simultaneous differential equations. The complexity of the equations depends both on the complexity of the system and on the assumptions made in deriving the mathematical model; they may range from simple linear differential equations with constant coefficients to non-linear equations that may even be beyond the scope of formal mathematical analysis other than by trial and error methods. These same features are characteristic of an electrical network, the analysis of which, using the normal circuit laws, gives rise to differential equations connecting voltages and currents in different parts of the network. As with other physical systems, the complexity of the circuit equations is dependent not only on the complexity of the system but also on the assumptions made and the second order effects ignored in the analysis. The usefulness of electrical networks as analogues of physical systems lies primarily in the fact that components are available with accurately determined parameter values and with parasitic effects several orders of magnitude smaller than the intended effects over a useful (although not unlimited) range of frequencies. In principle, therefore, it should be possible to build a network whose equations fit the system under study, and then, by injecting into the network an appropriate disturbance in the form of a voltage or current change, to observe the behaviour of the system in the form of the resulting changes in current or voltage at other points in the network. Currents are inconvenient to manipulate and measure, so that it is the universal practice to use voltages as the analogue variables, and to arrange the network in such a way that voltages in different parts of the network are constrained to obey the system differential equations.

2.2 Standard mathematical operations

Rather than designing a complete analogue network as a single unit, it is much more convenient to work with smaller standard bricks, each able to perform a relatively simple mathematical function, and then to synthesize the overall system by suitable interconnections among the basic units. To this end, the first requirements for a general purpose analogue computer may be defined in terms of two fundamental mathematical operations:

(*i*) the formation of a weighted linear sum

$$y = \sum_{i=1}^{n} a_i x_i \tag{2.1}$$

(*ii*) the formation of the time integral

$$y = b \int x \, dt \tag{2.2}$$

where $x_1, \ldots, x_n, y$ are to be voltages appearing at the inputs and outputs of computing units, and $a_1, \ldots, a_n, b$ are constants.

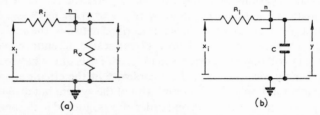

(a) (b)

Fig. 2.1. Approximate computing circuits. The grouped connection symbol indicates that there are *n* circuits, all identical in form, joined together at point *A*. Each circuit has the form indicated by the typical circuit shown (in this case, a resistor with an independent input connected to it).
(a) An addition circuit.
(b) A circuit that gives the integral of the sum of the inputs.

Consider first the circuit shown in figure 2.1(a) in which *n* input voltages $x_1, \ldots, x_i, \ldots, x_n$ are applied to *n* resistors $R_1, \ldots, R_i, \ldots, R_n$ the other ends of which are all joined together. Between the common point and earth a single load resistor R_0 is connected, and the output, *y*, is taken across R_0.

Applying Kirchhoff's current law at node *A*, we have

$$\sum_{i=1}^{n} \left(\frac{x_i - y}{R_i} \right) = \frac{y}{R_0} \tag{2.3}$$

$$\therefore \sum_{i=1}^{n} \frac{x_i}{R_i} = \frac{y}{R_0} + \sum_{i=1}^{n} \frac{y}{R_i}$$

$$\therefore y = \frac{R_0 \sum\limits_{i=1}^{n} \dfrac{x_i}{R_i}}{1 + R_0 \sum\limits_{i=1}^{n} \dfrac{1}{R_i}} \tag{2.4}$$

If now we can arrange that

$$R_0 \sum_{i=1}^{n} \frac{1}{R_i} \ll 1 \tag{2.5}$$

then we may use the approximate relationship

$$y \simeq R_0 \sum_{i=1}^{n} \frac{x_i}{R_i} \tag{2.6}$$

Thus, if $R_0/R_i = a_i$, we have

$$y \simeq \sum_{i=1}^{n} a_i x_i$$

so that this circuit gives an approximate realization of the first required mathematical relationship, expressed in equation 2.1. In deriving this expression we have made not only the explicit assumption of equation 2.5, but also the implicit assumption that any succeeding circuit connected to point A will have an input impedance that is so large that the current it takes will be negligible with respect to that flowing in R_0.

The significance of our original assumption may be assessed by comparing the exact equation 2.3 with the approximate equation 2.6. We then see that the approximation amounts to saying that

$$y \ll x_i \text{ for all } i$$

or, since x_i (the signal) can clearly not conveniently be made indefinitely large, y needs to be vanishingly small if the approximation is to be valid.

Consider now the circuit shown in figure 2.1(b), which is the same as figure 2.1(a) except that the resistor R_0 is replaced by a capacitor C. Applying Kirchhoff's law as before we have

$$\sum_{i=1}^{n} \frac{x_i - y}{R_i} = C \frac{dy}{dt}$$

or
$$y = \frac{1}{C} \int \sum_{i=1}^{n} \frac{x_i - y}{R_i}\, dt. \qquad (2.7)$$

If in this circuit also we can assume that

$$y \ll x_i \text{ for all } i$$

then we may say that

$$y \simeq \int \sum_{i=1}^{n} \frac{x_i}{CR_i}\, dt$$

or
$$y \simeq \int \sum_{i=1}^{n} b_i x_i\, dt \qquad (2.8)$$

where $b_i = \dfrac{1}{CR_i}$.

Thus, by comparing equations 2.8 and 2.2, we see that a circuit of this type with a single input gives an approximate realization of the second of the required fundamental mathematical operations.

2.3 Operational amplifiers

The restriction that has been placed on circuit conditions – that the output must be very small compared with the inputs – is clearly not acceptable for a practical computing system. Vanishingly small signals would get lost in the noise in the system, and would in any case be unable to drive the input to a second computing element. This suggests that we need an arrangement of the kind shown in figure 2.2, where between computing elements there is a buffer stage consisting of a linear amplifier with a high gain so that the vanishingly

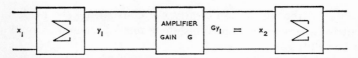

Fig. 2.2. A buffer amplifier connected between computing stages improves the signal levels.

small output y_1 from the first element can give rise to a signal Gy_1 large enough to act as the input x_2 to the second element. Since the inputs x_i in equation 2.6 could all be constant, in which case y would also be constant, it follows that the buffer amplifier must be directly coupled; in order to satisfy the implicit assumption mentioned above of negligible loading on R_0, the amplifier must have a very high input impedance; and if it is to be able to drive succeeding computing element inputs without in turn suffering from loading effects then it must have a very low output impedance. These conditions, together with the condition that the gain G should be very large, can all be met by a practical amplifier without too much difficulty; the objection to the system shown in figure 2.2 is that the numerical value of G appears in the computed results. This implies that G has to be accurately known and must be a real quantity whose magnitude is constant throughout the range of frequencies of operation of the computer. The gain must also remain constant with time to within our computing tolerance, which is typically of the order of 0·01 to 0·1 %. The gain stability requirements can be met with a practical amplifier only by the use of feedback. If to the input of the

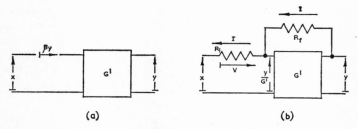

Fig. 2.3. (a) An amplifier with feedback to control the gain.
(b) One way of introducing feedback.

amplifier is added a further signal representing a fraction β of the output, so that the total input is $x+\beta y$ as shown in figure 2.3(a), then if the gain of the amplifier is G' the output is given by

$$y = G'(x+\beta y)$$

or

$$y = \frac{G'}{1-G'\beta} x.$$

Hence the net gain G of the amplifier with feedback is given by

$$G = \frac{G'}{1-G'\beta}. \tag{2.9}$$

If now $|G'\beta| \gg 1$ then we can say that

$$G \simeq -\frac{1}{\beta} \qquad (2.10)$$

so that

$$y \simeq -\frac{1}{\beta} x. \qquad (2.11)$$

Under these conditions, therefore, we can obtain an amplifier having an overall gain whose magnitude is dependent only on the feedback fraction, and this, being determined normally by passive circuit components, can be specified very accurately. Using this feedback amplifier in the circuit of figure 2.2 however still presents difficulties because of the requirement that G should be very large, and hence (from equation 2.10) that β should be very small. Thus, if $G = 10^4$ (so that equation 2.6 represents a good approximation) then $\beta = 10^{-4}$. But in order that equation 2.10 should be valid we require $|G'\beta| \gg 1 = 10^4$ say. In other words, even although the exact value of the gain of the internal amplifier is not important, it needs to be of the order of 10^8 or more at all frequencies from d.c. up to the highest computing frequency if all the assumptions made in the analysis are to be satisfied. There is also one further restriction on this amplifier that should be noticed. The Nyquist stability criterion may be expressed in the notation of equation 2.9 as $G'\beta \leqslant 1$, assuming that G' and β are both real. Thus, since $|G'\beta| > 1$, the amplifier can be stable only if $G'\beta$ is negative.

The requirement for very high gain over the entire computing frequency range would be a very difficult one to meet, but examination of equation 2.11 suggests that we might use an amplifier not merely to restore the signal level, but to implement equation 2.1 directly. In this case, since we would expect all working signals to be of the same order of magnitude, we would not require a high value of net gain, and so the internal gain of the amplifier would not need to be so large. A method of obtaining a suitable feedback signal in a circuit with a single input is shown in figure 2.3(b). The current, I, in the feedback resistor is given by

$$I = \frac{y - (y/G')}{R_f} = \frac{1}{R_f}\left(1 - \frac{1}{G'}\right)y.$$

This same current flows in the input resistor if no current is taken by the amplifier, so that the voltage V appearing across R_i is given by

$$V = IR_i = \frac{R_i}{R_f}\left(1 - \frac{1}{G'}\right)y$$

Thus, comparing this with figure 2.3(a) we have

$$\beta = \frac{R_i}{R_f}\left(1 - \frac{1}{G'}\right) \tag{2.12}$$

$$\simeq \frac{R_i}{R_f} \text{ if } |G'| \gg 1$$

Hence,

$$\frac{y}{x} = G = -\frac{1}{\beta} = -\frac{R_f}{R_i} \tag{2.13}$$

We have already seen that for this circuit arrangement to be stable, $G'\beta$ is required to be negative. Furthermore, from equation 2.12 it is clear that β is positive, and hence G' needs to be negative. Notice, however, that it is not the negative sign of G' that is responsible for the negative sign appearing in equation 2.13: this equation was derived from expressions in which terms such as $1/G'$ were neglected with respect to 1, and this approximation would be equally valid whatever the sign of G'.

An amplifier intended for this kind of application is usually called an *operational amplifier*, and is the fundamental building brick of an analogue computer. The detailed capabilities of operational amplifiers for use not only in analogue computers but also in many other applications will be considered in chapter 6; in the meantime the main properties of a computing amplifier may usefully be summarized as follows:

(a) The gain of the amplifier is negative at d.c. This implies that there is an odd number of amplifying stages.

(b) The gain is numerically very large (ideally infinite). It is often denoted by $-\mu$, where μ is commonly 10^8 or more at d.c. (The way the gain depends on frequency will be discussed in chapter 6).

(c) The input impedance is very large (ideally infinite) so that the current taken in operation is very small. Typically the maximum current taken is between $0\cdot1$ and 10 nanoamps.

(d) The output impedance is very low (ideally zero). In practice the output stage is an emitter follower giving an output impedance of the order of a few hundred ohms. This is further

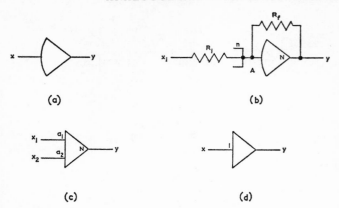

Fig. 2.4. (a) The symbol for an operational amplifier.
(b) The use of an operational amplifier for addition.
(c) The symbol for a summer: the gains shown against the inputs do not include the minus sign.
(d) An inverter.

reduced in operation by the overall negative feedback provided by the computing resistances, so that the net output impedance is reduced to a fraction of an ohm.

An operational amplifier is denoted by the symbol shown in figure 2.4(a), in which the common earth connection between input and output is omitted. The gain of the amplifier is always negative for the reasons suggested above so that the relationship between the input and output is

$$y = -\mu x$$

2.4 Summers and inverters

The circuit shown in figure 2.4(b) is a modified form of that shown in figure 2.1(a). Its operation may be analysed by applying Kirchhoff's current law at node A assuming that no current is taken by the amplifier itself. This gives

$$\sum_{i=1}^{n} \left(\frac{x_i - v_A}{R_i} \right) + \frac{y - v_A}{R_f} = 0 \tag{2.14}$$

where v_A is the voltage at A.
The equation of the amplifier is

$$y = -\mu v_A$$

Substituting this into equation (2.14) to eliminate v_A, and re-arranging the terms, gives

$$y = -\frac{R_f \sum_{i=1}^{n} \frac{x_i}{R_i}}{1 + \frac{1}{\mu}\left[1 + R_f \sum_{i=1}^{n} \frac{1}{R_i}\right]}$$

If now we can make the assumption

$$\frac{1}{\mu}\left[1 + R_f \sum_{i=1}^{n} \frac{1}{R_i}\right] \ll 1 \qquad (2.15)$$

then we obtain the approximate relationship

$$y \simeq -R_f \sum_{i=1}^{n} \frac{x_i}{R_i} \qquad (2.16)$$

or

$$y \simeq -\sum_{i=1}^{n} a_i x_i$$

where

$$a_i = \frac{R_f}{R_i}$$

Equation 2.16 is the same as equation 2.6 apart from the minus sign and so this arrangement also serves as an approximate realization of equation 2.1. The difference between the two systems lies essentially in the validity of the approximations used in deriving the equations. Comparing these approximations, as defined in equations 2.5 and 2.15, we can see that for the same set of computing resistors, the term that we neglect with respect to 1 is smaller when we use an operational amplifier by a factor of about μ. (For a detailed discussion of errors in computing circuits, see chapter 6).

An amplifier used with resistors as input and feedback elements as in figure 2.4(b) is called a *summer*, and point A, the junction of the input and feedback resistors, is called the *summing junction*. The complete summer, including the appropriate resistors, is represented by the symbol shown in figure 2.4(c). The number appearing inside the symbol in figures 2.4(b) and (c) is an identifying label to distinguish between different amplifiers in a computing programme. Alongside each input line is indicated the numerical value of the multiplying factor associated with that input; the negative sign associated with

c

the summation as a whole is not explicitly stated but must be taken into account when interpreting computer diagrams. Thus the equation implemented by the circuit of figure 2.4(c) is

$$y = -(a_1x_1 + a_2x_2).$$

It should also be observed that the summing junction voltage is $(-y/\mu)$ which is very small if μ is very large. For this reason the summing junction is often spoken of as a *virtual earth*. One special case of a summer that is very commonly used is one having a single input and with equal input and feedback resistors. This circuit, shown in figure 2.4(d), implements

$$y = -x$$

and is called an *inverter*. By the use of summers and inverters we can implement the general equation

$$y = \sum_{i=1}^{n} a_i x_i$$

where a_i can have any value, positive or negative, within the limits

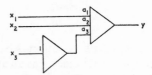

Fig. 2.5. Any weighted sum can be obtained with summers and inverters.

imposed by the approximation expression in equation 2.15. Thus in figure 2.5 we have

$$y = -a_1x_1 - a_2x_2 + a_3x_3$$

where a_1, a_2, and a_3 are all positive.

2.5 Integrators

If the feedback resistor, R_f, of figure 2.4(b) is replaced by a capacitor C we obtain the circuit of figure 2.6(a), which can again be analysed by taking the summing junction voltage to be $(-y/\mu)$ and assuming that the amplifier takes no input current. This gives

$$\sum_{i=1}^{n} \frac{x_i + (y/\mu)}{R_i} + C \frac{d}{dt}\left(y + \frac{y}{\mu}\right) = 0.$$

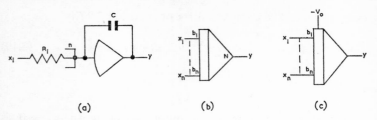

Fig. 2.6. (a) An integrator.
      (b) The symbol for an integrator. The gains shown omit the minus sign, as in the summer symbol.
      (c) The complete integrator symbol including the initial condition, which is also inverted. If the initial condition is zero, it is usually not shown.

If we can now assume that all the terms in $(1/\mu)$ are negligible – and this comes to the same thing as assuming that the virtual earth is a true earth – then we obtain the approximate relation

$$\sum_{i=1}^{n} \frac{x_i}{R_i} + C \frac{dy}{dt} = 0$$

or
$$y = -\frac{1}{C} \int \sum_{i=1}^{n} \frac{x_i}{R_i} \, dt. \tag{2.17}$$

As in the case of the summer, this is the same approximate equation (apart from the minus sign) as the one that applied to the simple basic circuit, but again the use of an operational amplifier reduces the magnitude of the neglected terms by a factor of nearly μ. The symbol for an integrator is shown in figure 2.6(b). As with a summer, only the magnitudes of the multiplying factors are given, the negative sign being understood. The equation that corresponds to figure 2.6(b) is thus

$$y = -\int \sum_{i=1}^{n} b_i x_i \, dt. \tag{2.18}$$

One point that has been ignored in deriving equations 2.7 and 2.17 is the effect of a charge being present on the capacitor before the inputs were applied. In fact, these equations as they stand must be incorrect: an indefinite integral does not have a specific value (because of the arbitrary constant of integration) whereas y is a voltage appearing at a point in a circuit, and must therefore have a defined magnitude at every instant. The complete form of equation 2.17 is

$$y = -\int_0^t \sum_{i=1}^n b_i x_i \, dt + V_0 \qquad (2.19)$$

where
$$b_i = \frac{1}{CR_i}.$$

V_0, the voltage appearing at the output terminal when $t = 0$, is called the *initial condition* of the integrator. An integrator is provided with a means of setting the initial condition to any desired value, but because of the way this circuit is built (see section 5.3) the voltage applied to the initial condition input has to be the negative of the required initial condition voltage. The complete function described by equation 2.19 is indicated on a computer schematic diagram by the symbol shown in figure 2.6(c). If, (as often happens in practice), the initial condition of a particular integrator is zero, this may be indicated either by putting a zero on the initial condition input, or, more commonly, by simply omitting the initial condition input altogether as in figure 2.6(b).

2.6 Principle of solution of a simple differential equation

Figure 2.7(a) shows a mass M hanging on an elastic string, the top end of which is attached to a fixed support. The unstretched length of the string is L, and it has a coefficient of elasticity S. When the mass moves, it is subject to air resistance, represented by a coefficient of friction D. The position of the mass at any instant is measured as a distance $(L+x)$ below the fixed support, so that the extension of the string is x.

The resultant force, F, acting on the mass is the algebraic sum of the gravitational force, the frictional force and the tension in the string so that

$$F = Mg - D\frac{dx}{dt} - Sx$$

The complete equation is obtained from Newton's Law of Motion, giving

$$M\frac{d^2x}{dt^2} = Mg - D\frac{dx}{dt} - Sx$$

or
$$\frac{d^2x}{dt^2} = g - \frac{D}{M}\frac{dx}{dt} - \frac{S}{M}x. \qquad (2.20)$$

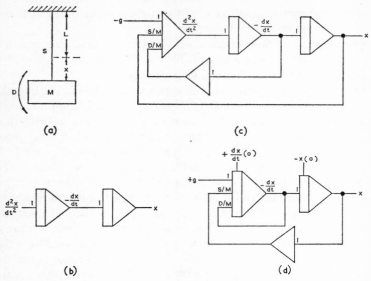

Fig. 2.7. (a) A mechanical system to illustrate the way analogue com-
           puter programmes can be developed.
        (b) First stage: a signal representing d^2x/dt^2 can be integrated
           twice to give $-dx/dt$ and x.
        (c) Second stage: signals representing dx/dt and x can give
           d^2x/dt^2 by satisfying the original equation.
        (d) If the acceleration is not required explicitly, one amplifier
           can be saved.

To understand how the solution to this equation is obtained on an
analogue computer we may consider the problem in two stages. First
we observe that if we have a signal representing d^2x/dt^2 we may
integrate it twice as shown in figure 2.7(b), to produce $-dx/dt$ and x.
Secondly, equation 2.20 tells us that we can generate d^2x/dt^2 by
means of a summer provided we have available signals representing
dx/dt, x, and g. The signal representing g would be, of course, a
constant voltage, which presents no difficulty. The other signals can
be obtained from the subsequent integration so that we can complete
the circuit by adding feedback loops to figure 2.7(b), using inverters
as necessary to get the signs right, giving the result shown in figure
2.7(c). This method of setting about the solution is fundamental
to all analogue computing; the essential steps may be summarized as
follows:

(a) Arrange the equation with the highest order differential co-efficient on the left hand side.

(b) Implement this equation with a summer, assuming that the necessary inputs are available.

(c) Integrate as many times as necessary.

(d) Feed back signals from the appropriate points in the integration chain to provide the inputs that were originally assumed.

We could economize on equipment in figure 2.7(c) by noticing that the addition and the first integration can be combined in a single amplifier, although such simplification is not of course possible if the acceleration is wanted specifically as a separate output. The elimination of an amplifier causes some changes of sign, and these have to be compensated for by a re-arrangement of inverters, giving the result shown in figure 2.7(d). In this figure is also indicated the need for initial conditions to be supplied to each of the integrators. This requirement for two initial conditions is to be expected from the form of the original equation 2.20: this is a second order equation, which can be solved completely only if two boundary conditions are known.

2.7 The use of potentiometers

Although in principle the schematic diagrams shown in figures 2.7(c) and 2.7(d) represent computer solutions of equation 2.20, in practice some modification would need to be applied before either could be set up on an actual computer. This is because of the need in a general purpose computer to be able to set the gain factors for each amplifier input, as well as the magnitudes of constant terms, to any value within a continuous range. Since an amplifier gain factor is obtained as the ratio of two resistances, or as the product of a resistance and a capacitance, it is clear that these components need to be extremely accurate, or at least accurately matched, and need also to have very good long-term stability if the computation is to yield meaningful results. Equally clearly, these accuracy and stability requirements cannot be satisfied except by the use of elaborate and expensive devices, so that both practical and economic considerations dictate that the gain factors obtainable from an operational amplifier by the use of computing impedances as defined in equations 2.16 and 2.17 should be confined to a few standard values only. The use of standard factors is universal in general purpose computers, and in fact most modern computers restrict the available gain factors to

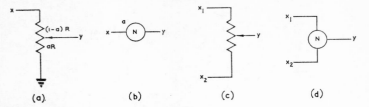

Fig. 2.8. Potentiometers are used to adjust coefficients.
    (a), (b) A two-terminal potentiometer, or attenuator, and its symbol.
    (c), (d) A three-terminal potentiometer and its symbol.

1 and 10. The required continuous range of values of gain factor is then obtained by using a potentiometer with one end earthed, as shown in figure 2.8(a). The input is applied to the other end, and the output, y, is taken from the wiper. If the total resistance of the potentiometer is R, and the resistance between wiper and earth is aR, then the potentiometer implements the equation

$$y = ax$$

where $$0 \le a \le 1.$$ (2.21)

A potentiometer used in this way is called a two terminal potentiometer, and is represented on a computer schematic diagram by the symbol shown in figure 2.8(b), where the number within the symbol is an identifying label. This is the commonest use of a potentiometer in computer circuits, but occasionally there is a need for a potentiometer with both ends free, as in figure 2.8(c). This is known as a three terminal potentiometer, and is represented by the symbol shown in figure 2.8(d).

Just as it is not practicable to use a continuous range of gain factors, so also it is not practicable to use a continuous range of direct voltage supplies to provide for all possible constant terms and initial conditions. The solution again is to use a few standard supplies, normally just one positive and one negative, and to have potentiometers available for setting the exact voltages required. A complete schematic diagram of a computer programme to solve equation 2.20 is shown in figure 2.9. We must assume that the required settings of the potentiometers satisfy the inequality in equation 2.21; methods of manipulating the problem so that these limits are observed will be dealt with in chapter 3.

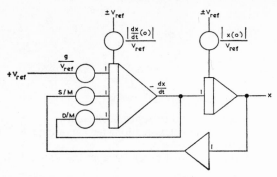

Fig. 2.9. Modified form of Fig. 2.7 (d) using potentiometers.

2.8 Differential analysers and simulators

The system that we have been discussing in the last two sections of this chapter was described at the beginning of section 2.6, but this description was not really complete. Equation 2.20, which is the mathematical form of the description, has a steady state solution to which it converges for all positive values of g, D, S and M (and negative values of these quantities are not physically realizable). In other words, this system will never move from its equilibrium position unless it is subjected to some kind of disturbance. This disturbance is represented in figure 2.9 by the non-zero initial conditions of the integrators; this representation, besides being rather indirect, is restricted to a disturbing force whose influence terminates at the beginning of the computation. A more complete model of the system might be as shown in figure 2.10(a), in which we suppose that the top of the string is subjected to some independent movement such that its position at any instant is y relative to a fixed datum. The position of the mass is also measured with respect to the same fixed datum, so that the equation of motion of the mass will now be

$$M \frac{d^2x}{dt^2} = Mg - S(x-y-L) - D\frac{dx}{dt}$$

or
$$\frac{d^2x}{dt^2} = \frac{S}{M}y - \frac{D}{M}\frac{dx}{dt} - \frac{S}{M}x + \left(g + \frac{SL}{M}\right) \qquad (2.22)$$

This could be mechanized (in principle at least) by the circuit shown in figure 2.10(b), where the input y is an externally generated signal representing the imposed movement of the top of the string. In

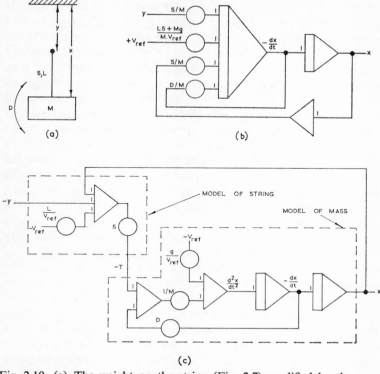

Fig. 2.10. (a) The weight on the string (Fig. 2.7) modified by the provision of an external disturbing force.
(b) A computer solution of the resulting equation (Differential
analyser approach).
(c) A computer model of the original system (Simulator
approach).

deriving this, what we have really done is first to form a mathematical
model of the system and then to manipulate this model to a form that
is convenient for a computer. In doing this, we have lost all structural
similarity with the original system and we have finished up with a
computer representation that is rather inflexible, being a representation of an equation rather than of a system. If, for example, we wanted
to assess the effect on performance of using a different mass, or a
string with a different length then we would be faced with an elaborate
calculation to obtain the new potentiometer setting. If a string of
different elasticity were to be used, then the settings of three potentio-

meters would have to be changed. These features may be of little account if the computer is being used purely as a mathematical device for solving differential equations, where all that is required is the overall solution – in this case the variation of x with time. The earliest analogue computers were in fact designed for this purpose, and were described as *differential analysers*; the method of investigating systems by way of a mathematical model that can be manipulated before being applied to the computer is termed a differential analyser approach. For many engineering applications, however, our interest goes far beyond a mathematical solution. In the system we have been considering for example, we might well be concerned to know the maximum value of the tension in the string, because a physical string will have a limit to the maximum tension it can support. Similarly, in many investigations of physical systems we will want to know about the behaviour of components of the system as well as being presented with the overall response. Such information is not easy to obtain from the circuit of figure 2.10(b); what is needed is an arrangement in which the physical components of the system are represented separately by identifiable groups of computer components. A computer used in this way is called a *simulator*: the method of studying a system by modelling each component of the system and retaining in the model a structural similarity to the original is termed a simulation. Figure 2.10(c) shows a simulation of the mass on the string, consisting of separate simulations of the component parts. The left hand part represents the string, with inputs of x and y and an output representing the tension, T, implementing the equation

$$T = S(x-y-L). \tag{2.23}$$

The right hand part of figure 2.10(c) represents the mass by the equation

$$M \frac{d^2 x}{dt^2} = Mg - D \frac{dx}{dt} - T.$$

The movement of the mass is also the movement of one end of the string, and the tension in the string is one of the forces determining the motion of the mass; these interconnections appear explicitly in the circuit. It should also be noticed that in the arrangement of figure 2.10(c) each parameter of the system appears as a setting of a single potentiometer, so that the effect of changing L, M, D, S, or g can be investigated readily. Alternatively we can adjust the potentiometers until a desired pattern of behaviour appears and then obtain the required system parameters from the settings.

2.9 Non-linear effects in practical systems

Simulation is now probably the most important application of analogue computers; by the use of these methods it is possible to obtain an insight into the workings of a system and to assess easily the effects on performance of changes in its components. Problems associated with the simulation of particular systems and system components will be dealt with later (mainly in chapters 8 and 11), but some preliminary observations can be made in connection with the mass and string example that we have been considering in this chapter. The string has been represented by equation 2.23, which is shown graphically as a function of $(x-y)$ in figure 2.11(a). This however is not an accurate representation of a physical string; a string cannot push, and so the tension can never be negative. A much more accurate simulation of a string would implement the relation shown in figure 2.11(b), which is described by

$$T = \begin{cases} S(x-y-L), & x-y>L \\ 0, & x-y<L. \end{cases} \qquad (2.24)$$

This is a simple form of a non-linear relationship; the inclusion of such non-linearities into a system equation makes the solution of the equation very much more complex, and, in complicated systems, can put the mathematical solution of the equation beyond the limits of

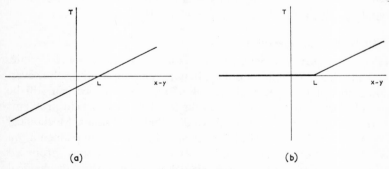

(a)   (b)

Fig. 2.11. Non-linearity in a simple practical system.
      (a) The tension-extension curve of the string as represented in
          the computer programmes of Fig. 2.10.
      (b) A more realistic characteristic.

available analytical techniques. This is where the analogue computer really comes into its own; equation 2.24 can be realized very simply by the addition of some further elements to the circuit of figure 2.10(c). The amount of extra equipment required depends on the accuracy demanded, and this in turn depends largely on the purpose for which the simulation is wanted. For the simplest form, only a single extra circuit component is needed. It is worth noticing that this simple realisation is possible only with the simulator circuit of figure 2.10(c) in which the tension T appears explicitly. It is also only in the simulator circuit that the deficiencies of the original linear model are made clearly apparent, for there is no mathematical reason why the equation 2.23 should not apply: it is only when we observe the behaviour of the string explicitly that we can readily see the physical shortcomings of the mathematics. Methods of simulating this and other non-linear effects in physical systems, and also methods of generating non-linear functions of all kinds, will be discussed in later chapters. For the moment it will suffice to say that non-linear equipment is a vital part of a general purpose analogue computer, and that the ability to produce non-linear functions easily is the main strength of analogue methods. In the system we have been considering, for example, we require not only a non-linear relationship to be implemented in forming T in accordance with equation 2.24, but also a generator that can produce an arbitrary waveform to represent y in equations 2.23 and 2.24, since the movement of the top of the string, being an external excitation, can in general be of any form. Methods of satisfying both these requirements will be dealt with in detail later (see chapters 8 and 10).

2.10 Notes and references

General purpose analogue computers are now invariably electronic, and all other devices are obsolete. In particular applications, however, some special non-electronic forms of analogue device can still be useful, particularly electrolytic tanks for the study of field problems and resistance nets for the study of distribution systems. Mechanical computation has historical interest as the earliest implementation of the techniques described in this chapter, originally proposed nearly a hundred years ago. A detailed description of these mechanical devices is given by Soroka, and an extensive account of other non-electronic analogue methods (such as conductive solids and liquids, and resistance networks) is given by Karplus, and Fifer also discusses a number of such systems at some length. A.c. computing, which is particularly suited to the study of sinusoidal steady state systems, is described by Nenadal and Mirtes.

A simple but clear introduction to the straightforward use of conventional analogue computers is given by Key, and a thorough practical introduction, with an emphasis on numerous numerical examples, is provided by Peterson. The programming of an analogue computer to solve linear and non-linear problems is discussed by Rekoff, who starts with the assumption of the existence of summers, integrators, and various non-linear units, and shows how to use them (including scaling and checking procedures) before describing how the units themselves are implemented.

An alternative way to set up computer programmes is the matrix method of programming. This method has found favour in some Eastern European countries, but does not seem to have become popular in Britain or the U.S.A. It is described by Borsky and Matyas, whose Czechoslovakian book is now available in an English translation.

The most authoritative book on all aspects of analogue computing, and a comprehensive source of references for the serious student of the subject, is the one by Korn and Korn. The density of information is such that it is not easy for the beginner to digest, but as a reliable and informative reference book it is unrivalled.

REFERENCES

BORSKY, V. and MATYAS, J. (1968). *Computation by Electronic Analogue Computers*, English translation ed. C. C. RITCHIE and G. F. MOXON, Iliffe, London.

FIFER, S. (1961). *Analog Computation*, 4 volumes, McGraw-Hill, New York.

KARPLUS, W. J. (1958). *Analog Simulation*, McGraw-Hill, New York.

KEY, K. A. (1965). *Analogue Computing for Beginners*, Chapman and Hall, London.

KORN, G. A. and KORN, T. M. (1964). *Electronic Analog and Hybrid Computers*, McGraw-Hill, New York.

NENADAL, Z. and MIRTES, B. (1968). *Analogue and Hybrid Computers*, English translation ed. R. J. M. GREW, Iliffe, London.

PETERSON, G. R. (1967). *Basic Analog Computation*, Collier-Macmillan, New York.

REKOFF, M. G. (1967). *Analog Computer Programming*, Merrill, New York.

SOROKA, W. W. (1954). *Analog Methods in Computation and Simulation*, McGraw-Hill, New York.

3 Scaling

3.1 Physical limitations on solutions

The methods suggested in chapter 2 for the programming of an
analogue computer to solve simple differential equations require
some modification in practice, because of inherent physical limitations
of the devices used in the computer. An understanding of these
limitations and of the ways in which they affect the solution of
problems is absolutely essential before even the simplest programme
can be applied to the computer.

Consider, for example, setting up a computer to solve the equation

$$\frac{d^2x}{dt^2} + \omega^2 x = 0 \qquad (3.1)$$

The procedure outlined in chapter 2 (see section 2.6) leads to the
patching diagram of figure 3.1. This represents in principle a satisfactory computer solution to equation 3.1; the limitations of this
circuit appear only when we insert actual numbers into the equation
and examine the required performance of each element in detail.
Analogue computing is in this respect different from many other
branches of electronic engineering, in that there is no such thing as

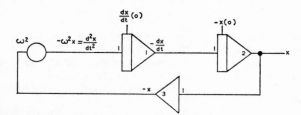

Fig. 3.1. Computer programme to solve a general undamped second order
equation.

32

a general solution to a general problem. Mathematically, we can write down the solution to equation 3.1 as

$$x = A \cos (\omega t + \phi) \tag{3.2}$$

where A and ϕ are dependent on the initial conditions. This is the general solution, valid for all values of ω, but figure 3.1 does not represent the general computer programme for generating the solution to equation 3.1. This is immediately apparent if we observe the requirement to set the potentiometer to the value ω^2. Since the setting of a potentiometer can never, for practical reasons, be larger than unity, it is clear that the range of problems that can be solved is severely restricted. The range can be extended a little by increasing the gains of the amplifiers; however, the maximum gain available is not likely to be more than about 30 (three inputs each with a gain of 10 connected together). This would increase the maximum value of ω^2 that could be accommodated to $2 \cdot 7 \times 10^4$, which represents a frequency of oscillation of only about 25 Hz. Many electrical and even mechanical systems are able to exhibit oscillatory changes at frequencies substantially above this limit, so that with the circuit as it stands a wide range of problems is excluded from consideration. Limitations also exist with very small values of ω; if $\omega = 10^{-2}$ for example the potentiometer would need to be set to 10^{-4} and although this is theoretically within the permitted range of variation, in practice it is clearly very difficult to adjust the position of a potentiometer wiper with the degree of precision necessary to avoid the possibility of a very large percentage error in the setting.

It might appear that these difficulties could be overcome by the use of additional elements in the loop. The high frequency range, for example, could apparently be extended by the inclusion of additional amplifiers in the loop so as to make up the required gain. This solution however, besides being expensive in equipment, is not normally open to us because of other fundamental practical limitations. The output devices commonly used with analogue computing systems for the purpose of observing and recording the behaviour of problem variables have severely limited ranges of operating frequency (see chapter 4). Even if we confine ourselves to the use of an oscilloscope, we can still not operate at very high frequencies because of the limitations of the amplifiers themselves; these limitations are very much more severe than one might expect from an electronic circuit (see chapter 6). Very low frequencies, on the other hand, are inconvenient in that problem solutions take a long time to appear (the simulation of a chemical plant, for example, will often involve time constants of the order of hours) and they also suffer from other accuracy limitations, mainly due to imperfections in the amplifiers (see chapter 6).

Further limitations in the circuit of figure 3.1 appear when we consider the signals that appear at the outputs of each of the amplifiers. If we suppose, for simplicity, that the initial conditions are given by

$$x(0) = 0; \qquad \frac{dx}{dt}(0) = \omega$$

then the solution (equation 3.2) becomes

$$x = \sin \omega t.$$

If we suppose further that $\omega = 40$ then the equation we have to solve (equation 3.1) becomes

$$\frac{d^2 x}{dt^2} = -1600x$$

which in the programme of figure 3.1 requires a potentiometer setting of 1600. The programme shown in figure 3.2 satisfies this equation by inserting gains of 10 in amplifiers 1 and 2 and a gain of 20 in amplifier 3 making a total gain of 2000, so that the required setting of the potentiometer is reduced by the same factor to give 1600/2000, or 0·8. If the output of amplifier 2 is x, the outputs of amplifiers 3 and 1 are $-20x$ and $-1/10 \, dx/dt$ respectively. These are all sine waves of the same frequency, but they differ in amplitude, having peak values of 1, 20 and 4. There are two practical difficulties attached to the use of amplifiers as computing elements apart from the frequency limitations mentioned above. The first is the obvious one that an amplifier can provide only a limited amplitude output (commonly $\pm 100V$ or $\pm 10V$). The second is that as the amplitude of the signal demanded from an amplifier decreases, then since the absolute accuracy with which the signal can be measured is approximately constant (limited by the output devices and by noise), the percentage accuracy falls.

If we examine the programme of figure 3.2 in the light of these remarks we see that the performance will not be optimal. If the computer is a 10-V one, then the demanded output from amplifier 3

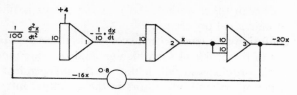

Fig. 3.2. An attempt to solve the equation

$$\frac{d^2x}{dt^2} + 1600x = 0; \quad x(0) = 0, \quad \frac{dx}{dt}(0) = 40.$$

This programme is not satisfactory.

exceeds the limit, while the output from amplifier 2 is too small for accuracy. A 100-V computer would not be troubled by saturation, but the 1-V peak output from amplifier 2 would be subject to very serious percentage errors, and the 4-V from amplifier 1 would be little better.

This difficulty can be avoided, as can the frequency problems mentioned earlier, by making use of the fact that when the variation of one variable, y, with another variable, t, is examined by the use of a graph of y against t, the size of the graph obtained is determined solely by arbitrary scale factors used on the axes. These scale factors themselves are determined only by mechanical convenience – the graph must be large enough to read, but small enough to fit on the page – and have no influence on the shape of the graph but only on its interpretation. In the same way, there is no reason why one second of time in the original problem should necessarily be represented by one second of time in the computer, or why one unit of amplitude of any variable need be represented by one volt. The difficulties discussed in this chapter so far are all overcome, or at least minimized, by the choice of suitable scale factors: an understanding of the methods of choosing and applying appropriate scale factors is essential before any problem can be set up on a computer.

3.2 Time scaling

The ideas behind scaling, and also the actual manipulations necessary to achieve it, are essentially simple; the difficulties that arise are almost entirely due to terminology and notation. No standards exist: the system that will be used here is the one that seems to the present author to be the most logical and convenient, but other systems

D

find favour with other authors, so that the choice is ultimately a matter of individual preference.

One confusion that tends to arise comes about because on the one hand most of the problems for which an analogue computer is used are dynamic problems in which time is the independent variable, while on the other hand integrators in the computer integrate with respect to time. If these two times are the same, we have what is known as a *real time simulation* and there is then no difficulty. If a time scale factor is introduced, however, the two times become different, and either could quite reasonably be called 'real time'. They will be distinguished here by calling the variable in the original problem 'problem time' denoted by t_p, and the variable in the computer 'computer time' denoted by t_c. The use of the term 'real time' will be studiously avoided, except in the phrase 'real time simulation'.

The two times with which we are concerned are related by the expression

$$t_c = kt_p. \tag{3.3}$$

In solving a problem involving time scaling we have to observe that the computer operates with respect to computer time, while the problem is stated and resu'ts are required in terms of problem time. In order to reduce the writing involved in setting down computer equations, it is convenient to denote differentiation with respect to computer time by using the D notation. From equation 3.3 we have

$$\frac{dt_c}{dt_p} = k$$

so that if f is any variable

$$\frac{df}{dt_p} = \frac{df}{dt_c}\frac{dt_c}{dt_p} = kDf.$$

Hence

$$\frac{d^n f}{dt_p^n} = k^n D^n f.$$

Thus if the problem is represented by a general linear differential equation

$$a_n \frac{d^n f_n}{dt_p} + a_{n-1}\frac{d^{n-1} f_{n-1}}{dt_p} + \ldots a_1 \frac{df}{dt_p} + a_0 f = 0$$

the effect of time scaling is to transform this to a computer equation

$$k^n a_n D^n f + k^{n-1} a_{n-1} D^{n-1} f + \ldots + k a_1 D f + a_0 f = 0.$$

Integrators operate with respect to computer time, so that the effect of an integrator is simply to reduce the power of D by one, and multiply by the appropriate gain factors as illustrated in figure 3.3.

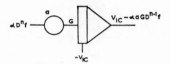

Fig. 3.3. The initial condition, which is known in terms of the problem variables, must be modified by the time scale factor before being applied to the amplifier.

The initial condition needs a little care, because the amplifier output when $t = 0$ is expressed in computer variables, but the problem data will include initial conditions expressed in problem variables. The time scale factor has therefore to be taken into account. The initial condition of the amplifier in figure 3.3 will be

$$V_{IC} = -\alpha a G \; D^{n-1} f(0) = -\frac{\alpha a G}{k^{n-1}} \frac{d^{n-1} f}{dt^{n-1}}(0)$$

Consider now the example we used before, in which the equation to be solved is

$$\frac{d^2 x}{dt^2} = -1600x$$

subject to the initial conditions

$$x(0) = 0; \qquad \frac{dx}{dt}(0) = 40.$$

We may choose as a convenient time scale factor

$$k = 100$$

so that the computer equation becomes

$$10^4 D^2 x = -1600x$$

or
$$D^2 x = -0\cdot16x \qquad\qquad (3.4)$$

with initial conditions

$$x(0) = 0; \qquad Dx(0) = \frac{1}{k}\frac{dx}{dt}(0) = 0\cdot4.$$

This equation may be implemented by the programme shown in figure 3.4, in which not only has the angular frequency of operation of

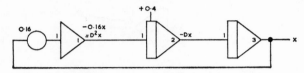

Fig. 3.4. A time scale factor of 100 applied to the programme of Fig. 3.2 avoids the high gains.

all components been reduced from 40 rad/sec to 0·4 rad/sec, but also the high gains of figure 3.2 have all disappeared and been replaced by unity gains. The programme, however, is still not satisfactory, because the amplitude problems remain.

3.3 Amplitude scaling

The solution to equation 3.4, with the initial conditions given, is

$$x = \sin 0\cdot4t \tag{3.5}$$

Hence, $\qquad\qquad Dx = 0\cdot4 \cos 0\cdot4t \tag{3.6}$

and $\qquad\qquad D^2x = -0\cdot16 \sin 0\cdot4t \tag{3.7}$

This means that the output of each amplifier in figure 3.4 is a sine wave of angular frequency 0·4 rad/sec, but the amplitudes of these waveforms are 0·16, 0·4, and 1 V respectively, so that amplitude scaling is necessary if reasonable computational accuracy is to be obtained.

As with time scaling, the principles and manipulative methods are not difficult, but poor notation can give rise to confusion. Again, the method to be used here is the one that seems easiest to the present author, but it would not find favour with everyone.

Since we require the output of each amplifier to extend over the largest possible fraction of its dynamic range, while making sure that the demanded output does not extend beyond the limit, we clearly need to know the maximum amplitude of each variable in the problem.

Operational amplifiers are always designed to have the dynamic range symmetrical about zero, so that the maximum amplitude in which we are interested is the maximum instantaneous value of the modulus of the variable. The optimum scaling factor will then be such that this maximum value corresponds to the maximum available output of the amplifier. In practice, the scaling factor chosen cannot usually be made equal to this optimum because maximum values are rarely known accurately beforehand, and also because the numerical interpretation of the results is made rather easier if the scaling factors are chosen to be round numbers.

The method of amplitude scaling to be used here avoids notational difficulties by working throughout with the original problem variables, making the assumption that one volt in the computer represents one unit of the problem variable. Thus in our harmonic oscillator example, which, after time scaling is described by equation 3·4, x may be a displacement measured (in the problem) in feet. In this case, an amplifier whose output is labelled x is taken to represent x on a scale of 1 V ≡ 1 ft and a signal marked Dx represents the rate of change of x with (computer) time on a scale of 1 V ≡ 1 ft/sec. The solutions to equations 3.4 for x, Dx, and D^2x are given by equations 3.5, 3.6, and 3.7; we see that as things stand the maximum signals are unacceptably small. If we have a 100-V computer, then we find the largest scale factors that can be used for each variable by dividing 100 by the maximum amplitude of the variable. This gives 100, 250, and 625 for x, Dx, and D^2x. Convenient values to choose in this case might then be 100, 200 and 500. We then rewrite the equation using as our variables $100x$, $200Dx$ and $500D^2x$, giving

$$500D^2x = -500 \cdot 0 \cdot 16 \cdot \left(\frac{100x}{100} \right)$$

$$= -0 \cdot 8 \, (100x). \tag{3.8}$$

In order to obtain the desired scaling factors for each variable we will also have to modify the integration operations, to give realizations of

$$-200Dx = -200 \int \frac{500D^2x}{500} \, dt_c$$

$$= -0 \cdot 4 \int (500D^2x) dt_c \tag{3.9}$$

and
$$100x = -100 \int -\frac{200\,Dx}{200}\, dt_c$$

$$= -0.5 \int (-200\,Dx)dt_c \qquad (3.10)$$

The computer programme based on equations 3.8, 3.9, and 3.10 is shown in figure 3.5, in which the initial condition has also been modified by the appropriate amplitude scaling factor.

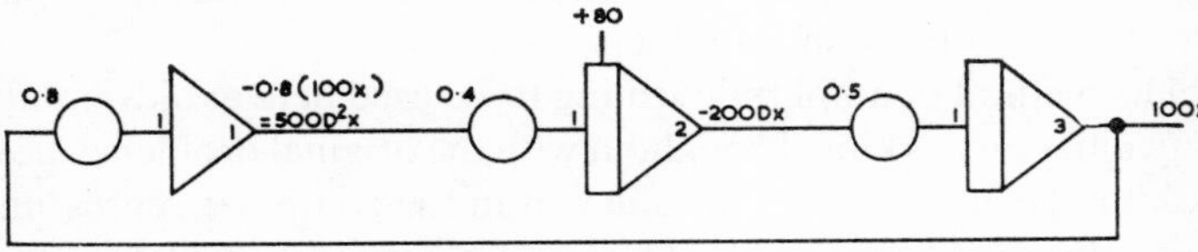

Fig. 3.5. By applying time and amplitude scaling to the programme of Fig. 3.4 a satisfactory solution is obtained.

3.3.1 *Parameter scaling*

One important area of use of an analogue computer is in system synthesis, where the aim is to investigate the effect upon overall performance of variations in certain parameters in the system, with a view to selecting optimum values for these parameters in the final design. It is desirable in this case that the parameters in question should appear as potentiometer settings, in order to simplify both the insertion of set values and the interpretation of adjustments that are obtained empirically. If a parameter is to appear as a potentiometer setting, then since this setting cannot exceed unity, there is, in general, clearly a need for a further magnitude scaling manipulation of the problem.

As with all amplitude scaling, there are two features of the equipment that need to be considered. The first, as has just been suggested, is that the setting of a potentiometer cannot exceed unity; the second is that if accurate results are to be obtained, the setting should not be allowed to fall below about 0.1. A fuller discussion of the difficulties of setting potentiometers and in particular of the difficulties of setting them to very low values, will be found in chapters 5 and 6; for the moment we need only observe that a parameter variation over one decade is all that can conveniently be accommodated with a potentiometer. If a larger range of variation is required a change can sometimes be made in one of the fixed gains in the computer programme. The change in this case would normally be a factor of ten, and this would then allow a further decade of parameter variation. If it is not possible to modify the computer programme, very low potentiometer settings may have to be accepted. In such a case, the special techniques mentioned in chapter 6 (see section 6.2) will have to be used when setting or interpreting the potentiometer readings.

Apart from this complication when dealing with large parameter ranges, the actual method of parameter scaling is quite straight-forward. Basically the potentiometer can be arranged to represent a normalized parameter; that is to say, the potentiometer setting can represent a fraction of the maximum of the range and of course this fraction cannot exceed unity. In practice it is often convenient to have a simple relationship between the parameter value and the potentio-meter setting, so that rather than performing the normalization with respect to the maximum of the range, it may be better to choose the next highest round number.

The procedure can be illustrated by considering a modification to the example we have used in the earlier sections of this chapter. The system equation was

$$\frac{d^2x}{dt^2} + 1600x = 0 \tag{3.11}$$

the solution to which is a pure sinusoidal oscillation. To investigate the effects of damping on this system we may modify the equation to

$$\frac{d^2x}{dt^2} + K\frac{dx}{dt} + 1600x = 0 \tag{3.12}$$

where K is a parameter that we will suppose to be able to vary over the range of values 5–80.

We notice first of all in this example that since more than one decade of parameter variation is demanded some special treatment will ultimately be called for. To start with, however, we will consider only the normalization necessary to enable the variation to be represented by a potentiometer. A scaling factor of 80 could be used since this is the maximum value of the parameter, but for simple conversion it would be preferable to use a factor of 100. If the para-meter variation required had been 8–80 then the smaller factor might have been justified to avoid entering a second decade, but since in this example we are already committed to using a second decade we have nothing to lose and a good deal to gain from using the larger factor. Equation 3.12 can then be written

$$\frac{d^2x}{dt^2} + 100\left(\frac{K}{100}\right)\frac{dx}{dt} + 1600x = 0 \qquad (3.13)$$

where $(K/100)$ can be set on a potentiometer since it does not exceed unity. The scaled version of equation 3.11 is given by equation 3.8; if the same scaling factors are used with equation 3.13 we have

$$-(500D^2x) = 2 \cdot 5(K/100)(200Dx) + 0 \cdot 8(100x) \qquad (3.14)$$

One implementation of equation 3.14 is shown in figure 3.6(a). If in a particular application it is not necessary to have D^2x available, then the summing and integrating properties of integrators can be used to produce the programme of figure 3.6(b), with a saving of one amplifier. In figure 3.6(a), potentiometer 3 is set to the value $(K/100)$, and can therefore be adjusted on successive computing runs

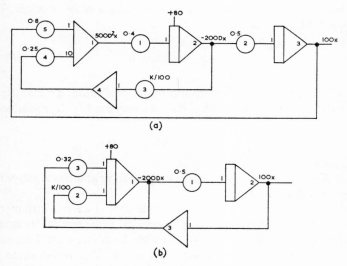

(a)

(b)

Fig. 3.6. Time and amplitude scaled solution of the equation

$$\frac{d^2x}{dt^2} + K\frac{dx}{dt} + 1600x = 0; \quad x(0) = 0, \quad \frac{dx}{dt}(0) = 40.$$

(a) Full programme with the second differential available.
(b) More economical programme when the second differential is not required.

to represent different values within the given range of variation of K. Since K varies from 5 to 80, $(K/100)$ varies from 0·05 to 0·8. For values of $K/100$ below 0·1, we can conveniently avoid the low settings of potentiometer 3 by setting this to $K/10$ instead of $K/100$ and compensating by reducing the following gain of amplifier 1 from 10 to 1. This possibility is not open to us in the programme of figure 3.6(b), so that even if D^2x is not required it might be convenient to use the larger programme.

In scaling this problem we have not so far mentioned the inverter amplifier in the feedback loop. It should, however, be observed that everything that has been said about the need for scaling applies as much to this inverter as it does to any other amplifier in the programme. Thus in figure 3.6(a) the gain of 10 in the inner feedback loop must appear in amplifier 1 and not in amplifier 4. If it were put into amplifier 4, then since amplifier 2 has been scaled to operate to a maximum of nearly its full permitted output, amplifier 4 would overload for any value of $K/100$ greater than about 0·1.

There is a slightly more subtle point in figure 3.6(b). Potentiometer 3 could be placed either between amplifiers 2 and 3 or between amplifiers 3 and 1, and at first sight there seems nothing to choose between these two arrangements. However, if potentiometer 3, set at 0·32, is put between amplifiers 2 and 3, then amplifier 3 will have an operating range of only about one third of that of amplifier 2. Connected as shown, the operating ranges of the two amplifiers are identical, so that the scaling that produces optimum operation of amplifier 2 also produces optimum operation of amplifier 3. If in the present example the potentiometer were put in front of amplifier 3 the difference in accuracy would probably not be great, but a smaller potentiometer setting could easily result in the range of operation of amplifier 3 being reduced below the minimum acceptable limits.

3.4 Choice of scale factors

So far in this chapter, we have considered the ways in which scale factors can be applied to an equation, but we have avoided any discussion of how we know what scale factors to apply. Clearly from what has been said this requires a knowledge of the maximum amplitudes of the various problem variables and also of the maximum frequency at which they will vary. Such information will not normally be available in advance, and cannot in general be calculated exactly, so that the first problem of scaling is the estimation of these maxima.

3.4.1 *Characteristics of second order differential equations*

A linear second order differential equation with constant coefficients commonly occurs in the description of physical systems or subsystems; moreover, other more complicated systems may sometimes be reduced as a first approximation to a second order system so that some observations regarding the behaviour of such systems may be useful here.

The general equation of a simple second order system is

$$\frac{d^2y}{dt^2} + a_1\frac{dy}{dt} + a_2y = F(t). \tag{3.15}$$

If a_2 is positive, this may be written in the more useful form

$$\frac{d^2y}{dt^2} + 2\zeta\omega_n\frac{dy}{dt} + \omega_n^2 y = F(t) \tag{3.16}$$

where ω_n is the undamped natural frequency and ζ is the damping factor. The solution to this equation consists of the particular integral, whose form depends on $F(t)$, and the complementary function, whose form depends on the solution of

$$\frac{d^2y}{dt^2} + 2\zeta\omega_n\frac{dy}{dt} + \omega_n^2 y = 0. \tag{3.17}$$

If $\zeta = 0$, the solution of equation 3.17 is a pure sine wave, of frequency ω_n. If $\zeta \neq 0$, then the solution of equation 3.17 depends on the solution of the characteristic equation

$$p^2 + 2\zeta\omega_n p + \omega_n^2 = 0. \tag{3.18}$$

If $\zeta > 1$, the roots of equation 3.18 are real and different giving the sum of two exponentials as the solution to equation 3.17.

If $0 < \zeta < 1$, the roots of equation 3.18 are complex, and the solution of equation 3.17 is a damped sine wave given by

$$y = Ae^{-\zeta\omega_n t}\sin(\omega t + \phi) \tag{3.19}$$

where
$$\omega = \omega_n\sqrt{(1-\zeta^2)}$$

and A and ϕ are constants depending on the initial conditions. If $\zeta = 1$ the system is critically damped, and the solution to equation 3.17 is exponential in form.

If in equation 3.15 either a_1 or a_2 is negative, then the solution will

contain exponentials with positive exponents, and this solution will
increase in magnitude with time. This corresponds to an unstable
system, and a computer simulation of such a system must result in
one or more of the amplifiers saturating. With a stable system, it is
clear from equation 3.19 that both the frequency and the amplitude
of this part of the solution are always less than they would be for
$\zeta = 0$. It may further be shown that the magnitude of each differential
coefficient of y with respect to t is also less than that of the corresponding quantity for the undamped case. Thus a conservative
estimate of the performance of an underdamped second order system
may be obtained by ignoring the damping term altogether. This
reduces equation 3.17 to

$$\frac{d^2y}{dt^2} + \omega_n{}^2 y = 0$$

which has as its solution

$$y = A \sin (\omega_n t + \phi).$$

This is the complementary function; the complete solution is obtained
by adding to it the particular integral, which depends on $F(t)$ in
equation 3.16. If we suppose that this is a step function of magnitude
F, then the complete solution for y is

$$y = Y + A \sin (\omega_n t + \phi)$$

where $$Y = \frac{F}{\omega_n{}^2}$$

$$\therefore \frac{dy}{dt} = A\omega_n \cos (\omega_n t + \phi)$$

i.e. $$y(0) = Y + A \sin \phi; \qquad \frac{dy}{dt}(0) = A\omega_n \cos \phi.$$

Hence, from the initial conditions we can find A, and so deduce
estimates of the maximum values

$$(y)_{max} = Y + A; \qquad \left(\frac{dy}{dt}\right)_{max} = A\omega_n; \qquad \left(\frac{d^2y}{dt^2}\right)_{max} = A\omega_n{}^2$$

This maximum value for y should be particularly noted. If the system
is initially at rest with $y = 0$, then it turns out that $A = Y$, so that

we then have $(y)_{\text{max}} = 2Y$. Since we are considering here an un-damped system, the solution in this case would take the form of a continuous oscillation. If the system were very lightly damped, it would reach a steady state at which $y = Y$, while the maximum value would still approach $2Y$. This estimate of the maximum as being twice the steady state value will appear again in the next section.

3.4.2 *Simplification of equations*

One valuable technique for estimating the natural frequencies and maximum amplitudes of variables appearing in a computer problem is that of making approximations in the equations so as to reduce them to a conveniently analytical form. This might involve ignoring non-linear terms so as to make the equation linear, or perhaps approximating complicated forcing functions by step or sine functions so as to simplify analysis.

Consider for example, a computer programme to solve

$$\ddot{y} + 9y = 10e^{-\alpha t} \tag{3.20}$$

with $\quad y = 0, \dot{y} = 50$, at $t = 0$.

The exact solution of this equation could be obtained analytically without too much difficulty, but the process is simplified considerably by assuming a step forcing function instead of the exponential. The general solution can then be written down by inspection as

$$y = \frac{10}{9} + A \sin (3t + \phi)$$

so that $\quad \dot{y} = 3A \cos (3t + \phi). \tag{3.21}$

Inserting the initial conditions then gives

$$A \sin \phi = -10/9$$

$$A \cos \phi = 50/3$$

$$\therefore A^2 (\sin^2 \phi + \cos^2 \phi) = A^2 = 100/81 + 2500/9 \simeq 2500/9$$

$$\therefore A \simeq 50/3$$

$$\therefore (y)_{\text{max}} \simeq 10/9 + 50/3 \simeq 17 \cdot 8$$

$$(\dot{y})_{\text{max}} \simeq 50.$$

These estimates suggest that time scaling would not be necessary (since $\omega_n = 3$ rad/sec), and that suitable amplitude scaling will be achieved if we take as working variables $(5y)$ and $(2\dot{y})$. A further scaling requirement in this particular example is for the forcing function, $10e^{-\alpha t}$. Methods of generating functions such as this will be dealt with in detail in chapter 10 (for the exponential function in particular, see section 10.3.1); for our present purposes we need only observe that a function generated in the computer almost invariably appears at the output of an operational amplifier, so that forcing functions need to be scaled in the same way as the outputs of other operational amplifiers. In the present example, the function $10e^{-\alpha t}$ has a maximum value of 10, so that in a 100-V computer it would be preferable to generate $100e^{-\alpha t}$. If $\ddot{y}$ is not required explicitly we mechanize the equation

$$-\dot{y} = -\int_0^t \ddot{y}\, dt - \dot{y}(0) \qquad\qquad (3.22)$$

so that inserting the scale factors into equation 3.20 and substituting into equation 3.22 gives

$$-2\dot{y} = -\int_0^t \left[\frac{2}{10}(100e^{-\alpha t}) - \frac{2\times 9}{5}(5y) \right] dt - (2\times 50)$$

and this leads to the patching diagram shown in figure 3.7. If $\ddot{y}$ is required, it will need to be scaled; an estimate of the maximum value can be obtained by differentiating equation 3.21 a second time giving

$$(\ddot{y})_{max} = 9A \simeq 150$$

so that a convenient quantity to form would be $(\ddot{y}/2)$.

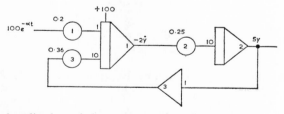

Fig. 3.7. Amplitude scaled programme to solve

$$\frac{d^2y}{dt^2} + 9y = 10e^{-\alpha t};\ y(0) = 0,\ \frac{dy}{dt}(0) = 50.$$

No time scaling is necessary in this example.

Scaling of simultaneous differential equations can also be estimated by making fairly gross approximations; in this case a major simplification can be obtained by replacing the cross-coupling terms by constants (preferably zero).

Consider for example, the equations

$$\left.\begin{aligned} 3\frac{dx}{dt}+2x+\frac{dy}{dt} &= 1 \\ \frac{dx}{dt}+4\frac{dy}{dt}+3y &= 0 \end{aligned}\right\} \tag{3.23}$$

with $\qquad\qquad x(0) = y(0) = 0.$

One assumption that can conveniently be made is that the cross-coupling terms remain constant at their initial values. These can be evaluated in this case by substituting $x = y = 0$ into equations 3.23, giving

$$\frac{dx}{dt}(0) = \frac{4}{11}; \qquad \frac{dy}{dt}(0) = -\frac{1}{11}$$

Equations 3.23 are then approximated as two independent first order equations

$$\left.\begin{aligned} \frac{dx}{dt}+\frac{2}{3}x &= \frac{4}{11}; \qquad x(0) = 0 \\ \frac{dy}{dt}+\frac{3}{4}y &= -\frac{1}{11}; \qquad y(0) = 0 \end{aligned}\right\} \tag{3.24}$$

The solutions to these equations can be written down by inspection as

$$\left.\begin{aligned} x &= \frac{3}{2}\cdot\frac{4}{11}[1-e^{-\frac{2}{3}t}] \\ y &= -\frac{4}{3}\cdot\frac{1}{11}[1-e^{-\frac{3}{4}t}] \end{aligned}\right\} \tag{3.25}$$

The maximum values can now be obtained directly from the equations 3.25 as

$$(x)_{max} = \frac{6}{11} \simeq 0\cdot55; \qquad (y)_{max} = \frac{4}{33} \simeq 0\cdot12;$$

$$\left(\frac{dx}{dt}\right)_{max} = \frac{6}{11}\cdot\frac{2}{3} \simeq 0\cdot36; \qquad \left(\frac{dy}{dt}\right)_{max} = \frac{4}{33}\cdot\frac{3}{4} \simeq 0\cdot09$$

where in each case the 'maximum' is as usual stated without regard to sign. A suitable set of working variables might then be chosen as

$$(100x), \quad (500y), \quad \left(200\,\frac{dx}{dt}\right), \quad \left(1000\,\frac{dy}{dt}\right).$$

Rewriting the original equation 3.23 in terms of these working variables gives

$$\left(200\,\frac{dx}{dt}\right) = \frac{1}{3}\cdot 200 - \frac{2}{3}\cdot\frac{200}{100}(100x) - \frac{1}{3}\cdot\frac{200}{1000}\left(1000\,\frac{dy}{dt}\right)$$

$$= 66\cdot 7 - 1\cdot 33\,(100x) - 0\cdot 067\left(1000\,\frac{dy}{dt}\right)$$

and $\qquad \left(1000\,\frac{dy}{dt}\right) = -\frac{3}{4}\cdot\frac{1000}{500}(500y) - \frac{1}{4}\cdot\frac{1000}{200}\left(200\,\frac{dx}{dt}\right)$

$$= -1\cdot 5\,(500y) - 1\cdot 25\left(200\,\frac{dx}{dt}\right)$$

A computer programme implementing these equations is shown in figure 3.8. The true maximum values of the variables in this problem can be found analytically (or experimentally by connecting up the

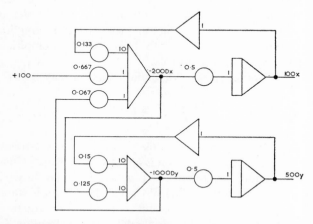

Fig. 3.8. Simultaneous equations could be manipulated to give separate equations of higher order, but it is generally more satisfactory to programme the original equations directly.

circuit of figure 3.8) and turn out to be

$$(x)_{\text{max}} = 0{\cdot}5 \qquad (y)_{\text{max}} = 0{\cdot}04$$

$$\left(\frac{dx}{dt}\right)_{\text{max}} = 0{\cdot}44; \qquad \left(\frac{dy}{dt}\right)_{\text{max}} = 0{\cdot}09.$$

The full analysis even of these simple equations is a slightly cumbersome affair; the approximations of equations 3.24 can be solved at sight, and yield estimates of the maxima that are quite good enough for initial scaling purposes.

3.4.3 n^{th} order differential equations – the equal coefficient rule

First or second order equations can provide approximations to very many systems or sub-systems, but higher order equations may sometimes be inevitable. We may notice in passing that higher order equations for describing complex systems are often derived by mathematical manipulation of a set of simultaneous lower order equations. In analogue computer terms, it is both unnecessary and undesirable that this mathematical manipulation should be performed; it is far easier to scale a series of relatively simple equations which can often (as in the example of equations 3.23) be approximated as independent equations, and then to simulate the whole system by cross-coupling the sub-systems appropriately. However, even with these simplifications we may be left with an equation of order greater than two. One useful way of estimating the maximum amplitude of the variable and its derivatives is to make use of an empirical rule known as the equal coefficient rule.

A general n^{th} order linear differential equation may be written

$$a_n \frac{d^n x}{dt^n} + a_{n-1} \frac{d^{n-1} x}{dt^{n-1}} + \ldots + a_1 \frac{dx}{dt} + a_0 x = F(t). \qquad (3.26)$$

The behaviour of a system with this equation may be estimated by assuming that the forcing function is a step of magnitude F and that all the initial conditions are zero. In practice, F can be chosen as the maximum expected value of $F(t)$. Provided the system is stable, the steady state value of x is F/a_0. As in the second order equation (see the comments at the end of section 3.4.1) we should allow for the existence of a very lightly damped mode of oscillation, which would give rise to a maximum excursion of x of twice the size of the step input; we therefore use as our estimate

$$(x)_{max} = |2F/a_0| .$$

The remaining estimates are then obtained from the rule of thumb

$$\left(\frac{d^r x}{dt^r}\right)_{max} = \left|\frac{F}{a_r}\right|$$

Working variables could then be chosen, in principle, as

$$\left(100 \left|\frac{a_r}{F}\right| \cdot \frac{d^r x}{dt^r}\right), 1 \le r \le n$$

assuming a 100-V computer.
Equation 3.26 then becomes

$$\frac{a_0}{100}\left|\frac{2F}{a_0}\right|\left(100\left|\frac{a_0}{2F}\right|x\right) + \sum_{r=1}^{n}\frac{a_r}{100}\left|\frac{F}{a_r}\right|\left(100\left|\frac{a_r}{F_r}\right|\cdot\frac{d^r x}{dt^r}\right) = F(t) \quad (3.27)$$

The rule derives its name from the fact that the coefficients of all the working variables in the summation in equation 3.27 are equal in magnitude; the coefficient of the undifferentiated term is numerically twice that of the others.

The procedure can best be illustrated by an example. Consider

$$\dddot{x} + 2\ddot{x} + 9\dot{x} + 18x = 36.$$

The estimates of the maxima obtained by the equal coefficient rule are

$$(x)_{max} = 4, \quad (\dot{x})_{max} = 4, \quad (\ddot{x})_{max} = 18, \quad (\dddot{x})_{max} = 36.$$

The true values, obtained analytically, are

$$(x)_{max} = 3 \cdot 02, \quad (\dot{x})_{max} = 3 \cdot 85, \quad (\ddot{x})_{max} = 10.34, \quad (\dddot{x})_{max} = 36$$

One important restriction has to be applied to this rule. The results are valid only if the estimates obtained are in descending or ascending order of magnitude. This restriction has to be applied in order to avoid difficulties with vanishing coefficients a_r.

3.4.4 Choice of time scale

In order to make a choice of an appropriate time scale for any problem, it is necessary to estimate the highest frequency component of the solution. This is not an easy matter with a high order differential

E

equation, and the results obtained are liable to be much more approximate than the amplitude estimates.

When dealing with the nth order system described by equation 3.26, one method of obtaining a rough estimate of the system natural frequency is to use the relationship

$$\omega_n^{tn} \simeq \frac{a_0}{a_n}.$$

This expression is exactly true for an undamped second order system, but can be very wide of the mark in other cases; it does, however, serve as a preliminary indication. An important point that should be borne in mind is that the solution will contain components due not only to the system dynamics but also to the characteristics of the forcing function. The highest frequency in the forcing function should therefore also be estimated, and time scaling should be carried out on the basis of both of these two component frequencies.

Another aspect of time scaling, which has not been mentioned before in this chapter, and which is often overlooked, is that the transformation expressed by equation 3.3 is only one of many possible ways in which computer time can be made to represent a problem variable. There are two other general kinds of transformation that are worth mentioning here.

In order to solve a second order differential equation, it is necessary to know two boundary conditions. The solution on an analogue computer requires that these conditions should be the values of the dependent variable and its differential coefficient at $t = 0$, but mathematically the problem is equally well specified, and equally easily solved, if these values are known for $t = T$. An analogue computer can be made to solve this equation in this case by adopting a time transformation

$$t_c = k(T - t_p)$$

in which case the boundary conditions become 'initial' conditions in the computer programme, and the solution is then generated with time running backwards. This method of solution will not work if the boundary conditions are given at different instants of time (the split boundary problem): a way of dealing with this kind of problem will be discussed at some length later (see section 5.9).

The final observation that we may make about time scaling is that any ordinary differential equation in which the independent variable is not time can still be solved on an analogue computer by using the time scale transformation

$$t_c = kx$$

where x is the independent variable and k is a positive or negative scale factor.

3.5 Changes of scale factors

After using all the variations on inspired guesswork outlined in the preceding sections, the computer programme is patched up from the final scaled equation, and the computer solution is generated. The first run must always be regarded as a test run, in which the aim is not to obtain solutions to problems, but simply to check that the programme is correctly patched and correctly scaled. The first requirement is that no amplifier should overload; this is easily verified, because overload indicators are fitted on all computers. These take the form of a set of indicator lamps showing which amplifiers have reached the saturation limit, and there is also sometimes fitted an audible warning signal. More difficult to detect, but just as important, is the amplifier whose output varies over only a very small range, thus failing to make the best use of the dynamic range of the amplifier. We need also to make certain that the frequency of the computed solution is within the limits of operational efficiency of the computer and, more particularly, of the output recording devices. These limits will be discussed in later chapters (see sections 4.2 and 6.6): at the moment we need only note the possible requirement, in the light of preliminary computer runs, to change the time scale of the solution. These changes, both of amplitude and of time scalings, could, of course, be achieved by simply returning to the original equations and working out a new set of scaled equations, which could then be patched on the computer afresh. There are, however, easier ways of incorporating changes to the programme, without having to return to the beginning.

3.5.1 *Changing the amplitude scale*

We may illustrate modification methods by considering the implementation of

$$\frac{d^2x}{dt^2} + 2\frac{dx}{dt} + 16x = 1000 \tag{3.28}$$

with

$$x(0) = +20, \qquad \frac{dx}{dt}(0) = -100.$$

With a time scale factor of unity, we may estimate the maximum amplitudes of the variables by using the equal coefficient rule. This gives

$$(x)_{max} = 2 \cdot \frac{1000}{16} = 125$$

$$(Dx)_{max} = \frac{1000}{2} = 500.$$

We may now choose working variables of $(x/2)$ and $(Dx/5)$, and re-write equation 3.28 as

$$\left(\frac{D^2 x}{5}\right) = \frac{1000}{5} - 2\left(\frac{Dx}{5}\right) - \frac{16}{5} \cdot 2\left(\frac{x}{2}\right)$$

$$= 200 - 2\left(\frac{Dx}{5}\right) - 6 \cdot 4\left(\frac{x}{2}\right) \qquad (3.29)$$

If equation 3.29 is implemented on a computer, using the patching diagram shown in figure 3.9(a), it will be found that the maximum voltage appearing at the output of amplifier 1 is about 27 V, corresponding to 135 ft/sec (assuming that x is a displacement measured in feet), and that the maximum output from amplifier 2 is about 42 V, corresponding to 84 ft. This indicates that better scaling will be achieved if we take as working variables x and $(Dx/2)$. The circuit modifications needed to bring about these changes of variable will not involve any change of layout, but only alterations to the gains: this is why it is so much easier to change the wrongly scaled programme than to work out a new one from the start.

The first change required in figure 3.9(a) is in the gain between amplifiers 1 and 2; instead of being $\frac{1}{2} \div \frac{1}{5} = 2 \cdot 5$ it must become $1 \div \frac{1}{2} = 2$, so that potentiometer 4 must be set to $0 \cdot 2$. The other changes of gain that need to be made can now be worked out by using the fact that the equation being solved is still the same as it was originally; this implies that the total gain around any computing loop must be the same in the modified programme as it was in the original one. In the outer loop in figure 3.9(a) the total gain (neglecting minus signs) is $0 \cdot 25 \times 10 \times 1 \times 0 \cdot 64 \times 10 = 16$. Thus, taking into account

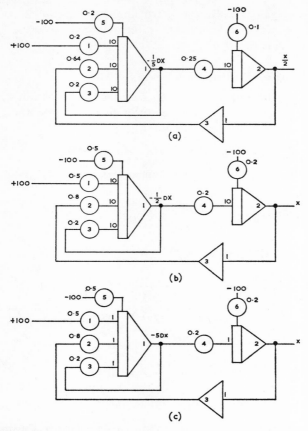

Fig. 3.9. Method of changing amplitude and time scales without having
to recalculate the whole problem.
  (a) Programme using unity time scale factor; working variables
      $x/2$ and $Dx/5$.
  (b) Modified programme using working variables x and $Dx/2$.
  (c) Further modification, changing the time scale by a factor
      of ten. The only effect on the programme is to change all the
      integrator gains by the same factor.

the gain of 2 between amplifiers 1 and 2, we need a gain of 8 between
amplifiers 3 and 1; potentiometer 2 must therefore be set to 0·8.
Potentiometer 3 needs no modification, because although amplifier
1 now has a different label on its output, there must still be no change

in the loop gain. Finally, the external input and the initial conditions must be altered to take account of the modified variables. The final programme is shown in figure 3.9(b).

3.5.2 Changing the time scale

If we consider again the system described by equation 3.28, and this time implement it with a ten times change of time scale, we will obtain the computer equation

$$100D^2x + 20Dx + 16x = 1000. \tag{3.30}$$

Using the maximum values obtained experimentally (as in section 3.5.1)

$$(x)_{max} = 90; \qquad \left(\frac{dx}{dt_p}\right)_{max} = 180 \qquad \therefore (Dx)_{max} = 18.$$

We may rewrite equation 3.30

$$5D^2x = \frac{5 \cdot 1000}{100} - \frac{20}{100}(5Dx) - \frac{16}{100} \cdot 5(x)$$

$$= 50 - 0 \cdot 2(5Dx) - 0 \cdot 8(x).$$

The initial conditions become

$$(5Dx)(0) = \frac{1}{10} \cdot 5 \cdot \frac{dx}{dt_p}(0) = -50$$

$$(x)(0) = 20.$$

Thus the programme becomes as shown in figure 3.9(c). The important feature of this as compared with the programme of figure 3.9(b) is that apart from the gains of the integrators the two are identical in every respect, including the independent inputs and the initial conditions. The interpretations of the variables are changed, such that each differential coefficient is with respect to the new time variable, and its multiplying factor is changed by the same factor as the time scale change. No changes are necessary in summers or inverters and the only change in integrators is a gain change equal to the time scale factor. The simplicity of this result is remarkable; the more so when we observe that a very convenient way of simultaneously changing the gain of all inputs to an integrator is simply to change the feedback capacitor. Many modern computers have a built-in facility to permit the feedback capacitors of all the integrators to be changed automatically by operating a central control switch (see section 5.5). This allows problems to be investigated at relatively high speed while preliminary results are obtained – permitting the use of an oscilloscope to display a repetitive solution – and also at much slower speed to obtain final results, the change of speed being effected by a single control. It should however be noticed that external inputs are unaffected only if they are constants. If a time-varying forcing function appears in a problem, then it also will have to be changed to take account of a change of time scale; this change will not be brought about by the computer time scale control unless the function is itself generated within the computer.

3.6 Notes and references

Scaling is, of necessity, dealt with in every book on analogue computing, and the reader who finds the treatment in this chapter obscure will have no difficulty in obtaining other explanations. Very full descriptions are given by Peterson and by Stewart and Atkinson, in each case including a number of worked examples and many additional exercises. An alternative approach to the subject, in which scale factors are carried right through the calculations, is advocated by Paul, but has not been used here because it involves the use of variables with multiple subscripts, and this seems more confusing than the method described in the chapter.

The equal coefficient rule was suggested without proof by Jackson. It certainly appears to provide very satisfactory estimates in most practical examples, and even when the conditions for the rule are not met it provides the basis for a reasonable first guess to enable a preliminary run to be made.

A very detailed discussion of all scaling methods is given by Levine, who also describes various tricks such as running time backwards. Of particular interest is the section on variable scaling techniques, which are designed to cater for problems in which a variable varies over a very wide range. In such problems, a scale factor that allows the largest values to be accommodated within the dynamic range of an amplifier would cause the smallest values to be lost in noise, so that if these small values need to be examined with any precision the scale has to be changed during the course of the computation.

REFERENCES

JACKSON, A. S. (1960). *Analog Computation*, McGraw-Hill, New York.

LEVINE, L. (1964). *Methods for Solving Engineering Problems Using Analog Computers*, McGraw-Hill, New York.

PAUL, R. J. A. (1965). *Fundamental Analogue Techniques*, Blackie, London.

PETERSON, G. R. (1967). *Basic Analog Computation*, Collier-Macmillan, New York.

STEWART, C. A. and ATKINSON, R. (1967). *Basic Analogue Computer Techniques*, McGraw-Hill, New York.

4 Input and Output Equipment

After having performed all the necessary manipulations on the form of a problem so that it is suitable for the computer, and after having also completed the scaling exercise as described in the last chapter, we are left with the practical problem of physically connecting up the computer elements in accordance with the final patching diagram. We need to consider how these connections are made in practical computers; how the computation is started and stopped; how the initial conditions are inserted into the integrators; and how results can be extracted in a useful form. This chapter considers the methods used to insert the problem and to extract the results. The techniques and equipment concerned with the control of computing operation are so important that they have been allocated a separate chapter (chapter 5).

4.1 Patchboards

In general purpose computers it is the universal practice to make permanent connections from the inputs and outputs of all the computing elements (amplifiers, computing resistors and capacitors, potentiometers and non-linear units) to a single area of the machine, and to obtain the required circuit for any particular problem by making direct connections between the appropriate terminals. In practice the computing elements terminate directly or indirectly in a matrix of sockets known as a *patchboard* and the interconnections are made by means of *patchcords* each of which is simply a wire with a plug on each end, used to short circuit a pair of sockets. When two adjacent sockets are to be connected together the normal practice is to use a bottle plug, which is a rigid or semi-rigid block fitted with two appropriately spaced plugs. A bottle plug is easier and quicker to patch than cords and also has the advantage that it is less likely to obscure the patchboard markings. One important consideration when designing the layout of the patchboard is that the most commonly occuring computer configurations should be able to be patched as much as possible with bottle plugs.

In any problem whose complexity is sufficient to justify the use of a computer at all, the number of computing elements employed is necessarily quite large. A medium size computer will have 50–100 amplifiers together with potentiometers and non-linear equipment, while the largest systems can have 500 or more amplifiers. The actual patching of a machine of this magnitude inevitably takes a long time, and it is clearly uneconomic to keep the whole machine standing idle for this period. Moreover, the results of any particular computer run will often need to be analysed and used as the basis for further computer runs incorporating minor modifications or additions to the programme or slight variations in the measurements made. Again it would be uneconomic to keep the machine standing idle while the analysis of the results is carried out, but to allow another user to run a separate programme would be unacceptable if it meant that the first programme would subsequently have to be repatched from the beginning.

The solution to this dilemma lies in the detachable patch panel or patchboard, in which the computer component terminations and the patchcord sockets are made physically separate. Different problems can then be applied to the computer by changing patchboards; these can be stored complete with the patchcords and the bottle plugs without the necessity of making any alteration to the patched programme. The provision of this facility makes the computer so much easier and more convenient in use that in practice nearly all modern analogue computers, even including some very small instructional machines, are fitted with detachable patchboards.

The construction of patchboard assemblies presents a number of problems, all of which have been solved by different manufacturers in slightly different ways. The basic problem is that we need to make simultaneously a large number of connections; the number of holes on the patchboard is not normally less than a hundred even for a very small machine, while in a big installation it can be several thousand. Every time that the patchboard is removed and replaced we required that each individual connection between a patchcord on the board and the corresponding fixed contact on the rear frame assembly must be firm and reliable, and have minimal contact resistance. Other mechanical constraints on the design are that the process of changing patchboards must not require undue physical strength and that inserted patchcords must be secure against displacement both during use and in storage. The main electrical constraint is the requirement for isolation between adjacent contacts both on the board and on the rear frame assembly and also for the avoidance of cross-talk in the cables connecting the rear frame assembly to the computing components themselves.

The extent to which these various specifications can be met depends to a large extent on the price we are prepared to pay for the patching system, and this in turn depends on the use to which the computer is to be put. The cheapest and simplest type of patching system, while quite adequate for many special purpose applications and for instructional or demonstration computers is not good enough for the more demanding problems for which a general purpose high speed computer is likely to be used.

Patching systems can be broadly divided into screened and unscreened systems. Screened systems use earthed metal patchboards to provide complete isolation between adjacent patching positions. In this case each cord is made of screened wire, and the screen is connected to the earthed part of the patchboard when the plug is pushed home. Screened systems are extremely expensive, and it has been found possible with modern materials to make insulated patchboards whose electrical properties are so good that screened patchboards are used only for a few of the most elaborate computers.

The general arrangement for fitting patchcords into the board are similar in all patching systems. The patchboard itself is invariably simply a support for the plugs, the connections being made directly between the tip of the plug and the termination in the rear frame assembly; it is in the way in which these two are brought together that the main differences between different systems lie. Perhaps the simplest of the systems (and certainly the cheapest) is illustrated in figure 4.1. The plug is held into the patch panel by a spring-loaded ball bearing, and the whole board is held in place in such a way that each plug presses against a spring loaded terminal. This arrangement ensures that there is an individual pressure exerted at each contact, but it is not ideal because with a simple pressure contact dirt and corrosion can intervene between the plug and the terminal, producing a high resistance connection. A better arrangement is to make a wiping contact, and this is done on the more elaborate patchboard

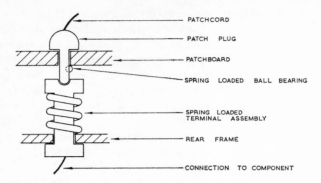

Fig. 4.1. A simple patchboard assembly. More elaborate systems arrange for a wiping contact between patchcord and rear frame.

systems by providing a two-directional movement of the board relative to the rear frame. The rear frame contacts then take the form of a set of springs, rather like relay springs in appearance and function. The patch panel is first moved onto the face of the rear frame, and then moved parallel with it so that each patch plug wipes against its corresponding spring. In this way, we again finish up with a positive pressure between plug and spring, as in the previous system, but over a long term the wiping action involved in this arrangement gives much better contacts than just pressure alone. The mechanical arrangements for each of these systems need to be quite elaborate: each position on the patch panel has to line up exactly with its corresponding rear frame terminal, and also a considerable total pressure has to be exerted on the whole panel in order to force it into its operating position against all the individual spring pressures. In some machines having very large patch panels, an electric motor is used to drive the panel into place; other machines have some kind of manually operated lever system. Either way, the complete patching assembly needs to be a precision made piece of equipment and is therefore very expensive.

Quite apart from its mechanical and electrical properties, an extremely important design feature of the patch panel is its layout. This has to be such as to simplify as far as possible the patching of the more usual circuits, and also needs to be marked in such a way that the functions of the components terminated at the patch bay are as far as possible obvious to the user. Some kind of pictorial layout is generally used, and there is also invariably a liberal use of colour in an attempt to make the whole system self-evident. The extent to which any particular machine actually achieves these ends is a matter of opinion: all have some merits, and none is without any ground for criticism. The ultimate truth of the matter is that no user can readily find his way round any patch panel until after he has spent some time actually operating the machine. The more complicated the machine the more true this is, but even the simplest requires some time for familiarization.

4.2 Output devices

A further important feature of a computer installation is the available range of devices for observing and measuring the results obtained from the computing components. The characteristics of these devices have important implications, as for example in determining the permissible range of frequencies in a signal that is to be recorded, and hence in limiting the choice of time scale in a problem.

4.2.1 *Oscilloscope*

The most important general purpose instrument in a computer laboratory is the oscilloscope. Its usefulness lies not so much in its ability to measure the final results of a computation as in its versatility in respect both of sensitivity and of frequency. Preliminary or trial runs are invariably made with the aid of an oscilloscope, which is able to give, in a very convenient form, an indication of the general shape of the solution and of the orders of magnitude of any or all of the computer variables. The results obtained from an oscilloscope would often not be sufficiently accurate for them to be used as the final results, but would certainly be more than adequate for the purpose of checking the patching and scaling of the problem. In addition, the oscilloscope is essential for detecting high frequency oscillations in the computer programme (see chapter 6) and for maintenance and adjustment purposes. Some computers have their oscilloscopes built in but this arrangement does not seem to have found favour with any of the larger manufacturers in this country.

The characteristics required of an oscilloscope that is to be used with a computer installation are not difficult to obtain from a normal commercial instrument. It is, however, essential to verify with any particular instrument that all the necessary or desirable features are available in a form convenient for use with computing circuits. The main points to watch out for may be summarized as follows.

(a) The upper end of the range of time base speeds needs to cover the high frequencies that are of interest in detecting possible parasitic oscillations or unstable loops in solutions (see sections 6.3 and 6.7).

(b) The lower end of the time base scale is often less well catered for than the upper end. It is desirable that a trace length of 10 sec or more should be obtainable; to allow a waveform of this length to be visible a long persistence screen is needed. Although the spread of repetitive methods of computation (see section 5.6) will eventually make the slow end of the time base range less important, the facilities are still very useful at present.

(c) The problem of synchronizing the time base to the computer waveform presents several difficulties. The easiest solution is often to produce the time base waveform within the computer, in which case it can be precisely controlled not only with respect to its time of starting but also with respect to its speed of travel. To be able to work in this way requires that the oscilloscope should be fitted with an 'external X' input facility; while this facility is in fact provided in very many oscilloscopes, some are rendered almost useless for computing purposes by having this input a.c. coupled to the X amplifiers.

(d) Quite apart from providing a time base from within the computer, it is often desirable to view plots of one computer variable against another. When simulating a position control servomechanism, for example, a phase plane plot (position plotted against speed) is of interest. To be able to do this conveniently requires not merely an external X input terminal but a complete X amplifier with calibrated gain settings and zero adjustments. Some double beam oscilloscopes incorporate a facility allowing one of the Y amplifiers to be used for this purpose, and the ultimate in convenience is to be provided with a switch on the front panel to permit immediate conversion from one mode of operation to the other.

(e) The final facility that is sometimes useful is that of intensity modulation of the spot (sometimes known as Z modulation). This facility is again often provided, but frequently requires a connection to be made to the rear or underneath the instrument. A front panel connection is preferable.

4.2.2 *Recorders*

The main difficulty that may be encountered in the use of an oscillo-scope to observe the output is that of displaying very slow waveforms extending over perhaps 30 sec. Even with a long persistence tube, such signals are difficult to see, and if there is likely to be any fine detail in the waveform, the necessarily cramped scale can cause it to be almost invisible. For observing waveforms over a long period, therefore, and for obtaining measurements of instantaneous values of particular signals, a recording device needs to give a permanent record of indefinite length.

The most straightforward form of recorder satisfying these requirements is the pen recorder, which in its simplest form consists essentially of a galvanometer movement with a pen mounted on the coil. The paper is driven past the pen by a motor at a speed that can be varied over a wide range by selection of different mechanical gearing. A diagrammatic view of this simple type of pen recorder

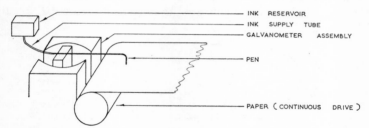

Fig. 4.2. Basic ink-writing pen recorder. Note that the pen gives a curved trace.

is shown in figure 4.2 and its most important characteristics are listed below.

(*a*) All curves obtained are necessarily plotted as functions of time. To obtain functions of variables other than time it is necessary to use an $X-Y$ plotter (described in section 4.2.3).

(*b*) Multiple traces are generally obtainable, up to eight pens being fitted in a single machine. The use of a large number of simultaneous recordings, however, usually means that each recording is very small, since, for mechanical reasons, overlap of the traces is not permissible.

(*c*) The co-ordinate system in the direction of the paper motion is curved because the pen tip moves through an arc of a circle. This makes the interpretation of simultaneous records a little more difficult than they would be when displayed on normal rectilinear co-ordinates.

(*d*) The use of ink as a writing medium brings with it a number of small but annoying practical complications concerned with keeping the ink supplies topped up, and the pens and supply tubes clear.

(*e*) In common with most electromechanical systems, the frequency response of this device is poor. Signal frequencies cannot be allowed to exceed about 10 Hz if recording accuracy is to be maintained within 1 %.

(*f*) Pen recorders have to be precision built mechanisms, and as such are inevitably very expensive.

The first and last of these characteristics are shared by all forms of strip chart recording device, but the other features are modified to a greater or lesser extent in some particular instruments.

One alternative form of pen recorder is illustrated in figure 4.3. The paper feed arrangements are the same as in figure 4.2, but the

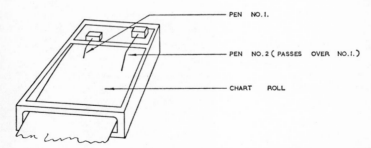

Fig. 4.3. A rectilinear multi-channel recorder in which each pen can write over the whole width of the paper, but the traces have to be slightly displaced to allow the pens to pass each other.

pens are mounted in linear runners and are positioned by servomechanisms. This arrangement produces rectilinear recordings, and by having the pens slightly staggered so that they are able to pass each other, allows full width recording on each trace. This however is achieved at the expense of having the traces offset along the time axis.

Another method of obtaining rectilinear motion is to use a rather complicated mechanical linkage to couple the galvonometer mov ment to the writing tip. This method is used, and works very well, but not surprisingly results in the instrument being even more expensive than the normal one.

The use of heat sensitive paper eliminates the use of ink and also gives rectilinear traces as shown in figure 4.4. The heated element

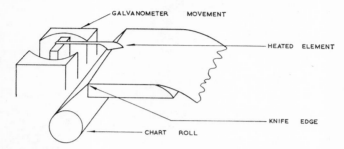

Fig. 4.4. A strip chart recorder using heat sensitive paper. The resulting recording is rectilinear.

marks the paper where it touches along the sharp straight edge placed perpendicular to the direction of paper movement. Heat sensitive paper, however, has its own problems; in particular, it is easily marked by mechanical handling, so that it is not ideal as a permanent record.

The poor frequency response inherent in mechanical systems has led to several attempts to work with lower inertia devices. One method in fairly common use is to use light sensitive (or ultra-violet sensitive) paper with a light spot deflected by a very small mirror. These instruments are usable at a frequency of 1 kHz or more. A second method that is sometimes used is to write on ordinary paper with a jet of ink. The nozzle, which is the only part that has to be moved, is again a very much smaller and lighter object than a pen and coil, but this system suffers from severe phase errors at fairly low frequencies. In many applications this may be less important than the amplitude response.

4.2.3 X–Y plotters

The problem of plotting one computer variable against another can be solved only by the use of an X–Y plotter (or plotting table). The principle of operation of the commonest type of plotter is shown in figure 4.5(a). The pen, together with its ink supply, is mounted

F

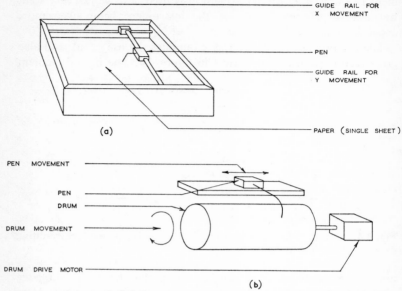

Fig. 4.5. $X-Y$ recorders allow any computer variable to be plotted as a function of any other computer variable.
(a) The most common form of $X-Y$ plotter.
(b) An alternative form, in which the driving systems for both axes are attached to the main frame.

above the writing surface on a bar, along which it can be positioned by a servomotor which is also mounted on the bar. Movement in the direction perpendicular to that of the bar is achieved by a second servomotor which moves the complete bar including the pen and the first servomotor system. As a result, the two inputs are very dissimilar with respect to frequency response because of the large difference in mass of the two servo systems.

An alternative form of plotter is illustrated in figure 4.5(b). This is similar to the recorder of figure 4.3, except that the paper is a single sheet wrapped round the drum rather than a continuous roll, and that the drum is driven by a servomotor rather than a continuous drive so that the drum can be positioned at will. This system has the advantage that the smaller servomotor is attached to the main frame of the instrument rather than being on a movable cross bar, but has the disadvantage that it is more awkward to change the paper. The most commonly used plotters are of the type shown in figure 4.5(a), although a modified form is quite often adopted, with a chart drive mechanism added. This allows the instrument to be used as a strip chart recorder as well as simplifying the process of changing the paper between recordings. An instrument of this form can also be used, with some additional equipment, for various non-linear function generation applications (see chapter 9).

4.3 Notes and references

The problems encountered in the construction of analogue computer components are discussed at length and in detail by Howe. Although his book was written some time ago much of it is still directly relevant today, especially his very lucid account of the merits of various patching systems.

Output equipment does not seem to receive much attention in the literature. Most books mention it briefly (as indeed this one has) but few devoted much space to it. The best accounts are to be found in Fifer (see Volume 2) and Korn and Korn, but for detailed explanations of the performance obtained, one has to rely on manufacturers' literature.

REFERENCES

FIFER, S. (1961) *Analog Computation*, 4 volumes, McGraw-Hill, New York.
HOWE, R. M. (1961). *Design Fundamentals of Analog Computer Components*, Van Nostrand, New York.
KORN, G. A. and KORN, T. M. (1964). *Electronic Analog and Hybrid Computers*, McGraw-Hill, New York.

5 Synchronous and Asynchronous Control of Computer Operations

The most significant advance in analogue computing in recent years has been due to the incorporation of high speed switching devices into the system. This has led to the adoption of asynchronous control methods which increase enormously the power and flexibility of the computer. These refinements are all based on the synchronous control systems used in conventional analogue computers; the workings of these systems will be discussed first.

The need for a computer control system is easily explained: the output of an integrator with a non-zero input is time-dependent, so that in order to obtain meaningful results we need some mechanism by which integrators can be started under the control of the operator. Provision must also be made for some convenient method of setting the initial conditions into the integrator before the computation is started and there must also be a way of setting potentiometers and of measuring settings obtained by trial and error. All these requirements are met by providing for various modes of operation of the computer, the selection of the mode being made by applying appropriate voltages to the coils of control relays or to electronic switches. This can be done either manually from a central control panel, or automatically by generating the control signals electronically. Electronic mode control becomes particularly important when we come to deal with iterative and hybrid systems; it is, however, important even in the simplest system to appreciate the differences between the various modes, and to understand what changes in the computer circuit take place as we switch from one mode to another.

There is unfortunately no universal standard terminology to describe the various modes, and variations on the names given here will be met with in practice, but for the principal modes at least current usage seems to be becoming uniform amongst the major manufacturers.

5.1 POTSET mode

Potentiometers for computer use are usually ten turn helical potentiometers with linearity of 0·1 % or better. These can be set mechanically by reference to the scale consisting of a turns counter and a fine scale divided into 100 divisions; this setting can readily and repeatedly be made to one part in a thousand. This would be perfectly acceptable were it not for the problem of potentiometer loading.

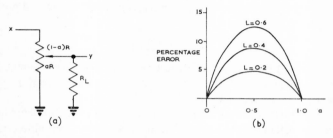

Fig. 5.1. The effect of loading a potentiometer is to make the electrical setting differ from the mechanical setting.
(a) A potentiometer with loading.
(b) Variation of fractional error with $L(= R/R_L)$.

Figure 5.1(a) shows a potentiometer, total resistance R, with a load of R_L attached to the wiper. If the mechanical setting is a, then we may assume that the potentiometer resistance is divided by the wiper into two parts aR and $(1-a)R$. The output, y, for an input x is then

$$y = [R'/(R'+(1-a)R)]x \qquad (5.1)$$

where R' is the equivalent resistance of R_L and aR in parallel.

$$\therefore R' = aRR_L/(aR+R_L). \qquad (5.2)$$

Substituting equation 5.2 into equation 5.1 gives

$$\frac{y}{x} = \frac{aRR_L}{aRR_L+(1-a)R(aR+R_L)}$$

$$= a/(1+a(1-a)L) \qquad (5.3)$$

where $L = R/R_L$ which is a measure of the loading. This shows that the electrical and mechanical settings, y/x and a, differ by an amount depending not only on the load applied but also on the setting itself.

The fractional error in setting may be obtained as

$$\epsilon = \frac{1}{a}\left[a - \frac{y}{x}\right] = 1 - \frac{1}{1 + a(1-a)L}$$

$$= \frac{a(1-a)L}{1 + a(1-a)L} \qquad (5.4)$$

By differentiating equation 5.4 with respect to a, we may show that the maximum value of the fractional error occurs at the mid position; this maximum has the value

$$\epsilon_{max} = L/(4+L) \qquad (5.5)$$

Figure 5.1(b) shows the variation of ϵ with a for various values of L, and it indicates that the errors obtained are far from negligible unless L can be made very small.

In the most common computer circuit, the potentiometer is used to set a coefficient at the input to an operational amplifier, so that R_L in figure 5.1(a) will be the input computing resistance. This resistance will almost never exceed 1MΩ even in 100-V computers, and we must certainly allow for it to be 100 kΩ. (In low voltage machines all the values are smaller, but the argument remains the same.) The only hope, therefore, of making L small is to make R, the overall potentiometer resistance, small. However, since this is the load on the previous computing element, there is obviously a limit to how much current can be supplied and this implies that a compromise has to be reached. The value of potentiometer resistance commonly chosen is in the range 25–50 kΩ: this means that values of L of 0·25–0·5 may be expected, and this (from figure 5.1(b)) would give rise to intolerable errors if the mechanical setting was taken as equal to the electrical setting.

The solution to this difficulty is to ignore the mechanical reading altogether for setting purposes, and to use instead a direct electrical measurement of the output at the wiper with the appropriate load connected and with the reference voltage applied to the top of the potentiometer. In making this measurement we must ensure that no additional loading is imposed on the potentiometer by the measuring equipment; one way of meeting this requirement is to use a Wheatstone Bridge arrangement as shown in figure 5.2(c), in which, in accordance with convention, the switches are shown in their un-operated positions. With both switches unoperated, the circuit is

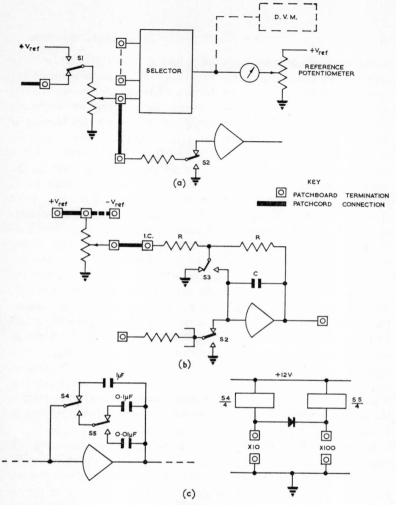

KEY

⊡ PATCHBOARD TERMINATION
▬ PATCHCORD CONNECTION

Fig. 5.2. Methods of providing the basic control requirements in an analogue system. Each switch is shown in the unoperated condition.

(a) Potentiometers are set by measuring the electrical setting. The mechanical setting (obtained from a calibrated dial and turns counter) is used only for general indication purposes.

(b) Integrators have three operating states, selected by the two switches.

(c) One form of TIME SCALE facility: integrators can be selected in groups of four for a change of capacitor. The value is changed by a factor of 10 or 100 depending on the patching.

connected in accordance with the patching, with the potentiometer acting as an attenuator in the usual way. When both switches are operated, switch S1 connects the top of the potentiometer to the positive reference supply, while switch S2 connects the summing junction to earth. This makes a negligible difference to the loading of the potentiometer since the summing junction is itself a virtual earth, but it is a necessary precaution against the risk of overloading the succeeding amplifier. The wipers of all the potentiometers in the machine are taken by way of a selector mechanism, which in its simplest form is a straightforward mechanical switch but in a more elaborate computer can be a diode switching matrix, and the output of the selector mechanism is connected through a centre-zero galvanometer to the wiper of a reference potentiometer. The setting procedure for this system is then to set the reference potentiometer to the desired ratio using the mechanical scale, and then to adjust the working potentiometer until a null is obtained on the galvanometer. At this point there is no load on the reference potentiometer, and so the electrical setting of this is the same as the mechanical setting, and because there is a null on the galvanometer, it follows that the electrical setting of the working potentiometer is also at the correct value although this will not be the same as its mechanical setting because of the load. If we need to measure the setting of a potentiometer that has been adjusted experimentally, then the procedure is worked in reverse: the reference potentiometer is adjusted to give a null reading and its mechanical setting is then taken as the required value.

This system has the merits of simplicity and cheapness, and can achieve surprising accuracy. It is however, a little cumbersome in use – particularly as we need to adjust two potentiometers for each setting. A more elegant arrangement than the use of a reference potentiometer is to fit a digital voltmeter (which is itself a form of Wheatstone Bridge) to read the output from the selector directly, the rest of the system remaining the same. Since digital voltmeters are very expensive, they are not normally fitted in small instructional computers, but their convenience and usefulness is such that they are standard equipment in all medium and large size general purpose computers.

The operating mode in which the switches S1 and S2 in figure 5.2(a) are both operated is called the POTSET mode. It is often also arranged that when this mode is selected the reference supplies are disconnected from the patch bay. In this case the patch bay terminations, which are exposed when the patch panel is removed, are made safe; for this reason POTSET mode should be selected not only when setting coefficient potentiometers but also prior to removing the patch panel and when doing patching with the panel in place. This instruction is almost invariably disregarded by operators, although the experience of putting a finger between the positive and negative 100-V supplies (each stabilized to give one or two amps at full voltage) can have a salutory effect. Two other points are worth noticing about this mode. Firstly, since all amplifier inputs are removed there is no possibility of overloads developing even if the patching is incorrect. This is, therefore, the right mode to enter if there are signs of trouble in any other mode. The second point to notice is that since the upper end of the potentiometer is disconnected from the patchboard, cascaded potentiometers cannot be set in this mode because the load on the first potentiometer would not then be correct (see section 6.2).

5.2 RESET mode

The next requirement for operating the computer is a facility for inserting the initial conditions into the integrators. The mode that provides for this is usually called the RESET mode, or sometimes INITIAL CONDITION mode, and the circuit employed is shown in figure 5.2(b). With the two switches S2 and S3 unoperated, the circuit is that of a normal integrator; with the two switches operated the circuit operation can be calculated in the same way as for summers and integrators (see section 2.4) by applying Kirchhoff's Law at the summing junction.

This gives

$$CR\frac{dy}{dt}+y = -V$$

where V is the voltage applied at the initial condition terminal, and y is the output of the amplifier. The solution to this is given by

$$y = -V(1-e^{-t/CR})$$

This represents an exponential approach to the value $-V$, which is the initial condition voltage inverted. The output is within 1 % of its final value after five time constants and within 0·01 % after ten time constants. Common values of C and R for a 100-V computer are 1 μF and 100 kΩ, so that in this case the output of the amplifier has to all intents and purposes reached the value $- V$ about one second after switching to RESET.

The setting of potentiometers associated with initial condition circuits is normally done with the computer in RESET rather than in POTSET. We can then look at the output of the amplifier directly with the digital voltmeter or the bridge circuit; this removes any discrepancy due to mismatching of the two resistors, and also provides a check that the initial condition is correct in sign as well as in magnitude, whereas in POTSET the top of the potentiometer is connected to the positive reference supply regardless of the way in which it is patched.

5.3 COMPUTE mode

With all the switches in figures 5.2(a) and 5.2(b) unoperated, the amplifiers and potentiometers are all connected as in the patching diagram so that the problem solution is then being generated. This is the COMPUTE mode, sometimes known as OPERATE or NORMAL.

5.4 HOLD mode

If in figure 5.2(b) S2 is operated and S3 is unoperated, the integrator is in the HOLD mode, in which the operational amplifier is left with no inputs but with its capacitor still connected between input and output. With an ideal capacitor (no leakage conductance) and an ideal operational amplifier (no input current) there is no path for any charge to flow from the capacitor. In this ideal situation, therefore, the output voltage of the amplifier would remain indefinitely at whatever value that it had had immediately prior to the selection of the HOLD mode. In practice the leakage paths that exist allow the capacitor to discharge exponentially, but with normal computing components the time constant of this decay can be anything up to an hour or more. This mode allows a solution to be halted at any point while perhaps readings are taken. A return to the COMPUTE mode will then cause the solution to continue from the point at which it had been interrupted.

5.5 Subsidiary modes: SLAVE and TIME SCALE

The three modes, RESET, COMPUTE, and HOLD, are the basic operating modes, and these, together with the setting up mode, POTSET, represent the essential control conditions that must be provided on any computer. Other modes provided are either variations on the basic modes, or else facilities that improve operating convenience.

When it is required to tackle a problem that needs more equipment than is available in a particular computer it may sometimes be possible to use a second computer to provide the additional components. For this arrangement to work, it is necessary to provide for a single overall control facility so that all the equipment in use in the two computers can be operated in synchronism. This is achieved by designating one of the computers as the 'master', whose control circuits will operate the whole system, and by putting the other computer, whose control circuits then become inoperative, into the SLAVE mode.

The provision of a TIME SCALE facility takes advantage of the fact that a given change in time scale of a computer solution can be accomplished as shown in chapter 3 simply by making the same change in the gain of each input to each integrator in the problem (see section 3.5.2). This is most easily achieved by changing all the feedback capacitors; the TIME SCALE mode provides for this by automatically switching all the amplifiers, or in some cases by switching some number of amplifiers as determined by the patching. Figure 5.2(c) shows the time scale circuit of one particular computer, in which groups of four integrators together can be selected for a time scale change of either ten or a hundred times by changing the capacitor value from 1 μF to 0·1 μF or 0·01 μF respectively.

5.6 Automatic mode selection: REPOP and ITERATIVE modes

A common requirement in analogue computation or simulation is to observe the effect on the overall system performance of changes in a particular parameter. This is achieved essentially by carrying out the computation repeatedly, changing the parameter between runs. A very convenient instrument for observing the qualitative effect of such changes is an oscilloscope, but for the most satisfactory results this requires a repetitive signal generated at a relatively high speed (a complete solution 10 or more times per sec) rather than a series of separate slow solutions. The change of speed is provided for by the TIME SCALE facility, and the repetitive generation of solutions can be obtained by using the REPOP facility.

The requirement in this mode of operation is that the computer should switch automatically from RESET to COMPUTE, remain in COMPUTE for some preset time, and then return to RESET to repeat the cycle. The time spent in RESET is usually fixed, and must be long enough to allow the integrators to take up their initial conditions; this time is normally determined by the values of the computing capacitor and the initial condition input resistor, although it may be necessary to allow longer RESET times if amplifiers are liable to overload (see section 6.6.4). The time spent in COMPUTE simply determines what length of solution is generated, and this time is set manually by a potentiometer on the control panel. The use of an oscilloscope in conjunction with the REPOP facility thus enables the overall effect of changes in a parameter to be seen at a glance by changing the appropriate potentiometer manually while the computer is running; detailed quantitative results can be obtained subsequently using the basic operating modes described above together with more accurate measuring instruments.

A more elaborate form of repetitive facility is provided on some computers in which a set of switching signals is generated (usually by a digital clock) to switch the computer through the cycle RESET – HOLD – COMPUTE – HOLD – RESET. . . . The increased elaboration of this facility (called ITERATIVE) compared with the REPOP facility consists not only of the inclusion of HOLD periods in the cycle but more significantly in the fact that the time spent in each of the modes is independently controlled by the operator. There may also be incorporated a counter that will stop the operation after a preselected number of compute periods. These features are of value in iterative computer operations but before this can be discussed we must first consider some additional facilities that can be obtained by other forms of mode control.

5.7 Summary of operating modes

Before developing the more elaborate variations on computer control, it is convenient to list the standard control modes already described, since these form the basis for the elaborations.

All the modes commonly met with in modern computers are amongst those described above. Some variations in nomenclature will be met with, and in some cases there will be additional modes – BALANCE and CHECK are two that have found favour in the past, but seem to be less popular now. The most important modes are summarized below, with reference to the control circuits shown in figure 5.2. It should be appreciated that the switches in these diagrams are in practice remotely controlled, taking the form of either relays or solid state switches.

COMPUTE
(Alternatives:
OPERATE: NORMAL)
All switches unoperated. Computer in state shown by patching diagram, with solution being generated.

RESET
(Alternative:
INITIAL CONDITION)
S2 and S3 operated; other switches unoperated. Integrators making exponential approach to initial condition voltage.

HOLD
S2 operated on integrators only; other switches unoperated. Summers connected normally. Computation 'frozen' with integrators holding their last values.

POTSET
S1 and S2 operated on all amplifiers; other switches unoperated. Potentiometers are correctly loaded, provided the load is not another potentiometer. Cascaded potentiometers and initial condition potentiometers should be set not in POTSET but in RESET.

SLAVE
All control functions of slave computer inoperative; control exercised by the master computer.

TIME SCALE
A mode used together with one of the other modes. S4 operated on some or all of the integrators (as determined by patching) to give an overall time scale change of 10:1; S5 operated to give a time scale change of 100:1.

REPOP
Automatic sequencing between COMPUTE and RESET. RESET time usually fixed; COMPUTE time determined by a preset manual control.

ITERATIVE
A more elaborate form of REPOP, in which the length of time spent in each mode (COMPUTE, RESET, and HOLD) can be controlled individually.

5.8 Asynchronously switched amplifiers

In everything that has been said so far about the control of operations in a computer, it has been tacitly assumed that we are dealing with a set of purely analogue signals applied to a group of computing components all of which are switched together into one or another of the operating modes. With pure analogue computation this method of operation is used, the mode selection being performed synchronously, whether under manual or repetitive control. A desire to increase the available speed of repetitive operation led to the adoption of electronic switches, which are both faster and more consistent than relays, and this suggested that it would be possible, and might sometimes be convenient, to base the decision to change modes on some criterion calculated within the computation itself. As soon as we introduce the idea of an automatic decision, and combine it with the control of two-state devices, whether these take the form of relays or of any other kind of switching device, we are clearly paving the way for the incorporation of the whole range of logic circuits and digital techniques into the analogue computing system. Taking this a stage further, there is no reason why the mode switching of all the amplifiers should necessarily be performed synchronously; if the logic inputs to the switches of each amplifier are made available separately then it is possible to operate asynchronously with the mode of each amplifier controlled individually either by logic decisions reached during the computation or by a preset timing sequence using a digital clock, or some other form of sequential switching circuit.

The inclusion of logic operations and signals into an analogue computer programme increases the flexibility of the device, but also demands an extension of symbolism so that analogue and digital signals can be distinguished. In addition, amplifiers need to have their control schedules indicated as well as their circuit functions. A consistent symbolism for these purposes will be presented in the remainder of this chapter, although in this as in so many other aspects of the subject there is as yet no universally accepted standard.

A discussion of logic circuits and the manipulation of logic expressions is beyond the scope of this book; the salient features of Boolean algebra and a symbolism for logic elements (on which there is also no universal agreement!) are summarized in appendix 1. On computer patching diagrams, digital inputs to analogue circuit blocks will be distinguished from analogue signals by having arrows on them.

The simplest digital component that we need to consider in analogue systems is an on-off switch. This can take several physical forms, which can be divided into electro-mechanical and electronic switches. The relay is an extremely versatile device, with a better ratio of forward to reverse resistance than any electronic switch, but suffers from an inability to work at high speed. Post Office relays

have operate and release times in the range 10–15 msec, and for low
speed working in instrumentation and control they still find many
applications, particularly in view of their ability to perform several
changeover switching functions at once. Much faster operation
(about 1 msec) can be obtained with a reed relay, but this can provide
only one on-off or changeover function per device. In all the techniques that are described throughout the remainder of this book,
there is in principle no reason why we should not replace all switches
by relays provided only that the speed of the operations involved is
sufficiently low.

Electronic switches can themselves take many forms, usually
based on diodes or transistors (particularly field effect transistors).
A very simple diode switch is shown in figure 5.3(a); this forms the

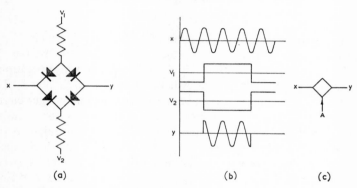

      (a)   (b)   (c)

Fig. 5.3. (a) A four-diode switch.
        (b) Waveforms in (a). The switching signals V_1 and V_2 are
            normally equal and opposite, with amplitude at least as
            large as the largest signal to be switched.
        (c) Symbol for a switch. A is a logic input, from which are
            derived the switching waveforms V_1 and V_2.

basis for the symbol that is commonly employed for all switches,
and which is shown in figure 5.3(c). In this diagram, A is a logic
signal having the value **0** or **1**; this represents the control signals
that need to be applied to make the switch operate. That is, if $A = \mathbf{1}$,
then the output is short-circuited to the input, while if $A = \mathbf{0}$, there
is an open circuit between input and output. The operation of the
simple form of diode switch (figure 5.3(a)) is illustrated in figure 5.3(b):
the circuit is analysed in detail in section 8.1.1.

The logic signals needed to drive switches can be obtained from two distinct sources. They can be generated from a purely digital source such as a sequential switching circuit operated by a digital clock. A clock and a quantity of logic circuitry is included as part of the complement of iterative and hybrid computers for the purpose of producing operating signals of this kind, but an important property of such computers is their ability to produce logic signals from an analogue computation. This ability to make decisions on the basis of some criterion computed as a continuous function within the analogue programme is vital to the execution of iterative procedures, and depends for its operation on a *Comparator*. This is a device that receives two analogue inputs x_1 and x_2 and gives a logic output, C, such that

$$\left. \begin{array}{l} C = 1 \text{ if } x_1 + x_2 > 0 \\ C = 0 \text{ if } x_1 + x_2 \leq 0 \end{array} \right\} \tag{5.6}$$

A comparator often takes the form of a Schmitt trigger circuit, so that the complementary output is normally available as well as the true one. A comparator action may also be produced using operational amplifiers: ways of doing this will be discussed in chapter 8. The effect of both the digital decision and its effect on an analogue circuit can be incorporated into a single device by using a relay on the output of an operational amplifier comparator. This is a convenient device provided the switching delays can be tolerated; for high speed applications an electronic comparator driving an electronic switch has to be used. Figure 5.4 shows the symbol that will be used for a comparator, whose output is defined by equation 5.6.

Fig. 5.4. A comparator gives a binary output which is 1 if the sum of the inputs is positive. The logic complement is also usually available.

The simplest way in which an electronic switch can be incorporated into an analogue computer programme is shown in figure 5.5(a). This switched summer, which is represented more compactly by the symbol shown in figure 5.5(b), produces the normal analogue output of $-\sum a_i x_i$ if, and only if, the logic signal $A = 1$. A variation of this idea is to incorporate the switch into some but not all of the input lines, The resulting device is symbolized in figure 5.5(c), where

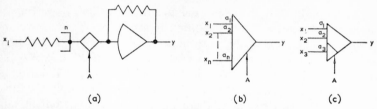

(a) (b) (c)

Fig. 5.5. A switch at the summing junction of a summer allows an analogue sum to appear under digital control.

(a) A switch controlling all the inputs.

(b) The switch can be symbolised by showing a logic signal entering the summer.

(c) If only some of the inputs are switched, while others are connected normally, the summer symbol may be partitioned.

the partition indicates those inputs that are affected by the logic signal.

All normal mode control, as has already been described, involves switching amplifiers in various ways. The three working modes, RESET, COMPUTE and HOLD, involve only integrators: summers are concerned only in POTSET. As indicated in figure 5.2(b), there are two switches essentially involved in the mode control of an integrator, and the usual practice is to arrange the circuit so that the normal (unoperated) states of both these switches corresponds to the COMPUTE mode. Logic signals are therefore required to switch the integrator to RESET or HOLD. We may indicate the logic signals by R and H and denote the integrator complete with its mode control logic inputs by the symbol shown in figure 5.6(a). Notice that the R

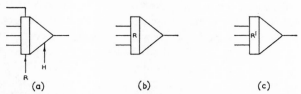

(a) (b) (c)

Fig. 5.6. Two logic signals are needed to control the operation of an integrator.

(a) The logic signals are distinguished by feeding the R signal to the rectangular part of the integrator symbol.

(b) A normal integrator operating under REPOP control is indicated by showing an R in the symbol.

(c) An integrator operated repetitively but with its control inverted is shown with R' in the symbol.

G

input goes into the rectangle of the integrator symbol, suggesting its association with the initial condition input. In one particular computer the operation of the integrator is such that if $R = 1$ it is in RESET; if $R = 0$ and $H = 1$ it is in HOLD; and if $R = H = 0$ the integrator is in COMPUTE. We might notice in passing, by referring to the switches in figure 5.2(b) that R and H are not simply the logic inputs to the two switches; there must be some logic circuitry in between.

For the control of normal analogue computer operations, the R and H logic inputs of all amplifiers are connected to busbars so that switching signals can be supplied simultaneously from the single central control switch. The same method is used when the computer is operated in the REPOP mode, except that the switching signals are generated electronically instead of being produced manually. In each case, as long as all the control is exercised synchronously, there is no notational problem, but because in an iterative computer the logic controls of each amplifier are available separately, we are no longer tied to synchronous operation, and it becomes necessary to distinguish not just between amplifiers performing different mathematical functions but also between amplifiers being operated in different ways.

The first class of integrators consists of those being operated in REPOP. These are indicated by having an R inside the rectangle of the symbol, as shown in figure 5.6(b). A simple variant of this is a 'complementary integrator' which has its R input driven by a signal that is the logic complement of the one used to drive the normal REPOP integrator. This has the effect of putting the complementary integrator into COMPUTE when the normal integrator is in RESET and into RESET when the normal integrator is in COMPUTE. In a computer fitted with ITERATIVE mode, where a HOLD period is incorporated into the iterative cycle, the R signal to the complementary integrator is modified so that all integrators enter HOLD together. This facility is necessary to enable the computer to have available a quiescent state in which all the integrators are held steady. A complementary integrator is denoted by the symbol shown in figure 5.6(c).

5.9 Iterative procedures

In order to understand the need for the other standard forms of synchronously switched amplifiers it is helpful to look first at a typical problem that can be tackled by the use of an iterative procedure,

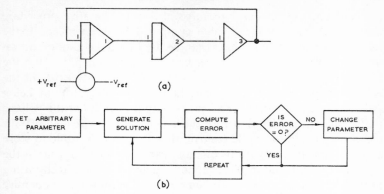

Fig. 5.7. (a) A split boundary problem, in which the initial condition of amplifier 1 is not known.
(b) The trial and error procedure used to find the initial condition.

so that the requirement for additional functional components will become clear.

A simple problem that can illustrate the techniques is represented by the equation:

$$\ddot{y}+y = 0$$
$$\left.\begin{array}{c} \ddot{y}+y = 0 \\ y(0) = 0, \quad y(T) = F \end{array}\right\} \quad (5.7)$$

with

Notice that this problem is fully specified – it can be readily solved analytically – but that the boundary conditions given are not in a form that allows the computer programme to be completely defined. The necessary programme is shown in figure 5.7(a); the difficulty lies in the fact that we do not know the initial condition of amplifier 1. This has to be determined by a trial and error procedure, modifying the potentiometer shown until the response curve $y(t)$ passes through the value F at time $t = T$. This could be done manually, using the procedure described in block diagram form in figure 5.7(b); this is a process of iteration – making successive modifications until the error is reduced to zero. A major function of iterative and hybrid computers is to enable such iterative procedures as this to be performed automatically.

5.9.1 *Analogue memory: the track-store amplifier*

One of the most important features of a digital computer, and one that accounts for a good deal of its usefulness, is its ability to store information. This ability is required also in the iterative procedure outlined above: the error value computed in one run has to be retained in some way so that it can be used to make a modification to the programme for the succeeding run. A device possessing the essential features of an analogue storage unit already exists in the conventional analogue computer, in that an integrator on being switched to the HOLD mode keeps its output (ideally) at the voltage that it had reached just before the mode change was made. With individual integrator mode control, therefore, it is possible to store any analogue quantity if this quantity can be made to appear at the output of an integrator. This cannot usually be done directly using normal integration; the most common requirement is that a quantity computed within the programme needs to be extracted and stored at some instant without interfering with the component amplifiers of the programme, as these are still required either to continue with the same computer run or to repeat the run after the parameter modifications have been made. The solution to this problem lies in the use of another operating mode: when the integrator is in RESET, the output of the amplifier makes an exponential approach to the initial condition voltage inverted. In normal operation the initial condition voltage is, of course, a constant, but there is nothing to prevent us from applying a varying voltage to the initial condition input. In this case the transfer function of the amplifier when in RESET is

$$\frac{y}{x} = -\frac{1}{1+CRs} \tag{5.8}$$

The output, y, will therefore follow the input, x, (with the usual inversion incorporated), provided that x varies slowly compared with the break frequency given by $\omega = 1/CR$. On switching to HOLD, the output will remain constant at its last value. An amplifier used in this way, following a varying 'initial condition' input and then storing the value reached at a particular instant, is called a track-store unit (or alternatively track-hold or sample and hold). Although the operation of the unit has been described in terms of the mode-switching of a standard integrator, this does not represent the ideal arrangement because of the relatively large time constant involved. A general purpose track-store unit while using the same circuit arrangement is normally a device separate from the integrators, typical values of C and R for a 100-V computer being 0·001 μF and 100 kΩ. Since only two modes are of interest in this device, a restricted

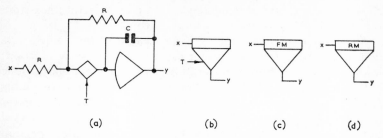

(a)   (b)   (c)   (d)

Fig. 5.8. Ordinary integrators can act as storage devices, but more
usually a separate device is used.
(a) The TRACK-STORE unit is switched by a single logic signal.
(b) A TRACK-STORE symbol is a rotated integrator with logic
input.
(c), (d) A TRACK-STORE element connected to the REPOP cycle
is called a forward memory (FM) if it is in TRACK when the
computer is in COMPUTE, and a reverse memory (RM) if it
is in STORE when the computer is in COMPUTE.

switching system is provided, as shown in figure 5.8(a) in which if
$T = 1$, then the amplifier is in TRACK with the transfer function given
in equation 5·8, while if $T = 0$ the amplifier is in STORE with the
output constant at the value that it had reached immediately before
T went from 1 to 0. A track-store amplifier is represented by the
symbol shown in figure 5.8(b). The use of an integrator symbol with
the input fed to the initial condition input emphasizes the essential
form of the circuit; having the symbol rotated indicates the different
purpose for which it is used. As has already been suggested a common
requirement for the track-store unit is to act as a memory device
working repetitively to store data obtained in one computer run so
that it can be used for a subsequent run. The two possible ways of
connecting the logic signals produced in the REPOP mode to the logic
input of the track-store unit result in the two basic elements shown in
figure 5.8(c) and 5.8(d). These two units are called forward and
reverse memories (denoted on the symbol by FM and RM respectively)
and their operation is defined as follows:

FM: TRACK when computer is in COMPUTE
     STORE when computer is in RESET or HOLD
RM: TRACK when computer is in RESET
     STORE when computer is in COMPUTE or HOLD.

It should be noticed that the STORE condition is not identical with the computer HOLD state; it is for this reason that the term track-store is preferable to track-hold so as to avoid confusion.

Although a separate amplifier is normally used for a track-store unit, a general purpose integrator can perform the same function; in this case a straightforward integrator with the input taken to the initial condition terminal and with no connections to the computing inputs will act as a reverse memory, while a complementary integrator connected in the same way acts as a forward memory. For general purpose integrators to be used successfully in this way the repetition speed needs to be kept low because of the generally longer time constant of the initial condition charging circuit; this will be improved by putting the integrator into TIME SCALE, although it is not usually possible to obtain in this way a time constant as small as that provided in a special purpose track-store unit.

5.9.2 Ratchet circuits

Returning to the split boundary problem defined by equation 5.7, and considering now how the iterative programme outlined in figure 5.7(b) can be automated, we see that the initial condition for amplifier 1 must be adjusted after each computer run, the extent of the modification being determined in both magnitude and sign by the error between $y_c(T)$, the computed value of y at $t = T$, and F, which is the required value of $y(T)$ specified in the problem.

The easiest way of obtaining $y_c(T)$ is by choosing the length of the COMPUTE period in the repetitive cycle to be T. A summer can then be used to form the function

$$E = F - y_c(t)$$

continuously throughout the COMPUTE period; the value of E at the end of this period will be the error, which must then be used to modify the initial condition for the next run. If the value of E is tracked by a forward memory, then the error will be stored during the RESET period. When the computer returns to COMPUTE, the track-store unit returns to TRACK so that the error from the previous run is then lost. In order to be able to keep this information, a second track-store connected as a reverse memory is required, as shown in figure 5.9(a). This arrangement of complementary track-store elements is commonly required in iterative procedures and is called a *ratchet circuit*. The working of the circuit is illustrated in figure 5.9(b) which shows first the repetitive cycle of computer modes and the corresponding states

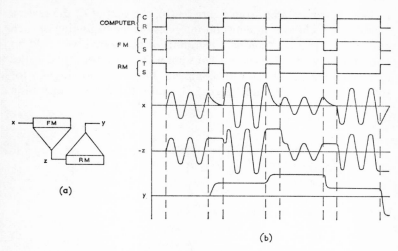

(a)

(b)

Fig. 5.9. To transfer information from one run to the next in iterative
programmes, it is necessary to use a ratchet circuit.
(a) A ratchet circuit consists of two memory elements.
(b) Waveforms illustrating the operation of a ratchet circuit.
The output of the forward memory is shown inverted. The
constant value of y during any given COMPUTE period is
equal to the value of x at the end of the preceding COMPUTE
period.

of the two memory amplifiers, and then the waveforms appearing at
each point in the circuit. The output of the forward memory is shown
inverted so that the tracking action of the amplifiers can be seen more
clearly.

In adjusting the parameter after each run, what is clearly required
is to make large changes when the error is large and small changes
when the error is small, so that it would seem reasonable to make the
change proportional to the error. We need therefore a device that will
retain the trial parameter value and add to it amounts proportional
to the successive errors, these being available in the form of a succes-
sion of step functions, as can be seen in figure 5.9(b). A device that
satisfies these conditions is a straightforward integrator; this main-
tains a constant output when its input is zero and generates a ramp
output in response to a constant input. The slope of this ramp is
proportional to the input so that if the integration is performed for a
constant time, the change of output is proportional to the input.

90   ANALOGUE AND ITERATIVE METHODS

In fact, as can be seen from figure 5.9(b), the output of the reverse
memory unit changes at constant intervals (at the beginning of each
RESET period); a continuous integration of this signal will yield an
output that eventually becomes constant when the error signal settles
to zero. Figure 5.10 shows a complete automatic programme for
solving equation 5.7, and figure 5.11 shows the detailed operation

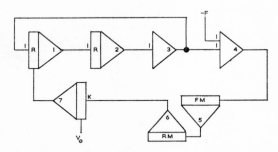

Fig. 5.10. A simple iterative programme to solve a split boundary
        problem. The COMPUTE time in the repetitive cycle is made
        equal to T.

of the circuit, with the output of amplifier N denoted by V_N and with
alternate outputs shown inverted. Note that a first approximation
can be applied in this problem by supplying an initial condition to
amplifier 7. There are several points of interest illustrated by this
programme:

(a) The change of sign of $\dot{y}(0)$ (V_7) during run 3 produces a 180°
    change of phase in the solution generated during run 4.

(b) The approach of V_7 to its final steady state has the appearance
    of a damped oscillation.

(c) The size of each modification is determined by K, the gain of
    integrator 7; the value chosen has to be a compromise between
    two unacceptable extremes. If K is increased, the damping of
    the oscillation of V_7 is reduced, and can become negative;
    if K is reduced, the damping is increased so that the time taken
    to reach the steady state value can be increased indefinitely.

(d) Integrator 7 is being used to accumulate the required value
    of $\dot{y}(0)$ on a trial and error basis, taking advantage of the fact
    that an integrator remains in a steady state when its input
    becomes zero. This enables it to be used in a closed loop

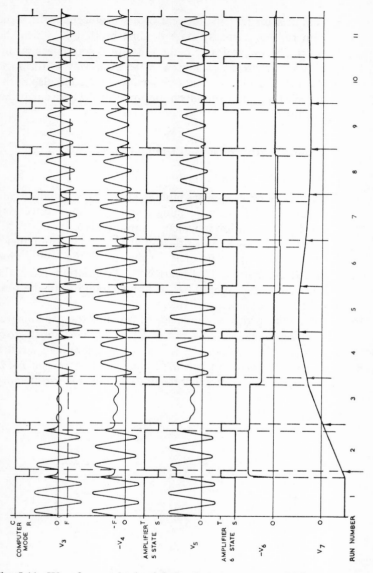

Fig. 5.11. Waveforms obtained from the programme of Fig. 5.10. V_n is the output from amplifier n. The outputs from alternate amplifiers are shown inverted so that the tracking actions are more easily seen.

system in a manner reminiscent of a servomechanism: if the system reaches a steady state it must be that in which the input to the integrator (c.f. the error in a servomechanism) vanishes. An integrator is used in the same way to form the basis of the backlash circuit (see section 8.5.2), and also in the solution of simultaneous algebraic equations, where equations of the form

$$\sum a_i x_i = 0$$

are converted to a pseudo-differential form

$$\sum a_i x_i = \dot{x}_i$$

In the steady state, $\dot{x}_i = 0$ so that the two sets of equations are identical. The integrator forming x_i from $\dot{x}_i$ is thus converging towards the condition in which its input is zero.

(e)   The value actually used for the initial condition of amplifier 1 on each run is the value of V_7 at the end of the reset period (marked in figure 5.11 by arrows). The output from the ratchet circuit, V_6, continues to be integrated until the next error signal becomes available.

In this particular problem the device of accumulating the answer in a free running integrator does not result in the most satisfactory solution because the modification made at the beginning of run n depends less on the error in run $n-1$ than on that in run $n-2$. Inspection of figure 5.11 shows that the output of the reverse memory

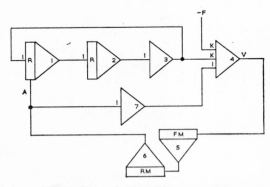

Fig. 5.12. An alternative solution to the split boundary problem, in which the required initial condition of amplifier 1 is accumulated directly in the TRACK-STORE unit (amplifier 6).

progresses in a stepwise fashion towards the target value of zero. If it can be arranged that the target value is itself the required initial condition voltage, then this signal can be used directly without the need for a further integrator.

A programme working on this principle is shown in figure 5.12; it will be seen that the parameter K, which determines the modification size, now appears at the input to amplifier 4. We can determine the effect of K in this particular problem by making use of the fact that it has a known analytical solution.

Since $y(0) = 0$ the solution to equation 5.7 is

$$y = A \sin t$$
$$\therefore \dot{y} = A \cos t$$

and so
$$\dot{y}(0) = A.$$

Thus the effect of altering the initial condition is simply to change the amplitude of the output waveform, as shown in figure 5.11. A change of sign of the initial condition, as noted in comment (a) above, results in a phase change of $180°$ – the solution becomes

$$y = |A| \sin (t+\pi).$$

If values computed on any computer run are denoted by the appropriate subscript, and if the final value of y (at $t = T$) is Y, then

$$Y_r = A_r \sin T$$

which may be written

$$Y_r = QA_r$$

where
$$Q = \sin T, \qquad (5.9)$$

which is a constant.

The error obtained is given by

$$E_r = F - Y_r$$
$$= F - QA_r$$
$$\therefore E_{r+1} = F - QA_{r+1} \qquad (5.10)$$

The output of amplifier 4 at the end of the computing run is

$$V_r = -[K(Y_r - F) - A_r]$$
$$= A_r + K(F - Y_r)$$
$$= A_r + KE_r.$$

This quantity is stored, and becomes the new initial condition for the following run, Hence,

$$A_{r+1} = A_r + KE_r \qquad (5.11)$$

Substituting equation 5.11 into equation 5.10 gives

$$E_{r+1} = F - Q(A_r + KE_r)$$
$$= F - QA_r - QKE_r$$
$$\therefore E_{r+1} = (1 - QK)E_r. \qquad (5.12)$$

If we are to approach a steady state value for A, then we require

$$|E_{r+1}/E_r| < 1 \text{ for all } r.$$

Hence, from equation 5.12

$$|1 - QK| < 1$$

or $\qquad\qquad 0 < QK < 2. \qquad (5.13)$

This confirms the intuitively reasonable supposition that if K is made too large then the value of A can oscillate increasingly about the target value instead of settling to a steady state. The other inequality expressed in relation 5.13, that QK must be positive, raises an additional point that is less obvious. From equation 5.9 it is clear that the sign of Q depends on the position of the boundary point, in accordance with the conditions

$$Q > 0 \text{ if } 2n\pi < T < (2n+1)\pi$$

$$Q < 0 \text{ if } (2n-1)\pi < T < 2n\pi$$

In the programme of figure 5.12 it has been assumed that Q is positive; if T had been specified such that Q is negative, an additional inverter would be required to satisfy the convergence condition. The analysis of the programme of figure 5.10 is less straightforward than that for figure 5.12 – equations 5.11 to 5.13 do not apply – but the qualitative conclusion is the same: the programme as it stands is correct provided Q is positive (as it is for the waveforms shown in figure 5.11) but requires an additional inverter for negative Q.

The final variation on computer control that will be dealt with here is needed when the solution is required over a period τ and the boundary value is quoted at time T where $T < \tau$. It is then not possible to use the simple ratchet circuit synchronized to the computer repetitive cycle. Instead, the ratchet must be controlled by specially

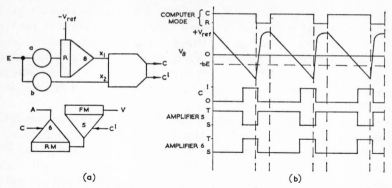

(a)　　　　　　　　　　　　　　　　(b)

Fig. 5.13. To extract a value other than at the end of the COMPUTE period requires a comparator to signal the appropriate time.
(a) Modification to the circuit of Fig. 5.12 for a COMPUTE time of τ, where $\tau > T$.
(b) Operation of this part of the circuit. Notice that the switching is reset at some indeterminate time within the RESET period.

produced logic signals so that the information transfer takes place at $t = \tau$ instead of at the end of the COMPUTE cycle. This is achieved by a comparator, as shown in figure 5.13(a), where the time is detected by generating a ramp

$$x_1 = V_{ref} - aEt$$

and comparing this with a constant

$$x_2 = bE.$$

The comparator therefore switches when

$$bE + V_{ref} - aEt = 0$$

or
$$t = \frac{bE + V_{ref}}{aE}$$

The operation of the circuit of figure 5.13(a) is shown in figure 5.13(b); the working of the remainder of the programme would be unaffected by the change.

5.10 Notes and references

The control of conventional analogue computers is described in nearly all computer books, although the details given differ from one book to another, probably reflecting the differences in construction of the various computers known to the authors. Normal mode control, however, is reasonably straightforward, and the differences between individual machines are not differences of principle but only of implementation. The interesting features of a computer control system are related, in fact, not to the way it is built, but to the way it is used.

The need for a REPOP facility in the solution of partial differential equations is well described by MacKay and Fisher. The first half of their book, describing the construction of a valve computer, is of little more than historical interest, but the computing procedures, and particularly the elegant display methods they developed, are still valid and useful.

Iterative methods in general receive surprisingly little attention in books. Ashley has a chapter describing the split boundary problem, and Paul gives a detailed discussion of iterative control methods and analogue memory elements, culminating in the formulation and solution of a number of problems in mathematics, ballistics, and structures. The most comprehensive general coverage of the topic is provided by Korn and Korn, who also include detailed solutions to various problems.

Iterative methods in the context of a particular machine (or series of machines) are very fully discussed in the programming manual produced by EAL. Dodds gives an introduction to the ideas behind the techniques, while Smith goes into more detail about implementation. This manual is potentially a valuable contribution to the literature, but unfortunately is spoilt by a very shoddy presentation (duplicated from a poor typescript) and complete lack of editorial effort (many misprints and no index). These faults, combined with a very high price, prevent the manual from realizing its potential.

The obvious extension of iterative techniques is to include not merely logic elements but a complete digital computer in the system. This requires a substantial increase in the complexity of the interface equipment, even apart from the large additional cost of the digital computer itself. The main problems are in analogue-digital and digital-analogue conversion, which have to take forms considerably more complicated than those suggested in this chapter. The problems are well described by Hoeschele, and there is also a useful section on the topic by Bekey and Karplus, who go on to describe the hardware and software necessary for the operation of full hybrid systems.

REFERENCES

ASHLEY, J. R. (1963). *Introduction to Analog Computation*, Wiley, New York.

BEKEY, G. A. and KARPLUS, W. J. (1968). *Hybrid Computation*, Wiley, New York.

HOESCHELE, D. F. (1968). *Analog-to-Digital/Digital-to-Analog Conversion Techniques*, Wiley, New York.

KORN, G. A. and KORN, T. M. (1964). *Electronic Analog and Hybrid Computers*, McGraw-Hill, New York.

MACKAY, D. M. and FISHER, M. E. (1962). *Analogue Computing at Ultra High Speed*, Chapman and Hall, London.

PAUL, R. J. A. (1965). *Fundamental Analogue Techniques*, Blackie, London.

EAL Staff: Advanced Techniques Manual: Programming Manual. Published by (and obtainable from) Electronic Associates Limited.
Chapter 7: DODDS, W. R. Introduction to Parallel Hybrid Computers.
Chapter 9: SMITH, R. Multispeed Computation.
Chapter 11: SMITH, R. Iteration and Optimisation.

6 Imperfections of Components

It has already been suggested in chapter 1 (see section 1.3) that interest in analogue computer circuits is not confined solely to their use as components in general purpose analogue computers, but that it is also concerned with their ability to perform useful functions as signal processing elements in instrumentation and control systems. These latter uses are becoming of increasing importance with the reduction in cost of transistors, and especially with the advent of integrated circuits. This has brought about a dramatic change in the economic feasibility of using analogue computer circuits for non-computational purposes: an amplifier that ten years ago cost anything up to £100 and occupied a volume of perhaps 1500 cm³ can now be replaced at a cost of under £10 by an amplifier having very similar performance but occupying a volume of less than 1 cm³. At the time of writing the cheapest operational amplifier known to the author costs less than £1. Admittedly the performance of this amplifier is not adequate for general purpose computing – the d.c. gain, for example, is only about 2000 – but it is quite good enough for many special purpose applications. An amplifier with a d.c. gain of 50,000 may be obtained for not much more than £3: these figures will almost certainly be further reduced with further advances in microcircuit technology. At this sort of price, data processing by analogue computation methods has become an attractive proposition, with the result that amplifiers varying widely in price and performance are produced not only by the manufacturers of computing components, but also by all the major semiconductor manufacturers. Some of the important characteristics and limitations of these amplifiers and of the circuits in which they are used will be discussed in this chapter: in particular, a potential user of amplifiers needs to understand the meaning of the various parameters used by manufacturers to specify performance.

The detailed circuit design of operational amplifiers however, is beyond the scope of this book and will not be discussed.

However operational amplifier circuits are to be used, whether in precision computing devices or in the generally less exacting applications in control, it is important to understand how the performance of the system is affected by the fact that the component parts have characteristics that depart from the ideal: it is essentially with errors in computing circuits that this chapter is concerned.

6.1 Transfer function of a general computing circuit

Perhaps the most straightforward way of looking at the question of errors in computing circuits is to compare the transfer function of any particular block containing its imperfect components with the transfer function that would have been obtained from an ideal block. To this end it is convenient to obtain a general transfer function from which the effects of various imperfections in the circuit may be deduced.

So far, all calculations involving operational amplifiers have represented the amplifier by the equivalent circuit of figure 6.1(a). This makes the implicit assumption that the output is zero when the input is zero. In practice it is not possible to obtain this condition simply by design, and all amplifiers have to be provided with balancing controls. In transistor amplifiers in particular there are two forms of unbalance possible: zero output is obtained only with a finite voltage at the summing junction and with a finite current being fed into the summing junction. These quantities, known as *offset voltage and current*, are provided for by means of additional inputs from the reference supplies to the first stage of the amplifier, and may be adjusted with preset potentiometers so that the output is truly zero when the signal inputs are all zero. These adjustments are not difficult, and the resultant unbalance can easily be reduced to an insignificant level; trouble with the arrangement arises because the offset voltage and current are not constant, but vary randomly with time and with ambient temperature. Offset current variations have to be supplied through the feedback impedance, and this results in further summing junction voltage drift; the two effects may thus be combined for the purpose of analysis, and represented by a single very low frequency random signal, e_d, appearing at the input to the amplifier as shown in the equivalent circuit of figure 6.1(b). This circuit also includes elements representing the finite input and output impedances of the

H

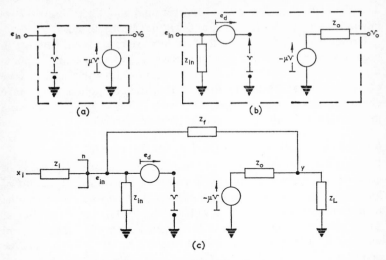

Fig. 6.1. A general computing amplifier circuit.
    (a) Model of an ideal amplifier.
    (b) A more realistic model.
    (c) The amplifier model incorporated into a computing circuit
       and driving a load. All the impedances, as well as the gain,
       are in general complex quantities.

amplifier. Amplifiers for use in computers are commonly drift-corrected (see section 6.5) but in special purpose applications this is not always necessary, especially with amplifiers having a field effect transistor input stage, but with valve amplifiers and with the cheaper types of transistor amplifier the problems are more serious, and frequent balancing may be necessary if the effects of drift are to be kept within acceptable limits.

Figure 6.1(c) shows a general computing circuit, consisting of an amplifier represented by its equivalent circuit, with input and feedback computing impedances connected, and supplying a load. It will be assumed that all the impedances are expressed in symbolic form as functions of s. This circuit can be analysed in the same way as were the idealized ones in chapter 2, by applying Kirchhoff's Law to the currents entering the summing junction. This gives

$$\sum_{i=1}^{n} \frac{x_i - e_g}{Z_i} = \frac{e_g - y}{Z_f} + \frac{e_g}{Z_{in}} \tag{6.1}$$

The amplifier has to supply the feedback and load impedances, giving a total output current of

$$i_0 = \frac{y - e_g}{Z_f} + \frac{y}{Z_L}$$

The output of the amplifier is related to its inputs by

$$y = -\mu v - Z_0 i_0$$

where

$$v = e_g + e_d$$

so that

$$y = -\mu(e_g + e_d) - Z_0\left(\frac{y - e_g}{Z_f} + \frac{y}{Z_L}\right) \qquad (6.2)$$

Eliminating e_g between equations 6.1 and 6.2 gives an overall expression relating the output to the inputs and the drift. Putting $Z_f/Z_i = G_i$ and $Z_f/Z_{in} = G_{in}$, this expression may be written

$$y = -\frac{\displaystyle\sum_{i=1}^{n} G_i x_i}{1 + \dfrac{1}{\mu}\left\{\dfrac{1 + \dfrac{Z_0}{Z_f} + \dfrac{Z_0}{Z_L}}{1 - \dfrac{Z_0}{Z_f}}\left[1 + G_{in} + \sum_{i=1}^{n} G_i\right]\right\}}$$

$$-\frac{1 + G_{in} + \displaystyle\sum_{i=1}^{n} G_i}{1 + \dfrac{1}{\mu}\left\{1 + \dfrac{Z_0}{Z_L} + \left(1 + \dfrac{Z_0}{Z_f} + \dfrac{Z_0}{Z_L}\right)\left[G_{in} + \sum_{i=1}^{n} G_i\right]\right\}} e_d. \qquad (6.3)$$

Equation 6.3 will be used to assess the errors arising in the basic computing circuits as a result of the imperfections that arise in practice. One point that should be particularly noted is that equation 6.3 is in vector form: in transfer function terms, all G values, and also μ, are functions of s, so that the performance at any frequency has to be determined from a complex expression representing both gain and phase shift.

6.2 Component tolerances and potentiometer settings

If the amplifier in figure 6.1 were ideal, it would have zero drift, zero output impedance, and infinite gain; substituting in equation 6.3

then gives

$$y = - \sum_{i=1}^{n} G_i x_i \qquad (6.4)$$

This is, not surprisingly, the same as the ideal relationship derived in chapter 2 and represents the target transfer function intended by the operator: it is mentioned here to draw attention to the fact that, apart from any other consideration, the transfer function realized depends for its accuracy on the values of the quantities G_i: these are in turn determined as products or ratios of the computing impedance values. Even if the amplifier is ideal, therefore, any departures from the nominal values of these impedances must represent errors in the transfer function.

The resistors used in general purpose computers have to be very high quality components; typically, high stability wirewound resistors with 0·0025 % tolerance, temperature coefficient of 0·0005 %/°C and long term variation within 0·0025 % over two years. It is much more difficult to obtain very low tolerance capacitors, so that it is the universal practice to provide trimming capacitors to enable the value to be set up by measurement. Temperature coefficients of capacitors also tend to be more difficult to keep within acceptable bounds, and this problem is often combatted by mounting all the computing capacitors in a temperature controlled oven. At the least, the capacitors must be protected from major temperature variations by keeping them well separated from power supplies and perhaps also by the use of fans to dissipate the heat produced in the computer.

For instrumentation purposes, the use of tight tolerance (and hence expensive) components may be avoided by matching to produce the required values of G_i, the final trimming being more conveniently performed with a potentiometer than with a capacitor. Similar trimming can also be used with summers to remove the static errors due to finite amplifier gain (see section 6.4).

Returning now to general purpose computers, a further accuracy limitation is imposed by the use of potentiometers to obtain the G values when they are not integral powers of ten. The problems of potentiometer loading effects was considered in chapter 5 (see section 5.1), and it was concluded that to obtain acceptable results potentiometers had to be set by direct measurement with the appropriate load connected. Under these conditions, settings can be made without difficulty to within 0·1 % of full scale. The uncertainty in the setting is related to the resolution of the potentiometer and of the measuring instrument, and so tends to be constant in magnitude, and independent of the required setting. This can lead to large errors if the setting is very small: an error of 0·001 (=0·1% of 1·0) would represent an error of 10% in a setting of 0·01. This is the reason why it was suggested earlier (see section 3.3.1) that very small settings should be avoided whenever possible. If, however, a small setting cannot be avoided, it is necessary to take steps to reduce the error.

One possible way of doing this would seem to be to use an amplifier with a reduced feedback impedance such that $|Z_f/Z_i| < 1$ in which case the amplifier itself would act as an attenuator. This method, however, is not as attractive in practice as it appears, because it imposes a very restricted range of operation on the amplifier: the errors due to noise and offset in an amplifier operating over 1% of its range could well be almost as great as those in setting a potentiometer to the corresponding ratio. The usual way to implement a very small potentiometer setting is to use two potentiometers in cascade; to obtain a setting of 0·01 for example, the two potentiometers could each be set to an electrical setting of 0·1. The uncertainty in each setting (0·001 as above) would then represent only about 1% of the setting, so that the total error even under the most unfavourable circumstances would not exceed 2%, as compared with 10% for the single setting.

An important point to observe if cascaded potentiometers are used is that the first potentiometer in the chain cannot be set correctly in the POTSET mode. This is because the load of the first potentiometer is the second potentiometer, which in POTSET is disconnected from the patchboard and connected to the reference supply (see section 5.1). The setting procedure has therefore to be more elaborate than usual: the second potentiometer can be set in POTSET in the normal way but the first potentiometer must then be set in RESET, with its input connected to the reference supply by patching.

6.3 Parasitic effects

As well as the departures of the computing impedances from their nominal values, which introduces amplitude (scaling) errors, we need also to consider the effects of parasitic impedances: the leakage resistance of capacitors and the stray capacitance in resistors. The changes that these effects introduce into the solution being generated are more difficult to deal with than a straightforward constant scaling effect: they produce unwanted phase shifts and gain changes both of which are frequency dependent.

6.3.1 *Capacitor leakage*

All practical capacitors suffer from leakage, with the result that a stored charge will gradually be dissipated. An integrator may thus be represented by the circuit of figure 6.2(a) in which R_f is a large but finite resistor shunting the feedback capacitor. Hence the value of Z_f is modified to

$$Z_f = R_f/(1+R_fCs).$$

Substituting this into equation 6.4 gives

$$\frac{y}{x} = -\frac{1}{R_iCs} \cdot \frac{R_fCs}{1+R_fCs}. \qquad (6.5)$$

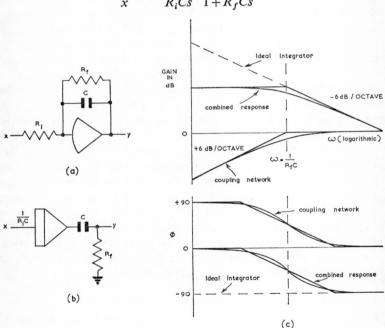

Fig. 6.2. The effect of capacitor leakage in an integrator.
    (a) Equivalent circuit (the amplifier is assumed ideal).
    (b) A more convenient form of equivalent circuit incorporating an ideal integrator.
    (c) Gain and phase responses of circuit (b).

The first term in equation 6.5 is the desired transfer function: an ideal integration with gain factor $1/R_iC$. The second term is equivalent to a C-R coupling network with time constant R_fC. The circuit can therefore be represented as shown in figure 6.2(b). The gain and phase responses of the integrator and of the coupling network are shown in figure 6.2(c) both individually and as a combined circuit. With present day materials leakage resistance is commonly of the order of 10^{11} Ω for a 1 μF capacitor, so that the break frequency is at about $\omega = 10^{-5}$ rad/sec. Thus the effect of leakage is felt only at extremely low frequencies, normally only with long periods of holding or integration. A somewhat more significant effect, however, is that of dielectric absorption. This can also be represented by a shunt resistor; in this case it is a frequency dependent resistor, with a value typically of the order of 10^{10} Ω at $\omega = 10$ rad/sec, falling to 10^8 Ω at $\omega = 100$. These values, however, are obtained only with high quality computing capacitors; in instrumentation applications, errors due to leakage and dielectric absorption can be significant if high quality components are not used.

6.3.2 *Stray capacitance of resistors*

The parasitic effects associated with resistors consist of the inductance of the element and the stray capacitance across its ends. In computing resistors, which are either 'non-inductive' wirewound or film resistors, the inductance is negligible at all computing frequencies so that we need consider only the capacitance effects. These have the effect of turning both input and feedback resistors into parallel R-C circuits,

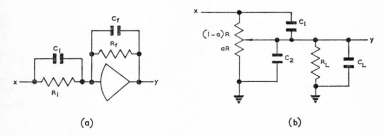

(a)   (b)

Fig. 6.3. Effects of stray capacitance.
    (a) In a summer the effects of stray capacitance can be cancelled by padding.
    (b) In a potentiometer exact compensation can be achieved only for a particular load and setting.

as shown in figure 6.3(a) giving an idealized transfer function for a summer of

$$\frac{y}{x} = -\frac{R_f}{R_i} \cdot \frac{1 + R_i C_i s}{1 + R_f C_f s}. \tag{6.6}$$

If $R_i C_i = R_f C_f$ then the transfer function of equation 6.6 is reduced to the ideal expression $-R_f/R_i$. This cancellation can be arranged by padding the resistors suitably; that is, by adding physical capacitors (perhaps 20 pF across a 1 MΩ resistor) so as to eliminate the effect of the strays. Padding of this kind is commonly incorporated with the computing components in general purpose computers: a significant improvement in the overall frequency response of a summer can be achieved in this way.

6.3.3 Potentiometer compensation

The stray capacitances associated with potentiometers are similar in origin to those associated with resistors, but are more significant in operation because they are more difficult to neutralize. Figure 6.3(b) shows a model of a potentiometer with a load represented by R_L and C_L, and the strays represented by capacitors between the wiper and each end of the track. The transfer function in this case depends in both magnitude and phase on the potentiometer setting, in accordance with the relationship

$$\frac{y}{x} = \frac{a}{1 + a(1-a)R/R_L} \cdot \frac{1 + (1-a)RC_1 s}{1 + \dfrac{a(1-a)RR_L}{R_L + a(1-a)R}(C_1 + C_2 + C_L)s}. \tag{6.7}$$

If $C_1 = C_2 = C_L = 0$, then equation 6.7 reduces to

$$\frac{y}{x} = \frac{a}{1 + a(1-a)R/R_L}, \tag{6.8}$$

which is the same as equation 5.3, and represents the effect of resistive loading: the electrical and mechanical settings are different. The methods of setting potentiometers, as previously discussed (see section 5.1), result in the electrical setting, represented by equation 6.8, being the same as the desired transfer function for the potentiometer. Hence, the only potentiometer error with which we need to be concerned now is that represented by the second term of equation 6.7, which shows that the stray capacitances introduce both a pole and a zero into the transfer function. These result in both phase lag and phase lead, the sign of the net phase change being a function of the loading and of the potentiometer setting. Examination of equation 6.7 shows that there is no simple means of compensating for the stray effects: we cannot make the pole and the zero coincide for all operating conditions. In instrumentation applications, in which a potentiometer may be used as a preset gain control with both the load and the setting fixed in operation, compensation can be applied by adding capacitance to either C_1 or C_2 as necessary to satisfy the condition

$$[R_L + a(1-a)R]C_1 = aR_L(C_1 + C_2 + C_L)$$

Typical values for a ten turn helical potentiometer are

$$R = 50 \, k\Omega, \qquad C_1 = C_2 = 200 \, \text{pF}.$$

If $a = 0.5$, $R_L = 1$ MΩ, $C_L = 200$ pF, then ideal compensation (within the limits of validity of the model of figure 6.3) is achieved by adding a further 200 pF between the wiper and the input end (across C_1).

Compensation of potentiometers for use in general purpose computers, in which neither the load nor the setting can be specified, is best achieved by using a tapped potentiometer in which fixed compensating capacitors are connected between the taps and the ends of the track. With nine taps it is possible to achieve a very good approximation to ideal compensation for all values of setting from 0.1 to 1.0, provided the load is constant.

An uncompensated potentiometer can easily give $\frac{1}{2}°$ phase shift at 1 kHz; with compensation, a 50 kHz square wave can be passed through the potentiometer without serious distortion – a rise time of perhaps 100 nsec compared with 5 μsec without compensation.

6.4 Finite gain and amplifier impedances

If in the general computing circuit of figure 6.1(c) the gain of the amplifier is not assumed to be infinite, then we see from equation 6.3 that the operating equation (still assuming zero drift and output impedance) becomes

$$y = - \frac{\sum\limits_{i=1}^{n} G_i x_i}{1 + \frac{1}{\mu}[1 + G_{in} + \sum\limits_{i=1}^{n} G_i]}. \tag{6.9}$$

Assuming that the second term in the denominator of equation 6.9 is small with respect to unity, we may write

$$y \simeq -\sum_{i=1}^{n} G_i x_i \left[1 - \frac{1}{\mu} \left(1 + G_{in} + \sum_{i=1}^{n} G_i \right) \right]. \qquad (6.10)$$

Hence the fractional error is given by

$$\epsilon \simeq \frac{1}{\mu} \left[1 + G_{in} + \sum_{i=1}^{n} G_i \right]. \qquad (6.11)$$

Equation 6.10 shows that the error depends not only on the open loop gain of the amplifier but also on the sum of the closed loop gains from each input to the output. We also see that in this respect the input impedance acts effectively as an additional input connected to the amplifier with a zero signal applied to it.

6.4.1 Summers with finite gain

If figure 6.1(c) represents a summer, Z_f is a resistor, so that all G_i are positive real numbers (neglecting parasitic effects). The resulting fractional error, as we can see from equation 6.11, is inversely proportional to μ and is a real quantity (provided μ is real). From this equation, we can obtain a numerical estimate of the amplifier gain required to keep the static error within any specified limits. For example, if an amplifier is being used as an inverter and we require $0 \cdot 1\%$ accuracy, then (ignoring G_{in} and Z_0 for the moment) we would require a minimum value of μ given by

$$\mu = \frac{1+1}{0 \cdot 1 \times 10^{-2}} = 2000.$$

If, on the other hand, the amplifier is required as a summer with two inputs at a gain of 10 and two at a gain of 1, the minimum amplifier gain required for the same accuracy becomes

$$\mu = \frac{1+22}{0 \cdot 1 \times 10^{-2}} = 23,000.$$

It should, however, be noticed that this error is simply one of scaling, and for a fixed purpose device the error could be removed completely by adjusting the computing resistors.

6.4.2 *Integrators with finite gain*

In an integrator, Z_f (and therefore each G_i) is a complex quantity so that the error terms in equation 6.11 represent changes not only in magnitude but also in phase. The effect is most easily illustrated by considering an integrator with a single input, for which equation 6.9 becomes (neglecting the input and output impedance terms again)

$$y = - \frac{\dfrac{1}{RCs} x}{1 + \dfrac{1}{\mu}\left(1 + \dfrac{1}{RCs}\right)}. \tag{6.12}$$

We may legitimately neglect $1/\mu$ with respect to 1 in the denominator of this equation, but at low frequencies $1/\mu RCs$ could become significant. Equation 6.12 can then be rewritten as

$$y = \left(-\frac{1}{RCs} x\right)\left(\frac{\mu RCs}{1 + \mu RCs}\right). \tag{6.13}$$

Equation 6.13 is identical in form with equation 6.5, and may be represented as an ideal integrator followed by a high pass filter network as in figure 6.2(b), for which the overall gain and phase characteristics are shown in figure 6.2(c). In this case the break frequency is given by

$$\omega_b = \frac{1}{\mu RC} = \frac{G}{\mu},$$

where G is the nominal closed loop gain.

With several inputs connected, the analysis shows that the effect is analogous to that represented by equation 6.13; an ideal integrator followed by a high pass filter, with the break point in this case at

$$\omega_b = \frac{1}{\mu} \sum_{i=1}^{n} G_i \tag{6.14}$$

As with the summer, therefore, the effect produced by the finite gain of the amplifier is dependent upon the sum of all the closed loop gains. Unlike the summer, however, this error is not a scaling error which can be compensated by adjusting the values of the computing impedance ratios, but a frequency dependent error which can be eliminated only by an appropriate choice of operating frequency. This effect is only at very low frequencies, and so determines the lower limit of operation of the integrator. The most significant feature of the effect is the phase change, which as pointed out in appendix 2 (see section A2.2), exceeds $\frac{1}{2}°$ for two decades either side of the break frequency. We may therefore use equation 6.14 to estimate the minimum gain required to keep the phase shift to below $\frac{1}{2}°$ at a given working frequency, ω, by assuming that the break frequency needs to be $0\cdot01\ \omega$. (The importance of phase shift to the operation of the circuit will be discussed in section 6.7: it will turn out that $\frac{1}{2}°$ phase shift can have serious consequences). This gives

$$\mu_{min} \simeq \frac{1}{0\cdot01\ \omega} \sum_{i=1}^{n} G_i.$$

For $\omega = 0\cdot1$ rad/sec and $\sum G_i = 20$, $\mu_{min} \simeq 20{,}000$.

6.4.3 Effect of finite input impedance

For both summers and integrators, as can be seen from equations 6.9 and 6.11, the input impedance contributes to the errors as though it were an additional computing input impedance.

The complete input impedance can be represented by a parallel combination of a resistance and a capacitance. Thus G_{in} may be expressed as the sum of two terms due to the two components R_{in} and C_{in}, giving

$$G_{in} = \frac{Z_f}{Z_{in}} = \frac{Z_f}{R_{in}} + Z_f C_{in} s. \tag{6.15}$$

The term due to the resistive component, Z_f/R_{in}, simply increases the effective value of $\sum G_i$, thus increasing the scaling error in summers and increasing the low frequency break point in integrators. In each case it can be interpreted as causing an increase in the minimum gain required to obtain a given performance. The value of R_{in} obtained in practice varies greatly depending on the kind of input stage used. The commonest range of values is 100 KΩ to 2 MΩ, although FET input stages have $R_{in} \sim 10^{11}$ Ω.

The capacitative component of the input impedance introduces new errors. In an integrator, for which $Z_f = 1/Cs$, the second term of the equation 6.15 is a real quantity C_{in}/C, which then represents a scaling error. This error is normally insignificant, since C is in the range $0\cdot01$ to 1 μf, while C_{in} can be anything from about 100 pF down to less than 5 pF for an FET input stage. Even if $C_{in} = 100$ pF and $C = 0\cdot01$ μF, this ratio is only $0\cdot01$, and from equation 6.11

we see that this would increase the resultant error by $1/\mu\%$.

In a summer, the existence of a finite C_{in} introduces a phase error. To a first approximation, the effect may be represented by

$$y = -\sum_{i=1}^{n} G_i x_i \cdot \frac{1}{1+\frac{1}{\mu} R_f C_{in} s}.$$

This is equivalent to an ideal summer followed by a low pass filter, the break point being at

$$\omega_b = \frac{\mu}{R_f C_{in}}.$$

The phase shift introduced by this is a high frequency effect which would set an upper limit to the working frequency, but with modern operational amplifiers this break point is at a higher frequency than other break points introduced by the amplifier itself (see section 6.6). The significant effect of this additional phase shift is that in conjunction with the amplifier phase shifts it can cause stability problems (see section 6.7).

6.4.4 *Effect of finite output impedance*

Examination of equation 6.3 shows that a non-zero output impedance effectively reduces the value of gain, μ. In practice, the value of Z_0, although finite, is still very small, and generally terms such as Z_0/Z_f and Z_0/Z_L have a negligible effect on the transfer function, appearing only as second order effects where they make marginal contributions to the static errors and low frequency break points. The effect of output impedance will not, therefore, be considered further.

6.5 Drift

The effect of drift on the output of a computing amplifier may be assessed by examining the second term of equation 6.3. We may invoke the superpostion principle to assert that the additional errors due to drift can be obtained by examining the circuit with all the inputs, x_i, put equal to zero. Thus the output due to drift (assuming zero output impedance) is given by

$$y_d = -\frac{1+G_{in}+\sum_{i=1}^{n} G_i}{1+\frac{1}{\mu}\left[1+G_{in}+\sum_{i=1}^{n} G_i\right]} \cdot e_d. \tag{6.16}$$

The first point that should be noticed from equation 6.16 is that even if the amplifier gain is infinite, the drift error is still finite. The drift voltage acts essentially as an input at a very low frequency, so that the amplifier gain is at its d.c. value; for most amplifiers it would be reasonable therefore to neglect the bracketed term in the denominator of equation 6.16, giving

$$y_d \simeq -(1 + G_{in} + \sum_{i=1}^{n} G_i) e_d. \tag{6.17}$$

In a summer, this error can be kept within bounds by balancing the amplifiers at reasonable intervals. Equation 6.17 can be used to provide an estimate of the necessary balancing interval: for example to keep a 10-V amplifier within 0·1 % if its drift rate is 50 μV/day and the total closed loop gain including the G_{in} term is 20, it is necessary to balance at intervals of

$$N = \frac{0·01}{21 \times 50 \times 10^{-6}} \simeq 10 \text{ days.}$$

This interval is further reduced by the offset current drift: in this case weekly balancing is clearly indicated.

In an integrator the error indicated by equation 6.17 is less easily disposed of: the second term represents an integration of the drift voltage during the computing period. During this period, the drift voltage can be taken as constant, so that the resultant output is a linearly increasing function of time. Thus, extending the example used above, if the drift has reached 0·5 mV, the maximum allowable integration time if the error is to be less than 0·1 % of 10 V is

$$t = \frac{0·01}{0·5 \times 10^{-3} \times 20} = 1 \text{ sec.}$$

Clearly a 6 % error after only 1 min of computation is not acceptable under any circumstances, and neither is the alternative of more frequent balancing, since to allow 1 min of computation with less than 0·1 % error requires the drift to be kept below

$$e_d = \frac{0·01}{20 \times 60} \simeq 8 \, \mu\text{V.}$$

Thus the amplifiers would have to be balanced every few hours – clearly an impracticable requirement even for a single amplifier;

in a computer installation containing many amplifiers it would mean that the computer would never be ready for use. When integrators are connected in computing loops, the situation is not quite as bad, because the drift tends to be cancelled by the feedback. Nevertheless, it is this basic difficulty that leads to the universal adoption in general purpose analogue computers of some form of automatic drift correction.

6.5.1 *Use of a.c. amplifiers*

Drift is essentially a d.c. phenomenon, representing the changes in the d.c. operating conditions of the circuit brought about by ageing of the components, temperature changes, and variations in the power supplies. Drift does not greatly affect an a.c. amplifier where the d.c. component of the output is removed by blocking capacitors so that the output is equal to zero when the input is zero independently of changes that occur in the working points of the individual amplifier stages. To be able to use such an amplifier for analogue computation with d.c. signals, a modulated carrier-system would have to be used, requiring a modulator, a.c. amplifier, and demodulator. The modulation can be achieved with a repetitively operated relay that connects the amplifier input alternately to the computing signal and to earth. This results in the signal being 'chopped' at the switching frequency; the relay is generally called a chopper relay. The chopped signal, after being amplified, can be demodulated by a second similar chopper synchronized to the first; this is achieved in practice by using a single chopper to perform both the modulation and the demodulation, as shown in figure 6.4(a). The waveforms obtained at various points in this system are shown in figure 6.4(b): it will be seen that the system is phase-sensitive, (that is, the sign of the output depends on the sign of the input) and it should be particularly noticed that there is an overall phase inversion from input to output although the gain of the a.c. amplifier itself is positive.

6.5.2 *Chopper stabilized amplifiers*

Although an a.c. amplifier of the kind described above can virtually eliminate drift, its use brings with it a compensating disadvantage. The low pass filter, necessary for the removal of the switching frequency component of the amplifier output, also has the effect of reducing the response of the system to higher frequency signals. In

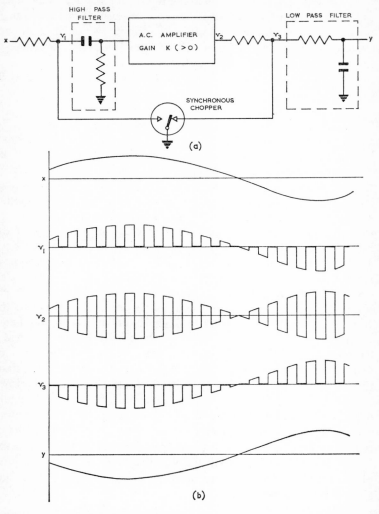

Fig. 6.4. D.c. amplification can be achieved without drift by using an a.c. amplifier with modulation and demodulation.

(a) A chopper amplifier, with a single vibrating relay contact performing both modulation and demodulation.

(b) Waveforms obtained from (a). Notice the inversion between input and output.

any case, the highest signal frequency that can be tolerated in the modulation system is perhaps 5% of the chopper frequency. The choppers commonly used are electromechanical, running at a frequency of not more than 400 Hz, so that a maximum signal frequency of about 20 Hz seems to be indicated. A solid state chopper operating at a very much higher frequency could increase the range of operation, but this brings further difficulties such as the need to eliminate switching spikes.

The method normally adopted, whereby we can obtain a substantial reduction in the drift without sacrificing the high frequency response, is to use the system shown in figure 6.5, in which an a.c. amplifier is used as an auxiliary amplifier whose sole purpose is to improve the drift characteristic, while a normal d.c. amplifier is used to maintain performance over a useful range of computing frequencies. The

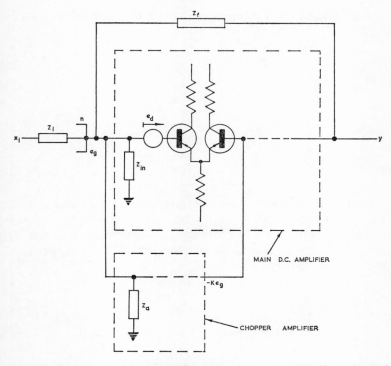

Fig. 6.5. A drift corrected amplifier using a chopper stabilizer channel with a differential d.c. amplifier.

I

chopper stabilizer is the system of figure 6.4(a), and is represented as having an input impedance Z_a and an overall gain of $-K$. The d.c. amplifier has a balanced differential input stage; the summing junction is connected to the inverting input, and the output from the chopper stabilizer is connected to the non-inverting input. The output of the amplifier, assuming zero output impedance, is thus given by

$$y = -\mu(e_g + e_d) + \mu(-Ke_g)$$
$$= -\mu(1 + K)e_g - \mu e_d$$
$$\therefore y = -\mu'(e_g + e_d') \tag{6.18}$$

where

$$\mu' = \mu(1 + K) \tag{6.19}$$

$$e_d' = \frac{e_d}{1 + K}. \tag{6.20}$$

Applying Kirchhoff's current law at the summing junction gives

$$\sum_{i=1}^{n} \frac{x_i - e_g}{Z_i} = \frac{e_g - y}{Z_f} + \frac{e_g}{Z_{in}} + \frac{e_g}{Z_a}$$

which may be written

$$\sum_{i=1}^{n} \frac{x_i - e_g}{Z_i} = \frac{e_g - y}{Z_f} + \frac{e_g}{Z_{in}'} \tag{6.21}$$

where

$$\frac{1}{Z_{in}'} = \frac{1}{Z_{in}} + \frac{1}{Z_a}. \tag{6.22}$$

Equations 6.18 and 6.21 may be compared with equations 6.2 and 6.1 respectively: it will be seen that with the assumption of zero output impedance they are identical in form, with μ', e_d', and Z_{in}' substituted for μ, e_d, and Z_{in}. Thus the output is given by the equation analogous to equation 6.3:

$$y = -\frac{\displaystyle\sum_{i=1}^{n} G_i x_i}{1 + \dfrac{1}{\mu'}\left[1 + G_{in}' + \displaystyle\sum_{i=1}^{n} G_i\right]} - \frac{1 + G_{in}' + \displaystyle\sum_{i=1}^{n} G_i}{1 + \dfrac{1}{\mu'}\left[1 + G_{in}' + \displaystyle\sum_{i=1}^{n} G_i\right]} e_d' \tag{6.23}$$

Substituting from equations 6.19 and 6.20 into equation 6.23 then gives

$$y = -\frac{\sum_{i=1}^{n} G_i x_i}{1 + \dfrac{1}{\mu(1+K)}\left[1 + G'_{in} + \sum_{i=1}^{n} G_i\right]}$$

$$-\frac{1 + G'_{in} + \sum_{i=1}^{n} G_i}{1 + \dfrac{1}{\mu(1+K)}\left[1 + G'_{in} + \sum_{i=1}^{n} G_i\right]} \cdot \frac{e_d}{1+K}. \qquad (6.24)$$

A comparison between equations 6.3 and 6.24 now enables us to assess the overall effect of incorporating a chopper stabilizer into the amplifier. The conclusions are:

(a) The errors due to finite gain are reduced by a factor $(1+K)$. This improves the static accuracy of summers (see section 6.4.1) and reduces the low frequency break point of integrators (see section 6.4.2).

(b) The drift voltage is effectively reduced by a factor $(1+K)$, although this is offset by an increase in G'_{in} compared with G_{in}. However, this increase is only of the order of unity, whereas K can be of the order of 1000.

It should be noticed that the gain of the chopper stabilizer channel falls with frequency due to the low pass filter until it is virtually zero at a comparatively low frequency (usually not more than a few Hz). The drift, being essentially d.c., suffers maximum effective attenuation, but it is only the *static* accuracy of summers that is improved: dynamic accuracy is still determined essentially by μ. It is the presence of a stabilizer channel that results in the very high d.c. gains ($\sim10^8$ or more) quoted for computing amplifiers (see section 2.3).

6.6 Limitations of operational amplifiers

Throughout the discussions of the performance of operational amplifier circuits, it has so far always been assumed that the gain of the amplifier could be represented simply by a negative real number, implying that the magnitude of the gain is constant and that the phase shift through the amplifier is always exactly 180°. We have also not considered any limitation on performance due to the finite power output capabilities of the amplifier. These limitations, together with the frequency dependence of the gain, have important implications in computation, and particularly need to be considered when choosing an operational amplifier for a special purpose application.

6.6.1 *Bandwidth*

As in virtually all other electronic circuits, the gain of an operational amplifier varies both in magnitude and in phase as a function of frequency. The d.c. open-loop gain is invariably specified as one measure of the performance, but the frequency dependence is, in many applications, of equal importance.

The change of gain with frequency is brought about by the existence of capacitance in the circuit. The impedance of a capacitive path to earth reduces as the frequency increases so that ultimately it acts as a virtual short circuit. Thus the magnitude of the gain tends towards zero while the phase lag increases from its d.c. value of 180° to a value determined by the effective number of capacitative circuits (*i.e.* the number of poles in the transfer function).

The capacitance in a single amplifier stage may be represented by the circuit of figure 6.6(a), in which the ideal amplifier producing a signal of Ax is connected to the output by way of a low pass filter

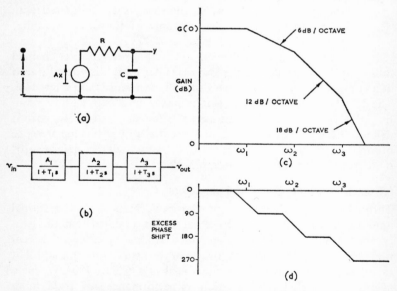

Fig. 6.6. Capacitative elements, either physical or parasitic, apply frequency limitations to amplifiers.
    (a) Simple amplifier model.
    (b) A multi-stage amplifier.
    (c), (d) Gain and phase reponses of (b). This system is unstable.

consisting of the output resistance R and the effective capacitance C. The response of the filter (see appendix 2, section A2.3), causes the amplifier gain to fall from its d.c. value A (which must, of course, be negative) at a rate of 6 dB/octave beyond the break point frequency given by $\omega = 1/CR$ rad/sec. It should again be noticed that the phase variation starts to become appreciable at a frequency more than two decades below the break point.

The importance of the variations of gain and phase with frequency lies in the fact that these amplifiers are intended for use in feedback circuits. The presence of extra phase shift in a feedback loop must always bring with it the possibility of instability, the limit being expressed by the Nyquist stability criterion. One form of stating this is that the total phase shift around the feedback loop must be less than 360° at all frequencies for which the gain is greater than unity (0 dB). For reasons of static stability (see section 2.3) operational amplifiers have 180° phase shift at low frequencies; the additional phase shift must therefore not be allowed to exceed 180° until after the gain has fallen below unity. In practice, if the amplifier response to a sudden change of input is to be free of undue overshoot and ringing, there must be an appreciable phase margin; a common design criterion is that the excess phase shift should not exceed 140°, and the most conservative designs impose a limit of 90°.

If the circuit of figure 6.6(a) were an adequate representation of the complete amplifier there would be no problem, since the phase shift added to the signal never exceeds 90° at any frequency. In practice, however, the overall performance is more accurately represented by the model shown in figure 6.6(b), in which each individual stage is taken to have a gain A_i and a break frequency $\omega_i = 1/T_i$. This gives an overall response of the form shown in figure 6.6(c), where the gain falls from its d.c. value $G(0) = 20 \log_{10} (A_1 A_2 A_3 \ldots)$dB, with a slope that gets progressively steeper as the successive break points are passed. The corresponding curve of excess phase variation is shown in figure 6.6(a); the amplifier as it stands would be unstable when used in a feedback circuit. The difficulty is overcome by introducing compensating and correcting networks that shape the frequency response. Essentially the various techniques used all depend for their operation on an ability to introduce new poles or zeros into the transfer function, or to move existing ones so as to ensure adequate gain and phase margins. Although a detailed treatment of amplifier design is beyond the scope of this book, it is worth while looking briefly at the effects produced on the frequency response by one or two simple networks.

Looking again at figures 6.6(c) and 6.6(d) showing the response of a series of *R-C* coupled amplifier stages, it will be seen that a phase margin of at least 45° (*i.e.* excess phase shift less than 135° when the gain curve passes through 0 dB), is bound to be obtained if the slope of the gain curve at that point does not exceed 6 dB/octave. This is because even if the next break point occurred exactly at the zero dB frequency, the gain contributed by it at that point would be only 45°. A convenient rule of thumb, therefore, is that for adequate stability the gain curve should cross the zero dB lines with a slope of 6 dB/octave.

One method that is sometimes used to help shape the response of an amplifier is known as *broadbanding*, and consists of adding to the circuit of figure 6.6(a) a resistive load R_L, as shown in figure 6.7(a). By the use of Thévenin's Theorem this may be converted to the equivalent circuit shown in figure 6.7(b), in which

$$A' = \frac{R_L}{R+R_L} A; \qquad R' = \frac{RR_L}{R+R_L} .$$

The effect of broadbanding one stage on the gain curve of a multi-stage amplifier is shown in figure 6.7(c). It will be observed that the phase margin has been increased, because the break point has been moved to a higher frequency, but that this has been achieved at the expense of a uniform reduction of gain at all frequencies, including d.c. Hence stability is in this case paid for by a reduction in static accuracy.

A way of retaining static accuracy while still reducing the slope of the gain curve over the critical frequency range is to use the *roll-off network* shown in figure 6.7(d). The capacitor in series with the resistor prevents the loss of d.c. gain, while at high frequencies the broadbanding effect is retained. Detailed analysis shows that the roll-off network replaces the pole of the original amplifier stage by two poles and a zero: the effect of this is also shown on the composite gain curve in figure 6.7(c).

The most conservative design requirement for an amplifier, as was mentioned earlier, is that there should be no slope exceeding 6 dB/octave above the zero dB line. This can be achieved in a number of ways, of which the simplest is that shown in figure 6.7(e), in which a capacitive load is added. This has the effect of changing the time

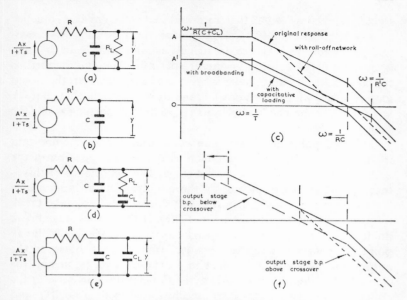

Fig. 6.7. The frequency response can be modified in various ways.

    (a) Broadbanding by adding a resistive load.

    (b) Thévenin equivalent of circuit (a).

    (c) Composite gain plot, showing the original amplifier charac-
teristic and the changes introduced by various compensation
schemes.

    (d) A roll-off network.

    (e) Capacitative loading can be used to 'submerge' the higher
break points.

    (f) The effect of capacitative loading at the output depends on
whether the output stage break point is above or below the
unity gain cross-over frequency.

constant of this stage from RC to $R(C+C_L)$, with a corresponding
reduction in the break frequency. By choosing the value of C_L
appropriately, the gain curve can be adjusted so that all the high
frequency break points are 'submerged' below the zero dB line, as
illustrated again in figure 6.7(c). It should be noticed that the requirement to keep the slope of the gain curve below 6 dB/octave while
above the zero dB line, whether it is satisfied by capacitative loading
or by some more sophisticated shaping network, implies that the
lowest break frequency is very small indeed; in practical amplifiers
it is often below 10 Hz. The conventional measure of bandwidth

sounds depressingly small therefore, and so it is the universal practice among amplifier manufacturers to quote instead the *unity gain cross-over frequency*, that is, the frequency at which the gain is unity (zero dB). This frequency is often rather misleadingly described as the bandwidth: if the amplifier is being used as an inverter, the closed loop response will be 3 dB down at the cross-over frequency, but for any other use the bandwidth in its conventional meaning is not the same.

One final point about the gain curve that can have important implications in the use of amplifiers is the relative position of the break frequency due to the output stage. The importance of this is that if the load to be driven by the amplifier has an appreciable capacitative component, then this will shift the output stage break frequency just as C_L does in figure 6.7(e). If the output stage break point occurs below the cross-over frequency, the change of break point will simply reduce the cross-over frequency; if, however, the output stage break point occurs above the cross-over frequency, the change due to loading can increase the slope of the gain curve at the critical point. These differences are illustrated in figure 6.7(f), and explain why some amplifiers have a limit to the capacitative load that they can drive.

6.6.2 *Common mode rejection*

The use of amplifiers with a differential input stage is essential in computers where chopper stabilization is to be used, but is also common in instrumentation applications. The use of a differential stage in which both transistors are on a single chip, or in the case of an integrated circuit amplifier occupy adjacent parts of the same slice, leads to a substantial degree of temperature stabilization, since both differential inputs are subject to very nearly the same temperature variations. Apart from this advantage, the differential facility is itself often useful, so that many operational amplifiers are of this form.

The two inputs to a differential amplifier are often spoken of as the inverting and non-inverting inputs, and the gain from each input to the output should be equal in magnitude and opposite in sign. Hence if signals x_1 and x_2 are applied to the inverting and non-inverting inputs respectively, the output is ideally

$$y = -\mu(x_1 - x_2). \qquad (6.25)$$

Implicit in equation 6.25 is the assumption that the output will be zero whenever x_1 and x_2 are equal, for all values of x_1 and x_2. In practice this is never true: it could be true only if the two input transistors were identical in all characteristics. The differences between the two halves of the input stage are reflected in a slight difference between the gains of the two channels, and this is specified in terms of the *common mode rejection*. If a signal is applied to both inputs simultaneously, this signal is spoken of as a common mode signal: ideally the output should be zero, but in practice a small output proportional to the input can be observed, so that a common mode gain can be measured. The ratio of the differential gain to the common mode gain is defined as the common mode rejection, which is often measured in dB. The common mode rejection is usually in the range 50–100 dB.

6.6.3 *Slewing*

No account has so far been taken of the power limitations of operational amplifiers. Part of the specification for any amplifier is the maximum output voltage and current, and in one way these define the power output capability. There is, however, an additional very important limitation which places a frequency dependent restriction on the power output. The reason for this is that when the output voltage changes, the amplifier has to supply not only the load that is connected, but also the capacitances in the circuit (both physical capacitances and strays). The more rapidly these capacitances are to be charged, the greater is the current necessary, and so the current capability of the amplifier determines a maximum rate of change of output voltage. This restriction is known as the *slew rating limit*, expressed in V/μsec, typically in the range 1–10 V/μsec.

The maximum frequency at which the amplifier will deliver the rated current at the rated voltage is also often quoted as a performance measure. This frequency, f_p, is related to the slew rate, S, since the maximum rate of change of a signal

$$y = V_0 \sin 2\pi f_p t$$

is given by

$$\left(\frac{dy}{dt}\right)_{max} = 2\pi f_p V_0$$

where V_0 is the rated output voltage.

Hence

$$S = 2\pi V_0 f_p$$

For a 100-V amplifier with a slew rate of 5 V/μsec, this gives a full power response frequency of about 8 kHz.

A very important implication of slew rate limiting is the frequency restriction that it places on integrators. This is because the feedback capacitor is much larger than any internal capacitances that may exist, so that the slew rate limit is really imposed almost entirely by the feedback. If a sinusoidal voltage of peak value V appears across a capacitor C, the current through it has peak value $\omega C V$. Thus for a 1 μF capacitor across a 100-V 50mA amplifier, the slew rate limit is given by

$$\omega \times 10^{-6} \times 100 = 50 \times 10^{-3}$$

or
$$f \simeq 80 \text{ Hz.}$$

Similar restrictions also apply to a summer driving a capacitative load.

6.6.4. *Overload*

The final feature of amplifier performance that needs to be considered is the way it reacts to overloads. Clearly the amplifier will not give the intended output if it is driven into saturation: the only way of avoiding these errors is by appropriate scaling (see chapter 3). Scaling, however, relies on estimates of maximum values and frequencies, and the only possible way of verifying these estimates is by making a trial run. In other cases, it may turn out that the system under investigation is unstable; a fact that emerges only when the computing run produces increasing signals leading to overloads. It is clear, therefore, that in operation overloads are inevitable from time to time, and that provision must be made for them to occur without damaging the amplifier. It is also essential to provide warning to the computer operator when overloads occur: an indicator lamp is always fitted to each amplifier and in larger installations there is an audible warning as well.

The signal used to activate the overload warning system could on the face of it be provided by some kind of threshold circuit at the output, but this would not in fact cover all forms of overload. Slew rate limiting, for example, can occur without the output voltage exceeding the rated maximum, and so can straightforward current overloads (attempting to drive a load beyond the output current capabilities of the amplifier). In cases like this a warning system based on the output voltage would not be activated, although the distortion and resulting inaccuracy could be just as serious as with a voltage overload.

Whatever kind of overload occurs, distortion arises basically because the output is unable to provide the feedback signal necessary to maintain the summing junction at its virtual earth potential. A significant departure of the summing junction potential from earth is therefore a much more powerful indication of overload than excess output voltage, and this is what is usually used. The summing junction potential itself, even under overload conditions, is still small and needs to be amplified to enable it to operate a warning system; the warning signal is therefore taken from the output of the first or second stage of the amplifier, or, in chopper stablized amplifiers, from the output of the a.c. amplifier.

After an overload condition has been removed, the amplifier should return to its normal state, and the warning indications should be extinguished. The time taken for this to happen is a further performance specification that should be quoted for any operational amplifier. With chopper stabilized amplifiers, the time involved is much longer than might be expected, due mainly to the long time constants in the filter networks either side of the a.c. amplifier (see figure 6.4(a)). Even longer time constants are encountered if, as is often the case, the direct input to the d.c. amplifier is taken through a blocking capacitor. These time constants have the effect of making the overload recovery time as much as fifteen to thirty seconds. This is particularly important in iterative operations, in which early runs in an optimizing programme may well produce overloads if the parameters are far from their target values. Error-computing amplifiers are particularly prone to this, because the final accuracy of the programme will depend on the ability to detect very small errors and so a large gain in the error amplifier is required. Very large errors therefore will overload the error amplifier, and so the RESET time in iterative operation must be made longer than the overload recovery time, or else, if this cannot conveniently be managed, then some more elaborate measures must be taken to prevent amplifiers from overloading at all. One way of doing this is to use limiting circuits (see chapter 8).

6.7 Effects of phase shifts

Repeatedly throughout this chapter, emphasis has been laid on the phase shifts that are introduced by the various effects discussed. Phase shifts have two main effects on computing circuits: they can cause the solution being generated to be a modified form of the desired solution, or they can cause it to contain a wholly new component that is unrelated to the problem being solved.

6.7.1. *Changes of solution*

The way in which phase shifts modify the solution being generated will be illustrated by considering a particular example. Figure 6.8(a) show a circuit consisting of a capacitor and an inductor connected across a current source. If the inductor is ideal, the circuit conditions are represented by the phasor diagram shown by solid lines in figure 6.8(b). At any particular frequency, the resultant voltage V is obtained as the vector sum of V_L and V_C. The resonance condition is obtained when $V_C = -V_L$, so that the net voltage across the circuit is zero. In this case the two terminals A and B could be shorted together, without disturbing the conditions in the circuit. The conditions that V_C and V_L are equal and opposite is given by

$$L\frac{di}{dt} = -\frac{1}{C}\int i\,dt$$

or
$$\frac{d^2i}{dt^2} + \omega_n^2 i = 0 \tag{6.26}$$

where
$$\omega_n^2 = 1/LC.$$

Equation 6.26 can be solved on a computer by the circuit shown in figure 6.8(c) (assuming that no scaling is necessary). If the open-loop response of this circuit is measured as in figure 6.8(d), the phasor diagram at any frequency is that shown by the solid lines in figure 6.8(e). In this case the total voltage across the circuit, V, is given by the vector difference of V_{out} and V_{in}, and with all ideal components this difference is zero at a frequency of ω_n. The loop therefore when closed to give the computer circuit of figure 6.8(c) will generate the desired solution for the circuit, given by

$$i_n = I \sin \omega_n t \tag{6.27}$$

provided the appropriate initial conditions are inserted.

With practical computer components, however, this idealized representation of the circuit performance is not always adequate. The phase shift introduced by each amplifier differs from the ideal $90°$ or $180°$ by amounts depending on all the effects mentioned earlier in this chapter, and depending also on the frequency ω_n. The open

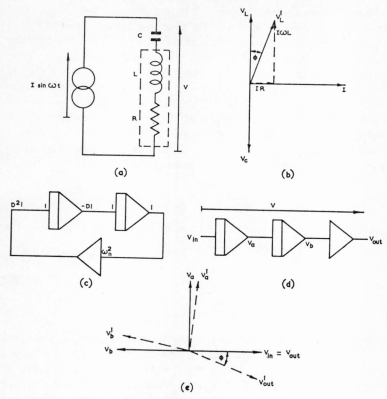

Fig. 6.8. The effect of phase shifts illustrated by a simple resonant circuit.

    (a) The circuit. With perfect elements, equal and opposite voltages appear across capacitor and inductor.

    (b) Phasor diagram for (a), showing both the ideal case and the change introduced by losses in the inductor.

    (c) Computer circuit for solution of the ideal equation.

    (d) Open loop test of the computer circuit in (c).

    (e) Phasor diagram of the open loop circuit, showing both the ideal case and the effect of unwanted phase shifts. These changes are analogous to those shown in (b).

loop phasor diagram at $\omega = \omega_n$ becomes modified as shown by the dotted lines in figure 6.8(e): a total net phase shift of ϕ is introduced, where ϕ can in general be positive or negative. The effect of this phase shift on the closed loop response – that is, the output obtained from the circuit of figure 6.8(c) – can be assessed by returning to the circuit of figure 6.8(a). If the inductor is no longer assumed to be ideal – that is, if R is assumed to be finite – the phasor diagram obtained is that shown by the dotted lines in figure 6.8(b). It will be seen that the effect is analogous to that of figure 6.8(e), so that the output of the computer circuit of figure 6.8(c) under these conditions will represent the current in the imperfect circuit with finite R rather than the desired solution given by equation 6.27. To make the analogy complete we need to allow for ϕ being positive or negative: this is mathematically simple if we allow R to take either sign.

The advantage of using this analogy is that the operation of an R-L-C circuit is well known. Its operating equation is

$$\frac{d^2i}{dt^2} + \frac{R}{L}\frac{di}{dt} + \frac{1}{LC}i = 0$$

and the solution (subject to the same initial conditions as before) is

$$i = Ie^{-\alpha t}\sin \omega t \tag{6.28}$$

where

$$\alpha = \frac{R}{2L} \tag{6.29}$$

$$\omega = \sqrt{\omega_n^2 - \alpha^2}. \tag{6.30}$$

Equation 6.28 indicates that the output obtained from the non-ideal circuit differs in both magnitude and frequency from the target function represented by equation 6.27, and that the extent of the error depends in each case on α. In order to relate α to ϕ, and so to estimate the errors as a function of ϕ, we must return to the phasor diagram of figure 6.8(b), from which we obtain

$$\tan \phi = \frac{R}{\omega L}. \tag{6.31}$$

If ϕ is very small, we may say that $\tan \phi \simeq \phi$, and so from equations 6.29 and 6.31 we obtain

$$\alpha = \frac{\omega \phi}{2}. \tag{6.32}$$

Hence, from equations 6.30 and 6.32,

$$\omega = \frac{\omega_n}{\sqrt{(1 + \phi^2/4)}}$$
$$= \omega_n(1 + \phi^2/4)^{-\frac{1}{2}}$$

or, for $\qquad\qquad \phi \ll 1, \quad \omega \simeq \omega_n(1-\phi^2/8).$ $\qquad\qquad$ (6.33)

Equation 6.33 enables an estimate to be made of the order of magnitude of the frequency error in a practical case. Thus, for

$$\phi = \tfrac{1}{2}^\circ = 8 \cdot 73 \times 10^{-3} \text{ rad}$$

$$\frac{\omega}{\omega_n} = 1 - 9 \cdot 5 \times 10^{-6}.$$

This represents an error of only about $0 \cdot 001\%$ for $\tfrac{1}{2}^\circ$ phase shift, or $0 \cdot 1\%$ for 50° phase shift, which implies that the frequency change will never be significant in practice.

Assuming, therefore, that $\omega = \omega_n$, we have from equations 6.27 and 6.28,

$$i = i_n e^{-\alpha t} = i_n \left[1 - \alpha t + \frac{(\alpha t)^2}{2} - \dots \right] \qquad (6.34)$$

Thus, if $\alpha t \ll 1$,

$$i \simeq i_n(1 - \alpha t) \qquad\qquad (6.35)$$

so that the fractional error is a linearly increasing function of time, the magnitude of the error depending on α, and hence on ϕ. This in turn depends on ω_n, the problem frequency, which is determined by the time scaling chosen by the operator.

After one cycle of the solution has been generated,

$$t = \frac{2\pi}{\omega_n}$$

and so, using equation 6.32 with $\omega = \omega_n$

$$\alpha t = \frac{\omega_n \phi}{2} \times \frac{2\pi}{\omega_n} = \pi\phi.$$

Hence, from equation 6.35, the fractional error per cycle is $\pi\phi$. If $\phi = \tfrac{1}{2}^\circ = 8 \cdot 73 \times 10^{-3}$ rad,

$$\text{amplitude error/cycle} = \pi \times 8 \cdot 73 \times 10^{-3} \times 100$$
$$= 2 \cdot 74\%.$$

This error is clearly unacceptable, which implies that a phase shift of as much as $\tfrac{1}{2}^\circ$ cannot be allowed. The maximum phase shift permissible if the amplitude is to be within 1% after 10 cycles is given by

$$\phi = \frac{0 \cdot 01}{10\pi} \times \frac{180}{\pi} \simeq 0 \cdot 018^\circ \simeq 1 \text{ min.}$$

This phase shift is produced by three amplifiers, so that it is clear that a very modest accuracy demand has resulted in a very stringent phase requirement. This requirement is met in practice by a choice of time scaling: 1 min of total phase shift implies that the working frequency must be about four decades from the high frequency (closed loop) break point, assuming that each amplifier contributes equally to the phase shift. This assumption in fact is not quite true because although each amplifier will have a phase lag due to the high frequency break point, each integrator has in addition a phase lead due to the finite gain error (see section 6.4.2). In theory it is possible to choose a working frequency such that the two effects cancel out; in practice the necessary working frequency turns out to be in the region of $\omega = 1$. For the usual range of working frequencies, therefore, the amplitude errors due to phase shifts are within tolerable limits; diffculties arise when working either with high frequencies or for long computing times. High frequency operation is often needed when using iterative procedures, and long computing times may be necessary in instrumentation and control applications: In these cases some form of compensation must be used to achieve accurate results (for an example, see section 10.3.2).

6.7.2 *Introduction of new solutions*

The possibility of new and irrelevant solutions being introduced into the computer output will be illustrated, as in the previous section, by a particular example.

Figure 6.9 shows part of a hypothetical computer programme in which N summers in series are connected in a closed sub-loop. With ideal amplifiers the loop gain of this part of the system ($V_{\text{out}}/V_{\text{in}}$) is

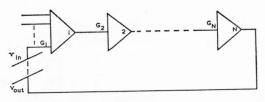

Fig. 6.9. A particular programme may call for several summers to be connected in a loop. This is termed an algebraic loop, and its stability can be assessed by finding the open loop transfer function.

simply a numeric; this is the intended loop transfer function and represents the correct solution. Because of the high frequency break point at $\omega_B = 1/T$ (assumed the same for each amplifier) the transfer function of each amplifier is given by

$$F_r(s) = -\frac{G_r}{1+Ts}, \qquad r = 1, 2, \ldots, N,$$

assuming that only one break point needs to be considered for each amplifier. The total transfer function therefore is

$$\frac{V_{\text{out}}}{V_{\text{in}}} = \prod_{r=1}^{N} F_r(s) = (-1)^N \frac{\prod\limits_{r=1}^{N} G_r}{(1+Ts)^N}$$

$$\therefore \frac{V_{\text{out}}}{V_{\text{in}}} = (-1)^N \frac{G}{(1+Ts)^N} \qquad (6.36)$$

where

$$G = \prod_{r=1}^{N} G_r,$$

which is the modulus of the intended gain. Hence, at any frequency, ω, the phase shift and gain are obtained from equation 6.36 as

$$\phi(\omega) = N[\pi - \tan^{-1}(\omega T)] \qquad (6.37)$$

and

$$\left|\frac{V_{\text{out}}}{V_{\text{in}}}\right| = \frac{G}{[1+(\omega T)^2]^{N/2}} \qquad (6.38)$$

If for any value of ω the phase shift is a multiple of 2π and the gain is greater than unity, the loop will be unstable; in other words a new solution unrelated to the problem will be generated. If n is even and $G > 1$, this condition will be satisfied at $\omega = 0$; all the amplifiers will be driven to saturation indicating either an unstable system or a programming fault. An even number of amplifiers is, however, permissible provided the loop gain is less than unity.

If N is odd, equation 6.37 shows that the phase shift will be a multiple of 2π if

$$N \tan^{-1}(\omega T) = \pi$$

or

$$\omega T = \tan\left(\frac{\pi}{N}\right). \qquad (6.39)$$

Substituting equation 6.39 into equation 6.38, we find that the gain

K

at this frequency is

$$\left|\frac{V_{\text{out}}}{V_{\text{in}}}\right| = \frac{G}{\left[1+\tan^2\left(\dfrac{\pi}{N}\right)\right]^{N/2}} = G\cos^N\left(\frac{\pi}{N}\right) \qquad (6.40)$$

The maximum intended loop gain, G, is therefore restricted if the system is to be stable, for if

$$\left|\frac{V_{\text{out}}}{V_{\text{in}}}\right| < 1$$

then from equation 6.40

$$G < \sec^N\left(\frac{\pi}{N}\right)$$

This requires the loop gain to be less than 8 for $N = 3$ and 2·9 for $N = 5$; if a particular computer programme violates this condition is must be re-arranged, because even although the oscillations produced would be at a frequency too high to influence most ouput recording devices, they would nevertheless make the computation meaningless through overloading the amplifiers.

6.8 Notes and references

It is perhaps not surprising that the subject of errors in computing circuits is ignored in many books, because many of the sources of error are often not significant in an analogue computer where the d.c. gain of an amplifier really is nearly infinite and the computing impedances are high stability high accuracy components with trimming and padding and often a temperature-controlled environment. It is possible therefore to solve quite a wide range of problems in an analogue computer without coming up against limitations imposed by imperfections of the equipment (apart from scaling requirements). Errors do, however, arise even in computer circuits, and can be particularly important in instrumentation applications.

A useful discussion of errors is given by Gilbert, who includes a very detailed section on the performance of operational amplifiers. Even though his comments are centred around valve amplifiers, the performance, limitations, and compensation methods are essentially very similar to those found in transistor amplifiers. For the same reason, the book by Jackson, although rather old, is still useful.

Rekoff includes a description of the redundant integrator problem, which is really a difficulty in problem formulation, but which can give rise to serious errors. Briefly, the problem is that an nth order system can be described by a number of simultaneous equations of total order greater than n. A third order system, for example, might be described by two simultaneous second order equations, and this would then require four integrators for the solution rather than three – hence the 'redundant integrator'. Where this arises, the problem may often be mathematically soluble: for example, in a circuit theory problem, it may be convenient for the current through a particular capacitor not to be defined as a problem variable, but to be obtained as the difference between two currents which are themselves problem variables. Computer solutions for these currents would then require one more integrator than there are storage elements in the circuit. Mathematically the order of the equations is reduced because a particular term appears on both sides of an equation and is therefore cancelled, but this is where the practical difficulty arises, in that these two cancelling terms will appear as two independently generated signals, and cancellation therefore requires that we have two identical integrators. Since this cannot be achieved, errors will arise, but as suggested earlier, the difficulty must be resolved at the problem formulation stage, by ensuring that the total order of the equations to be solved does not exceed the order of the system.

The best sources of information about the properties of operational amplifiers, and the ways in which they can be used in a wide variety of applications, are undoubtedly the applications manuals produced by the various manufacturers such as Philbrick, Burr-Brown, Texas, and RCA. These are all very inexpensive and full of useful circuits, and often contain valuable sections on the theoretical aspects as well. The only word of caution that is needed in connection with the manufacturers' specifications is that some of the performance measures are sometimes defined in a rather individualistic way, and this can have an important bearing when comparing the products of different manufacturers. The journal Simulation has made an attempt to standardize the measurements, but the extent to which these suggestions are followed by the manufacturers is not known, although two manufacturers at least (Analog Devices and Motorola) have published detailed statements of the ways that their measurements are taken (see papers by Stata and Blair).

The method of examining the effects of phase errors in a second order system by analogy with an R-L-C circuit was proposed by

Venning, who claims that the method can also be used in more complicated cases. The particular merit of this approach is not just that it is easy to relate phase error to change of performance, but also that a straightforward analytical solution is very complicated. In the example given, for example, an analytical approach would require each amplifier to be described by a transfer function incorporating a first order lag term, so that the complete solution of even this simple problem would involve a fifth order differential equation.

Other forms of error that are not mentioned at all in this chapter are those that appear in hybrid systems consequent on the analogue-digital conversion. These are discussed by Karplus and by Bekey and Karplus: sampling and quantization errors are probably as important as any when determining the limits to the speed and accuracy obtainable with these complex computing systems.

REFERENCES

BEKEY, G. A. and KARPLUS, W. J. (1968). *Hybrid Computation*, Wiley, New York.

*BLAIR, K. Getting More Value out of an Integrated Operational Amplifier Data Sheet. Application Note AN 273, Motorola Semiconductor Products Inc.

*Burr-Brown Research Corporation. Handbook of Operational Amplifier Applications.

GILBERT, C. P. (1964). *The Design and Use of Electronic Analogue Computers*, Chapman and Hall, London.

JACKSON, A. S. (1960). *Analog Computation*, McGraw-Hill, New York.

KARPLUS, W. J. (1968). Error Analysis of Hybrid Computer Systems, in *Simulation—the Modelling of Ideas and Systems with Computers*, Ed. J. MCLEOD, McGraw-Hill, New York.

*Philbrick-Nexus Research. Applications Manual for Operational Amplifiers.

*R.C.A. Linear Integrated Circuits.

REKOFF, M. G. (1967). *Analog Computer Programming*, Merrill, New York.

Simulation Council. Definition of Terms used to Specify General-Purpose Analogue Computers and Methods of Measurement, in *Simulation—the Modelling of Ideas and Systems with Computers*, Ed. J. MCLEOD, McGraw-Hill, New York.

*STATA, R. User's Guide to Applying and Measuring Operational Amplifier Specifications, *Analog Dialogue* 1 No. 3, (September 1967).

*Texas Instruments Semiconductor and Components Data Book 1.

VENNING, B. H. (1963). The Effects of Phase Errors on Analogue Computation, *Int. J. Elect. Eng. Educ.* 1, 223.

* Manufacturers' data sheets, manuals, and handbooks can be obtained direct from the manufacturers or their agents.

7 Linear and Non-Linear Systems

The systems dealt with so far in this book have been described by simple analytical expressions, and the problems considered have been confined to a study of the behaviour of these systems when released from an unstable initial condition (as in the example in chapter 2 of the weight on the end of a string) or when subjected to a step function disturbance (as in the differential equation example in section 3.5). Practical problems, however, are seldom as straightforward as this. Many systems cannot be adequately described by simple differential equations requiring just summers and integrators for their solution. It is also often necessary to determine the response of the system to prescribed complex forcing functions as well as to simple disturbances. As a result, there is a need for an extension of the range of available computing or simulation blocks: it is with the methods of producing these blocks that the next four chapters are concerned.

7.1 System analysis

The purpose of most analogue computer programmes, as discussed in chapters 1 and 2, is to construct a model of a system under study, in order to permit predictions of the response of the system to any specified input. The computer model is based essentially on a mathematical model, so that it is worth while to consider briefly some of the methods used in theoretical analysis. The ways in which systems are classified, and the analytical techniques available for systems and components of different types, bring out some important implications attached to the use of these components both in systems and in computers.

In its most general form a system can be regarded as a device with a number of inputs x_i ($i = 1, 2, \ldots, m$), and a number of

135

outputs y_j ($j = 1, 2, \ldots, n$). Each input is in general a function of time, and each output is a function of time and of the inputs. This can be expressed as a set of simultaneous equations

$$y_1 = f_1(x_1, x_2, \ldots, x_m, t)$$
$$y_2 = f_2(x_1, x_2, \ldots, x_m, t)$$
$$\cdot \quad \cdot \quad \cdot \quad \cdot \quad \cdot$$
$$y_n = f_n(x_1, x_2, \ldots, x_m, t)$$

This set of equations can be more conveniently and compactly expressed using vector notation as

$$\mathbf{y} = H(\mathbf{x}) \tag{7.1}$$

where $\mathbf{x}$ and $\mathbf{y}$ are the input and output vectors respectively, given by

$$\mathbf{x} = \begin{bmatrix} x_1 \\ x_2 \\ \vdots \\ x_m \end{bmatrix} ; \quad \mathbf{y} = \begin{bmatrix} y_1 \\ y_2 \\ \vdots \\ y_n \end{bmatrix}$$

and H is, in this case, a vector valued function given by

$$H = \begin{bmatrix} f_1(x_1, x_2, \ldots x_m, t) \\ f_2(x_1, x_2, \ldots x_m, t) \\ \cdot \quad \cdot \quad \cdot \quad \cdot \quad \cdot \\ f_n(x_1, x_2, \ldots x_m, t) \end{bmatrix} \tag{7.2}$$

In general, H is an operator that, when applied to the input vector $\mathbf{x}$, produces the output vector $\mathbf{y}$. This operator, which characterizes the system, determines by its form the classification of the system.

A system description of the kind discussed so far, in which inputs and outputs are expressed as functions of time, is said to be a time domain description, and the system function H is an operator involving differentiation and integration with respect to time as well as algebraic manipulations which may or may not be analytical in form. This method of description has in effect been used in the earlier chapters of this book: the operation of an integrator, for example, may be defined by the differential equation

$$\frac{dy}{dt} = x$$

which may be written, in terms of the differential operator, D,

$$D(y) = x \tag{7.3}$$

or

$$y = \frac{1}{D}(x).$$

This is a system with a single input and a single output, and a system function given by

$$H = \frac{1}{D}.$$

Another form of description, which has been used freely in chapter 6, relies on transforming the inputs and the outputs from functions of time to functions of a real or complex frequency. These methods, utilizing the Fourier and the Laplace Transformation respectively, result in system functions that do not involve calculus operations, but are algebraic functions of the frequency variable. Such a description is a frequency domain description, and for a one input – one output system, the system function is often plotted as a pole-zero pattern in the complex frequency plane since this pattern completely specifies the shape of the response of the system to any particular input.

7.1.1 *Classification of systems*

A number of important distinctions may be made amongst systems by applying a series of tests to the system function H as expressed by equation 7.1.

In order to emphasize that both x and y are functions of time, equation 7.1 may be rewritten as

$$\mathbf{y}(t) = H[\mathbf{x}(t)]$$

At a particular time $t = T$, the output vector is given in general by

$$y(T) = H[\mathbf{x}(t)]$$

indicating that the output at any instant depends on the system function and on the whole input waveform. If we further suppose that the output at time T depends on the inputs over the range

$$\tau_1 \leq t \leq \tau_2$$

several classifications depend on the limits τ_1 and τ_2. If $\tau_2 > T$, then the output at any instant depends not only on the past history of the input but also on future values. Such a system is termed *anticipatory*, and the importance of this classification lies in the fact that it cannot represent a physical system. All physical systems are *causal* (or non-anticipatory), that is $\tau_2 \leq T$: this fact can be used to deduce constraints on mathematical representations of systems.

If $\tau_1 < T$ then the output depends on past values of the inputs as well as on the present values. Such a system is said to possess a memory of length $T - \tau_1$. An integrator is such a system, since the system equation is

$$y(t) = -\int_0^t \sum_{i=1}^n x_i \, dt + y(0)$$

$$= -\int_{-\infty}^t \sum_{i=1}^n x_i \, dt$$

where
$$y(0) = -\int_{-\infty}^0 \sum_{i=1}^n x_i \, dt.$$

Thus an integrator has an infinite memory.

A causal system with a memory of zero length is defined by the limits $\tau_1 = \tau_2 = T$: the output of such a system at any instant depends only on the inputs at that instant, and not on past or future values of the inputs. This is an *instantaneous* system, an example of which is a summer.

The system function H is shown in equation 7.2 as a vector valued function of the inputs and of time. An important class of systems is that for which the system functions do not depend on time. These are called *stationary*, or time-invariant, as opposed to *time-varying* systems whose system functions do depend on time. The significance of this distinction is that in a stationary system the size and shape of the output is dependant only on the size and shape of the input and not on the time of application of the input. The formal test of a stationary system is that it satisfies the condition

$$H[\mathbf{x}(t - \tau)] = \mathbf{y}(t - \tau)$$

for all τ.

In many practical problems it is necessary to predict the performance of a system when subjected to inputs that are not well defined time functions, but can be described only in probabilistic terms. An autopilot system, for example, is required to keep the aircraft on the commanded course in the face of random wind disturbances. Just as the inputs (and hence the outputs) of a system might be described in a *probabilistic* rather than a *deterministic* manner, so also the system itself may be probabilistic, meaning that the output for a specified input may be definable only in this way. Adaptive (or learning) systems in particular are often of this form.

The form of the time variable itself provides the basis for a further classification of systems. Systems operating with inputs and outputs that are continuous functions of time are known as *continuous* systems; a very important class of systems, however, operates with signals that are defined only at discrete instants of time. These systems are called *discrete* systems, and are treated by mathematical techniques that are different from, although analogous to, those used for continuous systems. In particular, discrete systems are generally characterized by difference equations rather than by differential equations. It should be noticed that a system will be classified as discrete if its inputs and outputs are only observed discretely, even although the system itself operates continuously, since models can be constructed and predictions can be usefully made only on the basis of the discrete information. Many sampled-data and time-shared systems fall into this category.

The most important distinction of all that can be made amongst systems is on the basis of linearity. A *linear* system is defined as one that satisfies the superposition principle. This states that if the output vector is y_1 in response to an input vector x_1, and y_2 in response to x_2, then the response to an input vector $(a_1x_1 + a_2x_2)$ is $(a_1y_1 + a_2y_2)$, where a_1 and a_2 are any two constants. Using the symbolism of equation 7.1 the superposition principle may be expressed as

$$H(a_1x_1 + a_2x_2) = a_1H(x_1) + a_2H(x_2). \qquad (7.4)$$

A system is linear if, and only if, it satisfies equation 7.4 for all values of a_1, a_2, x_1, and x_2. This is a very stringent requirement, which strictly speaking is not truly satisfied by any physical system, just as the inevitable presence of noise ensures that no physical system is entirely deterministic. However, many systems can be treated as though they were linear by restricting operation to some specified working range or perhaps by considering only small deviations about a working point, and the effects of noise also can often be made insignificant; the whole exercise of scaling in an analogue computer, for example, can be regarded as a method of ensuring that each computing element operates in a region in which a deterministic linear model is a valid approximation.

Transform methods all rely for their operation on the superposition principle, and are thus valid only for linear systems. In fact, not even all linear systems can be dealt with; time-varying systems are particularly difficult. The importance of time varying and non-linear systems, especially in control theory, has therefore led to a shifting of attention away from the frequency domain methods of analysis back to time domain methods. This has not, however, been a simple return to the classical method of solution of the system differential equations, but has been based on the state space description of systems. This form of description can be linked conveniently with an analogue computer model.

7.1.2 State space and normal form

The state space approach to systems is based on the definition of a new set of variables, known as the *state variables*, that together define the state of the system at any given time. The state of the system and the output from the system at any time t are uniquely determined by the state at some earlier time t_0 (usually taken as zero time) and the history of the input functions between t_0 and t. The set of state variables forms a *state vector* which defines the state of the system at any instant as the position of a point in an n-dimensional *state space*. The movement of this point (the tip of the state vector) in the state space as a function of time is called the *trajectory*, and defines the response of the system to the particular input function when starting from a particular initial state.

Any deterministic continuous system can be described by a differential equation relating the outputs to the inputs. A system with a single input u and a single output y, for example, may be described by a general n^{th} order differential equation

$$f\left(\frac{d^n y}{dt^n}, \frac{d^{n-1} y}{dt^{n-1}}, \ldots, \frac{dy}{dt}, u, t\right) = 0 \tag{7.5}$$

which can be re-written as

$$\frac{d^n y}{dt^n} = f_n\left(\frac{d^{n-1} y}{dt^{n-1}}, \ldots \frac{dy}{dt}, u, t\right). \tag{7.6}$$

An analogue computer programme to simulate this system would take the form shown in figure 7.1, in which the first block denotes a unit whose output is related to its inputs by the function f_n (assuming that such a block is realizable). This function block, together with integrator N, implements equation 7.6; the remainder of the programme makes use, as usual, of the set of relationships

$$\left. \begin{aligned} \frac{d}{dt}\left(\frac{d^r y}{dt^r}\right) &= \frac{d^{r+1} y}{dt^{r+1}} \quad (r = 1, 2, \ldots n-2) \\ \frac{d}{dt}(y) &= \frac{dy}{dt} \end{aligned} \right\} \tag{7.7}$$

and

Many systems satisfying equation 7.5 would have their outputs completely determined by a set of values, at any particular instant, of y and its first $(n-1)$ differential coefficients, together with the subsequent input: in terms of figure 7.1, this is equivalent to saying that the behaviour of the system is uniquely determined by the input u and the initial conditions on the N integrators. If this is so, then by the previous definition these n quantities form a valid set of state variables. We may notice, in passing, that there may be, and usually is, more than one valid set of state variables. If we denote these variables by $x_1, x_2, \ldots, x_n$ we may rewrite equations 7.6 and 7.7 in state variable form as

$$\left. \begin{aligned} \frac{dx_1}{dt} &= x_2 \\ \frac{dx_2}{dt} &= x_3 \\ &\vdots \\ \frac{dx_{n-1}}{dt} &= x_n \\ \frac{dx_n}{dt} &= f_n(x_n, x_{n-1}, \ldots, x_2, x_1, u, t) \\ \text{where} \quad x_1 = y, \; x_2 = \frac{dy}{dt}, \; x_3 = \frac{d^2 y}{dt^2}, \ldots, x_n = \frac{d^{n-1} y}{dt^{n-1}} \end{aligned} \right\} \tag{7.8}$$

An alternative way of looking at this set of equations is that each one describes the operation of one of the integrators in figure 7.1, the state variables being the outputs of the integrators. This concept can then be extended to a more general scheme in which each integrator in the programme can receive multiple inputs. Every input to a particular integrator must therefore come (perhaps by way of a

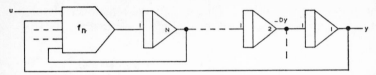

Fig. 7.1. The representation of a system in normal form is particularly suitable for analogue computer programming. Each integrator output is a state variable.

function block) either from the output of one of the other integrators (or indeed from its own output), or from the input. Equations 7.8 may therefore be generalized to give

$$\frac{dx_1}{dt} = f_1(x_1, x_2, \ldots, x_n, u, t)$$

$$\frac{dx_2}{dt} = f_2(x_1, x_2, \ldots, x_n, u, t)$$

$$\cdots \cdots$$

$$\frac{dx_n}{dt} = f_n(x_1, x_2, \ldots, x_n, u, t)$$

and this may be written in the more compact matrix notation

$$\dot{\mathbf{x}} = \mathbf{f}(\mathbf{x}, u, t). \tag{7.9}$$

The output in which we are interested need not in general be itself one of the state variables, but may be obtained through a further function block, giving

$$y = g(\mathbf{x}, u, t) \tag{7.10}$$

For a system with multiple inputs and outputs, equations 7.9 and 7.10 become

$$\left.\begin{array}{l} \dot{\mathbf{x}} = \mathbf{f}(\mathbf{x}, \mathbf{u}, t) \\ \mathbf{y} = \mathbf{g}(\mathbf{x}, \mathbf{u}, t) \end{array}\right\} \tag{7.11}$$

The sets of equations 7.11 are said to describe the system in *normal form*: basically an nth order system is then described by n simultaneous first order equations rather than by a single n^{th} order equation. In principle, equation 7.11 can form the basis for an analogue computer programme to simulate the system, although whether such a programme is directly realizable will depend on the form of the functions $\mathbf{f}$ and $\mathbf{g}$.

For many systems, equations 7.11 can be rewritten in the form

$$\left.\begin{array}{l} \dot{\mathbf{x}} = \mathbf{A}\mathbf{x} + \mathbf{B}\mathbf{u} \\ \mathbf{y} = \mathbf{C}\mathbf{x} + \mathbf{D}\mathbf{u} \end{array}\right\} \tag{7.12}$$

where $\mathbf{A}$, $\mathbf{B}$, $\mathbf{C}$, and $\mathbf{D}$ are matrices whose elements may be constant or time-varying (for linear systems) or may be non-linear functions. Analytical methods for the solution of equations 7.12 exist for the simple cases (in particular for linear systems), and various important features of the system (notably stability criteria) can be deduced from the form of the matrices $\mathbf{A}$, $\mathbf{B}$, $\mathbf{C}$, and $\mathbf{D}$ in linear cases without the necessity for solving the equations. Where solutions are required to non-linear problems, the use of a computer simulation is often the best, or even the only, method available.

Throughout this section, discussion has been limited to continuous systems. An analogous treatment applies to discrete systems, with differential equations replaced throughout by difference equations. The normal form in this case consists of a set of first order difference equations relating the next state of each state variable to the present state of each state variable and each input, and a set of output equations relating the outputs to the state variables and the inputs. These may be expressed as

$$\left.\begin{array}{l} \mathbf{x}_{k+1} = \mathbf{f}(\mathbf{x}_k, \mathbf{u}_k, k) \\ \mathbf{y}_k = \mathbf{g}(\mathbf{x}_k, \mathbf{u}_k, k) \end{array}\right. \tag{7.13}$$

where k is the discrete time variable.

Equations 7.13 are closely analogous to equations 7.11 for continuous systems: a matrix form analogous to equations 7.12 can also be obtained for some systems.

The simulation of either continuous or discrete systems on an analogue computer requires the provision of simulation blocks to implement the various elements of the matrices in equation 7.12 (or its analogous discrete form). If these matrix elements are anything other than constants, the simulation cannot be accomplished with the simple elements and techniques described in the earlier chapters.

7.2 System simulation and forcing function generation

Although the remainder of this part of the book is concerned only with simulation blocks designed to realize complex analytical functions or non-linear functions, it should not be assumed that the simple techniques of the earlier chapters are not necessary. There is, in fact, always a place for the simple techniques of summation and integration in any simulation or computation. In any system, for example, the position of a body moving in a straight line can be obtained as the integral of the velocity, and this in turn is the integral of the acceleration. By measuring the components of acceleration in three orthogonal directions, a position in space can be obtained: this is the principle of operation of an inertial navigation system.

There are two main purposes for which simulation blocks are required. The first is for the reproduction of a complex input-output characteristic possessed by some component of the system. This may be a non-linear characteristic, such as the tension-length curve of the string in chapter 2 (see section 2.9), or it may be a linear but complicated transfer function that for reasons of convenience or economy it is required to generate in a single unit. The second purpose for which simulation blocks are required is for the generation of forcing functions. These may be repetitive or may be 'one-shot' but in either case are essentially functions of time, whereas system blocks are required to produce specified functions of an arbitrary variable. Another way of looking at it is that a system block is passive in character, its output being a function of its input, while a forcing function generator is active in character, having an output with no input. A system block can always be used as a forcing function generator by feeding it with an input signal proportional to time (that is, a ramp function; see section 10.1) but forcing function generators cannot normally be used as system blocks.

7.2.1 *Types of simulation block*

An important distinction that can be drawn for either kind of simulation block depends on whether the characteristics of the block are fixed or can be adjusted. This distinction depends on the construction of the block, and can be regarded as being drawn between special purpose and general purpose devices. The choice in any particular application will be governed by the requirements of that application: a fixed (special purpose) device is normally cheaper, but a general purpose one has flexibility and for some purposes convenience in use that may well make the additional cost worth while. A general purpose device is also often considerably more bulky than a fixed one and, in particular, may require more patchboard space for the inputs and outputs. Even in general purpose computers, therefore, a compromise has to be reached between flexibility and space, and as a result fixed simulation blocks are usually provided for a number of commonly occurring functions.

7.2.2 *Methods of realization*

A further division of simulation blocks can be made according to whether the function characterizing the block is an exact or an approximate realization of the intended function. This division is not made on the basis of the accuracy of the block, which is an independent consideration, but only on the way in which the function is implemented. For example, a crossed fields multiplier (see section 9.2.2) uses the fact that the force on an electron in mutually perpendicular electric and magnetic fields is proportional to the product of the field strengths. Although the accuracy of a device built on this principle depends on various engineering constraints and limitations, the relationship itself is an exact one. This may be contrasted with the devices described in chapter 8, in which the characteristic of the block is built up as a piecewise linear approximation to the desired characteristic.

If the mathematical description of the desired characteristic of a simulation block is analytical in form, it may be easier to produce an exact simulation than an approximation. With forcing function generators in particular, it is often possible to obtain the required waveform as the solution to an appropriate differential equation. In this case the simulation takes the form of a number of normal summers and integrators solving the differential equation by the use of the standard techniques described in chapters 2 and 3, perhaps with some refinements to ensure accurate operation under the conditions of the problem (see chapter 10).

It can also be convenient to simulate a complete section of a physical system with a single block, using the transfer function of the section as the definition of the required characteristic. In this case large savings of equipment are possible, at the expense of an almost complete loss of flexibility (see section 7.3). Clearly the use of this technique requires a knowledge of the transfer function of the section of the system, and normally it results in an exact simulation, although in some cases an approximation to the ideal transfer function may be used for reasons of economy of equipment.

Approximate simulations are obtained in two main ways. One is the piecewise linear approximation which has already been mentioned.

The other is mathematical approximation, which may be developed by the use of power series: rapidly convergent series are known for many analytical functions, so that good approximations can be obtained, provided the various powers of the input variable can be generated (see sections 9.1.1. and 9.3.3).

A block for which no analytical description is available is simulated either by the use of a special purpose device in which the characteristic can be incorporated, or by the use of a piecewise linear approximation. Since virtually any characteristic can be constructed by a piecewise linear approximation, this method forms the basis of nearly all general purpose simulation blocks, and in modern computers it also forms the basis of many of the special purpose blocks as well. Piecewise linear methods are considered in detail in chapter 8, and the less versatile, but for some purposes more convenient, special purpose devices are discussed in chapter 9.

One very useful technique for extending the range of existing equipment is known as implicit function generation. The principle on which the technique is based is illustrated in figure 7.2. Amplifier 1, although without immediate feedback, has a feedback loop around it indirectly by way of the function block. As with all operational amplifiers in stable feedback circuits, therefore, the output is driven in such a way as to keep the summing junction at virtual earth.

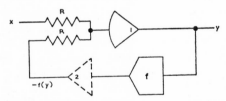

Fig. 7.2. Additional computing functions can be obtained from existing function blocks by the use of implicit function generation.

Amplifier 2 is shown dotted to indicate that it might or might not be necessary to include an inverter in the loop for static stability, depending on the form of the functional relationship represented by f. Since the two input resistors are equal, the equation satisfied by the circuit of figure 7.2 is

$$x - f(y) = 0$$

or
$$y = f^{-1}(x) \tag{7.14}$$

where $f^{-1}(x)$ is the inverse function compared with $f(x)$. For example,

if $$f(x) = \log x, \qquad f^{-1}(x) = \text{antilog } x$$

or if $$f(x) = x^2, \qquad f^{-1}(x) = \sqrt{x}.$$

7.3 Transfer function simulation

The purpose of a simulation is often to aid in the design of a sub-system required to control or operate in conjunction with a system that already exists, or that is already specified. A part of an autopilot, for example, may be required to control the position of a specific control surface (an aeleron or rudder) of a particular aircraft whose design has already been determined by other considerations. In this case, we need to simulate the characteristics of the control surface so that the performance of the autopilot can be assessed, but it is only the overall characteristics that are required rather than a detailed structural simulation of the kind mentioned in chapter 2 (see section 2.8). To put it another way, there is no merit in simulating the main system in such a way that experimental modifications are easily made, since we know that there is no interest in making such modifications. What is required is a block representing, in the most convenient or most economical way, the performance of the system, often expressed for this purpose in the form of a transfer function. The transfer function representation can be used only for linear systems, but is an adequate description of many practical systems (or parts of systems) over a working range.

An interesting extension of the idea of simulating system transfer functions is that the same techniques can be applied to the task of synthesizing a signal processing system to have a specified transfer function. Many communications and instrumentation systems require such specific filter networks, and designers are now making use of circuits incorporating operational amplifiers to produce what are known as active filters using techniques broadly based on the methods described in this chapter. Active filters as such will not be discussed further, except to remark that the amplifiers used for this purpose do not necessarily need to have the properties demanded from an ideal operational amplifier: amplifiers consisting of single transistors have been successfully used for particular filters.

7.3.1 *Basic single amplifier circuit*

The transfer function representation of an operational amplifier

L

with input and feedback impedances has already been used in chapter 6, and is given by

$$F(s) = \frac{y}{x} = -\frac{Z_f}{Z_i}.\tag{7.15}$$

It should be noticed that although we have so far considered such a circuit only for the cases in which Z_i is a resistor and Z_f is either a resistor or a capacitor, there is no reason in principle why we should not put any two two-terminal networks in these positions. Equation 7.15 still applies, with Z_f and Z_i then represented as complex impedances (functions of s) and the transfer function then also being in general a function of s. In practice inductors are inconvenient elements to incorporate into systems of this kind, so that interest is confined to R-C networks. This implies some restrictions on the forms of transfer function that can be realized: these restrictions are best expressed in terms of the allowable pole-zero patterns for the transfer function and for the individual networks.

Any R-C impedance has all its poles and zeros interlaced along the negative real axis, with a pole nearest the origin. If the transfer function $F(s)$ given by equation 7.15 is to be obtained as the ratio of two R-C impedance functions, therefore, all the poles and zeros of $F(s)$ must also occur on the negative real axis. It is convenient to express the transfer function in the form

$$F(s) = -\frac{F_Z(s)}{F_P(s)} = -\frac{F_Z(s)}{A(s)} \cdot \frac{A(s)}{F_P(s)}\tag{7.16}$$

where $F_Z(s)$ and $F_P(s)$ are polynomial functions of s whose roots are the zeros and poles respectively of $F(s)$, and $A(s)$ is a further polynomial function of s that can be chosen arbitrarily. By comparing equations 7.15 and 7.16, the problem is then reduced to finding input and feedback impedances such that

$$Z_f = \frac{F_Z(s)}{A(s)} \; ; \quad Z_i = \frac{F_P(s)}{A(s)}\tag{7.17}$$

and $A(s)$ must therefore be chosen in such a way that the two functions given by equations 7.17 are realizable as R-C impedances. It may be noted here that, because of the possible cancellation in equation 7.16 of poles and zeros in the impedance expressions to give the overall transfer function, the remaining set of poles and zeros do not necessarily interlace.

The manipulation of equations 7.17 into a form that allows them to be interpreted as *R-C* circuits is a standard problem of network synthesis, which is beyond the scope of this book. The simplest methods of synthesis consist essentially of the successive removal of terms representing identifiable circuit components or combinations of components in such a way that the remaining impedance function is simpler (in the sense of having fewer singularities) than the original. These methods result in a network consisting of a ladder network, or a series combination of parallel circuits, or a parallel combination of series circuits, as shown in figure 7.3.

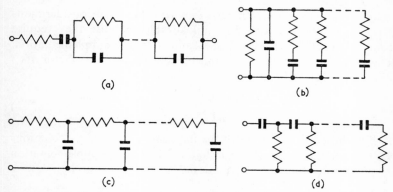

Fig. 7.3. R − C impedances can be implemented in many ways. Four basic forms are:
(a) series connection of parallel circuits.
(b) parallel connection of series circuits.
(c), (d) ladder networks.

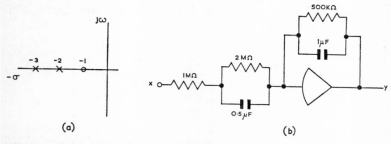

Fig. 7.4. An example of transfer function synthesis.
(a) The required pole zero pattern.
(b) One possible realization.

Consider, for example, the function

$$F(s) = - \frac{s+1}{(s+2)(s+3)} \qquad (7.18)$$

whose pole-zero pattern is shown in figure 7.4(a). We may choose Z_i and Z_f in several different ways, one of which is

$$Z_i = \frac{s+3}{s+1}; \qquad Z_f = \frac{1}{s+2}. \qquad (7.19)$$

Each of these functions satisfies the realizability conditions for an R-C impedance, so that there is in principle no need to introduce the cancelling factor $A(s)$ of equations 7.17. Practical considerations however make equations 7.19 unrealizable, because they require component values of the order of 1Ω and $1F$ for their implementation. This difficulty also can be overcome by using the arbitrary factor $A(s:)$ if it is a constant $1/A$, equations 7.19 become

$$Z_i = A \cdot \frac{s+3}{s+1}; \qquad Z_f = \frac{A}{s+2} \qquad (7.20)$$

If A is chosen to be 10^6, then the impedances defined by equations 7.20 lead to the circuit shown in figure 7.4(b) as one implementation of the transfer function of equation 7.18.

7.3.2 *Simulation of general transfer functions*

The limitations on the pole-zero patterns that can be realized by the simple circuit discussed so far can be avoided by using inverters and additional impedances as shown in figure 7.5. The transfer function of this circuit is obtained in the usual way by the use of Kirchhoff's Law at the summing junction, and is most conveniently expressed in

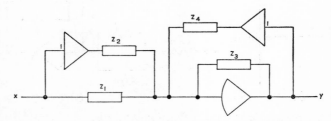

Fig. 7.5. With the use of additional amplifiers, any rational transfer function can be realised, using only R−C impedances.

terms of the admittances of the two-terminal networks as

$$\frac{y}{x} = - \frac{Y_1 - Y_2}{Y_3 - Y_4}. \qquad (7.21)$$

Equation 7.21 may be compared with the required transfer function given by equation 7.16, to obtain the two network equations

$$Y_1 - Y_2 = \frac{F_Z(s)}{A(s)}; \qquad Y_3 - Y_4 = \frac{F_P(s)}{A(s)} \qquad (7.22)$$

where again $A(s)$ is an arbitrary function chosen to enable equations 7.22 to be realized with R-C networks. The significant feature of equations 7.22 is the fact that each expression is made up as the difference of two admittances: this allows some terms in the expansion of $F_Z(s)$ and $F_P(s)$ to have negative or zero coefficients which would not be permissible if they were to be realized as pure passive networks. The realizability conditions can be summarized as follows.

(a) The poles of $(Y_1 - Y_2)$ and $(Y_3 - Y_4)$, which are the zeros of the arbitrary function $A(s)$, must lie on the negative real axis.

(b) The number of zeros of $A(s)$ must not exceed the number of zeros of either $F_Z(s)$ or $F_P(s)$ by more than one.

Since each of these conditions does no more than apply restrictions to the arbitrary function $A(s)$, it follows that any rational transfer function can be realized by the circuit of figure 7.5 using only R-C impedances.

The generality of this method may be combined with the economy of requiring only a single amplifier by using four terminal networks in the input and feedback branches of the circuit. This method uses more components than the three amplifier arrangement of figure 7.5, however, and with the continuing reduction in the cost of amplifiers the economic advantage is probably marginal.

7.3.3 *Simulation with standard computing components*

The methods mentioned so far are economical of equipment but require specific impedances to be made up for a particular simulation. This is acceptable for many cases, but it is sometimes convenient to be able to simulate a component specified by its transfer function using only the standard components available in an analogue computer. This can be done by returning to the original transfer function expression (equation 7.15) and introducing a dummy variable w so that we have

$$-\frac{F_Z(s)}{F_P(s)} = \frac{y}{x} = \frac{y}{w} \cdot \frac{w}{x}$$

This can then be broken down into two equations

$$F_P(s) \cdot w = x$$

and $$y = -F_Z(s) \cdot w.$$

Expanding $F_P(s)$ and $F_Z(s)$, both of which are polynomials in s, allows these equations to be rewritten as

$$(s^n + a_{n-1}s^{n-1} + \ldots\ldots + a_1 s + a_0)w = x \tag{7.23}$$

and $$y = -(b_m s^m + b_{m-1}s^{m-1} + \ldots\ldots + b_1 s + b_0)w \tag{7.24}$$

Equation 7.23 represents a straightforward differential equation with constant coefficients and a forcing function x. This is solved in the usual way, using n integrators and two summers as shown in the lower part of figure 7.6. Equation 7.24 is the output equation, which can be implemented using two additional summers, as shown in the upper part of figure 7.6. The potentiometers correspond to the coefficients a_0 to a_{n-1} and b_0 to b_m (some of which may be zero) so that time scaling must therefore be applied to the original function in order to make all these coefficients less than unity.

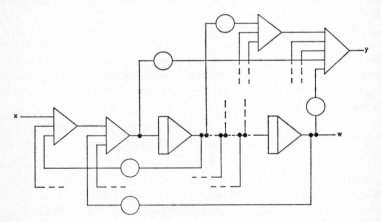

Fig. 7.6. General transfer functions can be realized with standard computing elements.

It will be observed that the computer programme of figure 7.6 can be used as it stands to implement equation 7.24 only if $m \le n$, since it would require further differentiation of w to give $s^r w$ for $r > m$. This limitation, however, is never significant, since for all physically realizable voltage or current transfer functions the number of zeros cannot be greater than the number of poles. The need for differentiation can arise in other ways, however, the implications of this will be discussed in the following section.

7.4 Differentiation

On the face of it, a desire for a differentiating circuit to complement the range of available circuit blocks does not seem unreasonable. With such a block available, a number of problems would be directly soluble. Consider, for example, a system described by the differential equation

$$\ddot{y} + a_1 \dot{y} + a_0 y = b_1 \dot{x} + b_0 x. \qquad (7.25)$$

An equation of this kind, whose significant feature is the inclusion of the differential of the forcing function, is not uncommon in control systems, where y is the controlled variable and x is an error

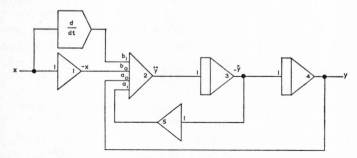

Fig. 7.7. Simulation of a second order system excited by a forcing function and its derivative. This programme contains a differentiator, which has undesirable characteristics.

signal. The left hand side of equation 7.25 then represents the dynamics of the control system, and the $b_1 \dot{x}$ term represents an error rate control added to the normal proportional control. If a differentiator were available, this system could be simulated by the circuit shown in figure 7.7, assuming that the differentiator introduces a sign change.

7.4.1 *Difficulties of differentiation*

One major reason why differentiators are not popular in computing programmes is the effect that such circuits have on noise. Noise is essentially a high frequency effect which does not itself generally interfere with computing signals, but can, if present in excessive amounts, overload amplifiers and other computing blocks. The effect that a differentiator has on noise can be appreciated by observing that

$$\left|\frac{d}{dt}(\sin \omega t)\right| = \omega \left|\sin \omega t\right|$$

In other words, high frequency noise signals will be increased in amplitude by a differentiating circuit.

A second objection to differentiating circuits arises because of the common use in control systems of step function excitations. The ideal response of a differentiating circuit to a step input is an impulse – an output that is infinite at the instant at which the step is applied and zero at all other times. Such an output cannot, of course, be realized by a physical circuit block, so that a differentiator is bound in such a case to give, at best, a very approximate substitute for the ideal output. Of more importance is the fact that the differentiator would overload, and this could lead to further difficulties due to overload recovery time (see section 6.6.4). Further differentiations of an impulse ideally yield doublet and higher order discontinuity functions with similar properties.

7.4.2 *Elimination of differentiators*

Even apart from the practical objections to the use of differentiators, the circuit of figure 7.7 would not be a satisfactory implementation of equation 7.25 because the outputs of the integrators do not in fact represent a valid set of state variables for this problem. States variables by definition (see section 7.1.2) must be such that the system output at any time t is uniquely determined by the state at the zero (reference) time t_0 and the history of inputs between t_0 and t. If the input contains a step which is passed through a differentiator this condition is not satisfied because impulse functions (and higher order discontinuity functions) would produce discontinuities in the state trajectory so that the state at that instant would not be uniquely defined.

Both the theoretical and the practical difficulties can be overcome if the differentiator can be eliminated from the programme. This can be done by re-writing equation 7.25 in the form

$$\ddot{y} - b_1 \dot{x} = -a_1 \dot{y} - a_0 y + b_0 x$$
$$= -a_1(\dot{y} - b_1 x) - a_0 y + (b_0 - a_1 b_1)x. \qquad (7.26)$$

By choosing state variables

$$q_1 = y; \qquad q_2 = \dot{y} - b_1 x \qquad (7.27)$$

equation 7.26 can then be converted to the normal form

$$\left.\begin{array}{l} \dot{q}_1 = q_2 + b_1 x \\ \dot{q}_2 = -a_0 q_1 - a_1 q_2 + (b_0 - a_1 b_1)x \end{array}\right\} \qquad (7.28)$$

which is implemented by the programme shown in figure 7.8(a).

An alternative way of setting about eliminating differentiators is to work directly from a computing programme. For this purpose it is less confusing if a preliminary block diagram is drawn without incorporating sign changes, as shown in figure 7.8(b). It is apparent from this diagram that the input signal that is passed through the

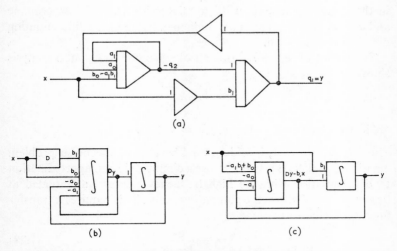

(a)

(b)   (c)

Fig. 7.8. It is often possible to eliminate differentiators by re-programming.
    (a) A programme based on a state variable approach.
    (b) The same problem programmed in block diagram form including a differentiator.
    (c) The programme of (b) modified to remove the differentiator.

differentiator is subsequently integrated: the elimination of the differentiator is accomplished by taking this input directly to the second integrator as shown in figure 7.8(c). If the output from the second integrator is to remain unchanged, therefore, the output from the first integrator must be modified to $(Dy - b_1x)$ so as to keep the total input to the second integrator as Dy. Removing the b_1Dx input will achieve this, provided the sum of the other inputs remains unaltered. One of these other inputs, however, is supplied from the output of the integrator itself, so that it has been modified from $-a_1Dy$ to $-a_1(Dy - b_1x)$: the extra term must therefore be removed by subtracting a_1b_1x. The resulting block diagram, shown in figure 7.8(c) may be compared with equations 7.27 and 7.28. More complicated systems, perhaps involving the second order differential of the input, can be treated in a similar way, always remembering that a change in the output of any one amplifier must be appropriately compensated wherever it feeds another amplifier.

7.4.3 *Differentiating circuits*

It occasionally happens that, despite the use of the techniques described in the preceding section, a differentiator is left in the programme and for some reason cannot be eliminated. In this case a differentiating circuit has to be used.

The circuit of figure 7.9(a) is an obvious one to try, and analysis shows that

$$y = -CR\frac{dx}{dt}$$

or, in transfer function terms, $y/x = -CRs$.

This circuit, however, is seldom used because of the noise problem mentioned earlier. It is better to use a circuit giving an approximation to differentiation with the high frequency response attentuated at frequencies well above the computing range. This requires a transfer function of the form

$$\frac{y}{x} = -\frac{as}{1+Ts} \tag{7.29}$$

The circuit of figure 7.9(b) has the transfer function given by equation 7.29 with $a = CR_f$, $T = CR_i$.

An alternative way of producing a differentiator is to make use of implicit function generation techniques. The circuit shown in

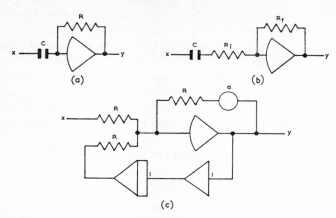

Fig. 7.9. If a differentiating circuit has to be used there are various forms that it can take.

(a) The simplest differentiator, which is very noisy.

(b) Noise problems can be reduced by attenuating the high frequency components.

(c) A more elaborate way of providing differentiation with high frequency attenuation, using only standard computing elements.

figure 7.9(c) is essentially the same as that shown in figure 7.2, with an integrator acting as the function generator in the feedback loop. The additional feedback serves the purpose of filtering out the high frequencies, giving an overall transfer function of

$$\frac{y}{x} = - \frac{s}{1+as}.$$

This circuit has the additional merit that it uses only standard computing elements.

7.5 Generalized integration

One basic feature of analogue processing methods, whether in computation or in instrumentation systems, is that integration is necessarily performed with respect to time. For most of the problems for which these methods are normally used this presents no difficulty because the problem is itself one of dynamics in which the only independent variable is time. In a number of other cases the problem involves an independent variable other than time, but provided that there is only one such variable appearing in the differential equations describing the system this also does not present any difficulty: it is then basically a matter of time scaling the problem (see section 3.4.4).

There are, however, occasions when a dynamic problem, in which it is necessary to have computer time corresponding to problem time, contains in its mathematical formulation differentiations with respect to some other variable. The problem that then arises is how to implement an integration with respect to this other variable: this is called generalized integration.

The normal method is to transform the equation

$$F = \int f(x) \, dx$$

to the equivalent form

$$F = \int f(x) \frac{dx}{dt} \, dt. \tag{7.30}$$

The full implementation of this equation requires the use of a multiplier: a device that receives two inputs x and y and gives an output proportional to xy. The symbol for this device is shown in figure 7.10(a); the scaling of multipliers is dealt with briefly in section

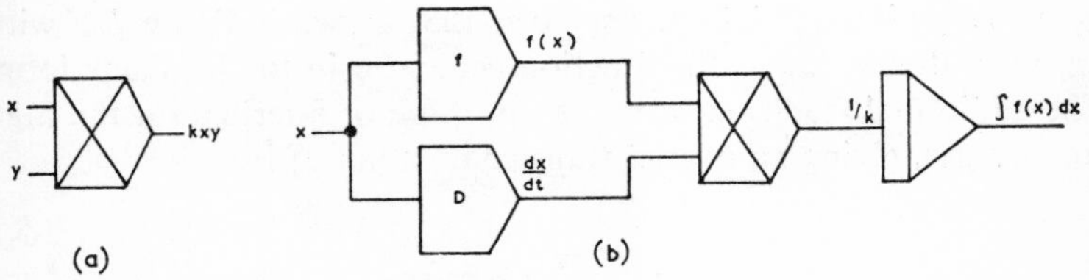

Fig. 7.10. (a) The symbol for a multiplier.
(b) The use of a multiplier to achieve generalized integration.

8.4.4. The full programme to implement equation 7.30, assuming that only x is available (as a function of time) is shown in figure 7.10(b). If x is itself generated within the computer from a differential equation, then dx/dt will be available without the need for a differentiator, but if it is a forcing function then this is one of the occasions on which the use of a differentiator cannot be avoided. This is so even although the differentiator is followed by an integrator, because linear and non-linear operations cannot be transposed.

7.6 Notes and references

The classification of systems and the state variable approach to systems analysis are discussed at length in most modern books on the theory of control systems. Among the many that could be cited are those by De Russo, Roy, and Close, and by Schwarz and Friedland. The latter, in particular, gives a very lucid account of the underlying theory, and also makes a good deal of use of analogue computer diagrams as a conceptual aid in analysing systems.

The use of operational amplifiers to provide specified transfer functions is discussed by Paul, who has worked extensively with analogue computers in connection with aerodynamic systems, and by Huelsman, who writes from the point of view of the manufacturer of amplifiers intending his products to be used in filter networks. The value of this technique can scarcely be over-emphasized. In his later book, Huelsman covers a wide range of active filter techniques, and cites a comprehensive list of references in each field.

REFERENCES

DE RUSSO, P. M., ROY, R. J. and CLOSE, C. M. (1965). *State Variables for Engineers*, Wiley, New York.

HUELSMAN, L. P. (1966). *Handbook of Operational Amplifier Active RC Networks*, Burr-Brown Research Corporation.

HUELSMAN, L. P. (1970). *Active Filters*, McGraw-Hill, New York.

PAUL, R. J. A. (1965). *Fundamental Analogue Techniques*, Blackie, London.

SCHWARZ, R. J. and FRIEDLAND, B. (1965). *Linear Systems*, McGraw-Hill, New York.

8 Piecewise Linear Techniques

The most important method of realizing non-linear simulation blocks relies on forming a piecewise linear approximation to the required characteristic. This means that instead of having a slope that varies continuously as the input varies, the characteristic consists of constant slope segments with step discontinuities of slope occurring at particular input values. These input values at which the characteristic changes from one segment to another are known as *break points*. The individual linear segments of the characteristic are then obtained by straightforward linear methods, and the choice of segment for any particular input is made by a switching circuit. The switching circuit can take various forms such as an electromechanical stepping switch (a uniselector), or an electronic rotary switch (a dekatron), but the most frequently used methods rely on the switching properties of diodes.

8.1 Diode switching methods

The simplest way to analyse a diode circuit is to represent the diode as an ideal switch. The output can then be calculated using normal linear methods, representing the diode first as closed circuit and then as an open circuit. Some care is needed in multiple diode circuits since not all the possible combinations of open and closed states are necessarily realizable. The transition point at which a particular diode switches over can be found by considering the current passing in the forward direction when the diode is conducting, and obtaining the condition for this current to fall to zero. Alternatively, we can find the reverse voltage across the diode when it is non-conducting, and obtain the condition for this voltage to fall to zero.

8.1.1 *Ring switches*

The operation of the ring switch shown in figure 8.1(a) is conveniently analysed by first assuming that all the diodes are conducting and then calculating the current flowing in each diode. Having replaced each diode by a short circuit representing its 'on' state, the circuit is then

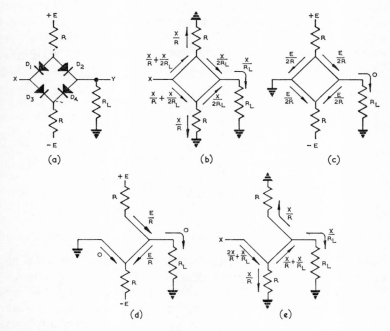

Fig. 8.1. (a) The diode ring switch in its simplest form.
  (b) Partial equivalent circuit with all diodes conducting and supplies at zero.
  (c) Second partial equivalent, with signal at zero. The total currents are obtained by superposition.
  (d), (e) Re-evaluation of currents if one diode is non-conducting.

linear and can be analysed using linear methods. In particular, the superposition principle can be used to simplify the calculations. The currents due to the signal can be obtained from the equivalent circuit shown in figure 8.1(b), where the switching supplies are replaced by earths; and the currents due to the switching supplies, E and $-E$, can be obtained from the equivalent circuit shown in figure 8.1(c), in which the signal X is earthed. In figure 8.1(b) the output must be zero because it is shorted by the diodes to the earthed input. Hence the current in the load must be zero and so by symmetry the supply currents (each equal to E/R) divide equally as shown. In figure 8.1(b), the four corners of the diode bridge are all at a potential of X, so that the currents in the three earthed resistors are obtained directly; these currents also are distributed symmetrically among the diodes. By adding the two current distributions in figures 8.1(b) and 8.1(c) we can now find the total current in each diode. Thus the forward currents are given by

$$
\left.
\begin{aligned}
i_{D1} &= \frac{E}{2R} - \left(\frac{1}{R} + \frac{1}{2R_L}\right)X \\[2mm]
i_{D2} &= \frac{E}{2R} + \frac{X}{2R_L} \\[2mm]
i_{D3} &= \frac{E}{2R} + \left(\frac{1}{R} + \frac{1}{2R_L}\right)X \\[2mm]
i_{D4} &= \frac{E}{2R} - \frac{X}{2R_L}
\end{aligned}
\right\}
\tag{8.1}
$$

The model on which this calculation has been based assumed that all the diodes were conducting; the model is valid therefore only if the net forward current in each diode is positive. From equations 8.1 we see first of all that if E is negative then for $X \geq 0$, i_{D1} and i_{D4} are both negative, while for $X \leq 0$, i_{D2} and i_{D3} are both negative. It follows therefore that for $E < 0$ the switch is open for all values of X. If E is positive then the model is clearly valid for $X = 0$, all four currents being positive, but if X is increased, i_{D1} and i_{D4} will fall until i_{D1} becomes zero when

$$
X = \frac{R_L}{R + 2R_L} E.
\tag{8.2}
$$

At this point the switch is still closed, because $D3$ and $D4$ are still conducting, but the model represented by figures 8.1(b) and 8.1(c) is no longer valid because $D1$ is cut off. To investigate the effect of a further increase in X, new equivalent circuits have to be drawn as shown in figures 8.1(d) and 8.1(e). The diode currents now become

$$i_{D2} = \frac{E}{R} - \frac{X}{R}$$

$$i_{D3} = \left(\frac{2}{R} + \frac{1}{R_L}\right)X \qquad (8.3)$$

$$i_{D4} = \frac{E}{R} - \left(\frac{1}{R} + \frac{1}{R_L}\right)X$$

From equations 8.3 it is clear that i_{D4} will fall to zero, cutting off $D4$ and so disconnecting the input from the output, if X reaches a value of

$$X = \frac{R_L}{R + R_L} E. \qquad (8.4)$$

The calculations can be repeated for negative values of X: diodes $D3$ and $D2$ cut off in turn at values of X that are numerically the same as those given by equations 8.2 and 8.4. If the switch is to remain closed for all input signals, therefore, the switching voltage must satisfy

$$E \geq \left(1 + \frac{R}{R_L}\right)X_{max} \qquad (8.5)$$

while if all the diodes are to remain conducting, then from equation 8.2,

$$E \geq \left(2 + \frac{R}{R_L}\right)X_{max}.$$

Thus, keeping all the diodes conducting, which has the advantage that it keeps the total resistance of the switch down to a minimum, requires the switching voltage to be nearly twice as large as it needs to be if one of the diodes is allowed to cut off.

8.1.2 Input switching

A common requirement in piecewise linear circuits is to switch a signal into an amplifier whenever the signal exceeds a threshold. This is conveniently achieved by taking advantage of the fact that the summing junction of an operational amplifier is virtually fixed at zero potential. The insertion of a diode between the input resistor and the summing junction, as shown in figure 8.2(a), ensures that current

M

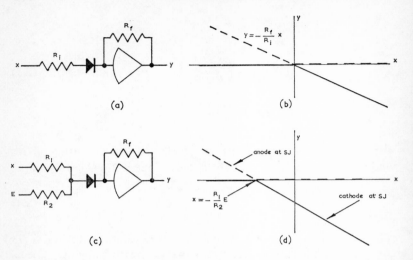

Fig. 8.2. (a) A diode connected between the summing junction and the amplifier input suppresses one part of the linear characteristic.

(b) The characteristic of (a) (solid line). Reversing the diode gives the characteristic shown dotted.

(c) The addition of a constant input moves the break point away from zero.

(d) The characteristic given by (c) (solid line). The broken line is the characteristic obtained by reversing the diode.

can flow in the input resistor only if $x > 0$. Thus, if $x > 0$, the amplifier operates as a normal summer, to give

$$y = -\frac{R_f}{R_i} x,$$

but the output is zero for $x \leq 0$. Reversing the direction of the diode interchanges the two limits. The two characteristics are shown in figure 8.2(b). To achieve a non-zero break point, a bias supply may be added as shown in figure 8.2(c). If the diode is non-conducting, the output is zero, and if the diode is conducting the output is

$$y = -\frac{R_f}{R_1} x - \frac{R_f}{R_2} E.$$

Switching occurs when the voltage at the junction of the two input resistors tends to become positive. The condition for the diode to conduct, therefore, is

$$\frac{R_1 E + R_2 x}{R_1 + R_2} \geq 0$$

or
$$x \geq -\frac{R_1}{R_2} E.$$

The transfer characteristic obtained from the circuit of figure 8.2(c) is shown by the solid line in figure 8.2(d); if the diode is reversed the equations of the two segments of the characteristic remain the same, but the conduction condition is reversed, giving the curve shown dotted in figure 8.2(d).

8.1.3 *Analogue logic circuits*

The circuit shown in figure 8.3(a) has to be analysed in a slightly different way because of the two independent inputs that are connected through diodes to a common point. In this case it is clearly impossible,

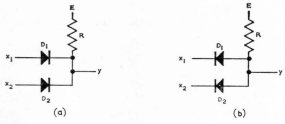

$$\text{(a)} \qquad \text{(b)}$$

Fig. 8.3. Analogue logic circuits.
(a) $y = \max [x_1, x_2, E]$
(b) $y = \min [x_1, x_2, E]$

if both the inputs are supplied from low impedance sources, to have both diodes conducting at once, apart from the special case when the two inputs are equal. It is, however, possible to have both diodes cut off, in which case the output, y, will be at a potential of E (assuming the circuit is not loaded). If both the diodes are to be reverse biassed, therefore, the inputs must satisfy the condition

$$x_1, x_2 < E. \tag{8.6}$$

If condition 8.6 is not satisfied, one of the diodes will conduct. If $D1$ is conducting, then $y = x_1$, and this is possible only if $D2$ is reverse biassed, that is, only if $x_1 > x_2$. Similarly, if $x_2 > x_1$ then $y = x_2$. The whole operation of the circuit can be conveniently expressed as

$$y = \max (x_1, x_2, E).$$

If the resistor R is the input resistor of a summer then $E = 0$ and the final output becomes

$$y' = - \frac{R_f}{R} [\max (x_1, x_2, 0)].$$

By reversing the directions of both the diodes, as shown in figure 8.3(b) the operation of the simple circuit becomes

$$y = \min (x_1, x_2, E)$$

and again the use of an operational amplifier gives a modified output

$$y' = - \frac{R_f}{R} [\min (x_1, x_2, 0)].$$

The circuits of figures 8.3(a) and 8.3(b) are identical to ones that can be used in digital systems to perform logic operations (see appendix 1, section A1.2.1); it is for this reason that they are often described as analogue logic circuits.

8.2 Limiters

Many piecewise linear approximations are based on circuits having a single switching action, so that the transfer characteristic consists of two linear segments separated by a single break point. Combinations of these units can be used to produce a wide range of composite characteristics by combining a number of different segments.

One type of switching action that is often needed either alone or as part of a more complicated characteristic, is one allowing normal summer (or integrator) action on one side of a break point, and a constant output on the other side. A device having this form of transfer characteristic is generally described as a limiter, since the output is limited to a particular value irrespective of the value of the input. The simplest forms of limiter characteristic are those for which the limiting value is zero and the break point is at the origin, as shown in figure 8.2(b). The circuit of figure 8.2(a) gives one of these transfer characteristics, and the same circuit with the diode reversed gives the other; this circuit is therefore often spoken of as a series limiter. An alternative way of producing this characteristic is by connecting a diode as a feedback path as shown in figure 8.4(a). If the diode is non-conducting, the amplifier acts as a normal summer; while if the diode conducts, the output is held at the summing junction potential, which is virtually zero. The transition occurs when the output tends to become positive, so that the break point is at the origin, giving the characteristic shown as the solid line in figure 8.2(b) (which is also

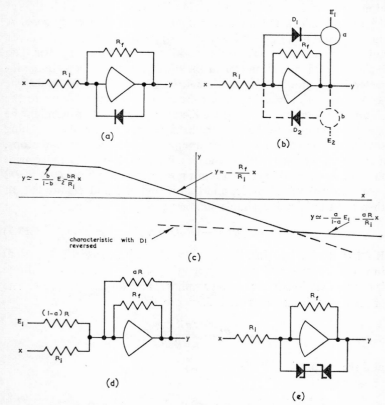

Fig. 8.4. (a) Simple shunt limiter which, with an ideal diode, would have the characteristic shown in Fig. 8.2(b).

(b) A limiter with adjustable break point. The complementary part of the circuit, shown dotted, allows an upper limit to be applied as well as a lower one.

(c) The characteristic of (b). Note that this is a 'soft limiter': the slope in the limiting region is not zero.

(d) Equivalent circuit of (b) when D1 is conducting.

(e) Limiting with zener diodes.

the characteristic given by the series limiter of figure 8.2(a)). The dotted line in figure 8.2(b) is the characteristic obtained from either of the circuits shown in figures 8.2(a) and 8.4(b) by reversing the diode.

The circuits of figures 8.2(a) and 8.4(a) are both restricted in their application by the fact that, although the break point can be shifted along the x axis by adding a biassing input, as illustrated in figures 8.2(b) and 8.2(d), the limiting output value is necessarily zero. A more general requirement is for a limiting circuit whose limit can be adjusted to any value within the working range of the amplifier. The inclusion of a potentiometer in the diode feedback loop (potentiometer 1 and diode $D1$ in figure 8.4(b)) allows this to be done. The second potentiometer in figure 8.4(b) applies a second limit to the characteristic as shown in figure 8.4(c); this characteristic might be used, for example, to simulate the behaviour of an amplifier reaching saturation, or of a movable component constrained by end stops. The transfer characteristic of the circuit can be derived in a piecewise fashion, first observing that it is not possible to have both $D1$ and $D2$ conducting simultaneously, and that if both $D1$ and $D2$ are cut off then the amplifier is a simple summer giving

$$y = -(R_f/R_i)x. \qquad (8.7)$$

If $D1$ is conducting, then the circuit can be redrawn as in figure 8.4(d) in which a is the setting of the potentiometer ($a = 0$ when the diode is connected directly across the amplifier) and R is its resistance. The effective feedback resistance, therefore, is

$$R'_f = \frac{aRR_f}{aR + R_f}$$

and the output is given by

$$y = - \frac{aRR_f}{(1-a)(aR + R_f)R} E_1 - \frac{aRR_f}{R_i(aR + R_f)} x. \qquad (8.8)$$

Normally, $aR \ll R_f$ (since $a \not> 0.5$, $R \sim 30$ kΩ, $R_f \sim 1$ MΩ) so that equation 8.8 may be rewritten

$$y \simeq - \frac{a}{1-a} E_1 - a \frac{R}{R_i} x. \qquad (8.9)$$

The third segment of the characteristic, when $D2$ is conducting, can be obtained in the same way, giving

$$y \simeq - \frac{b}{1-b} E_2 - b \frac{R}{R_i} x \qquad (8.10)$$

where b is the setting of potentiometer 2, which is assumed to have the same resistance, R, as potentiometer 1. The transition from equation 8.7 to equation 8.8 occurs when the potential at the wiper of potentiometer 1 attempts to go negative. The condition for this is

$$\frac{(1-a)Ry + aRE_1}{R} < 0$$

or
$$y < - \frac{a}{1-a} E_1.$$

It should be noticed that no restriction has been placed on the sign of E_1, so that the limit can be either positive or negative. Moreover, by reversing the diode, the transition can be made the other way, giving the characteristic shown dotted in figure 8.4(c). It should also be noticed from equations 8.9 and 8.10 that even though the diodes have been assumed to be perfect – switching from open circuits to short circuits – the slope of the characteristic in the 'limited' region is not truly zero. Taking typical values of $R = 30$ kΩ, $R_f = 1$ MΩ, the slope in the worst case, with $a = 0\cdot5$, is $0\cdot015$. The error introduced by this finite slope could theoretically, taking extreme conditions, rise to about 3 %, but in practical cases the error will seldom exceed 1 %, which is adequate for many applications. Methods of obtaining precision limiting characteristics for more exacting applications will be described in the next section.

In special purpose applications, where adjustment of the limits throughout a continuous range may not be required, the circuit of figure 8.4(b) can be simplified by replacing the potentiometers by fixed resistor chains. An even greater simplification is possible for some purposes by using Zener diodes to provide both the switching and the bias supply, giving the circuit shown in figure 8.4(e). The difficulty with this circuit is to obtain pre-defined limiting levels, since there is only a finite number of breakdown voltages for which Zener diodes can be obtained and these voltages drift appreciably with time and temperature. There are many occasions, however, when limiting is required not to simulate a system component but to provide protection for the amplifiers or other components of the simulation itself. In such cases, a 5% tolerance on the limiting level would normally be perfectly acceptable, and the circuit of figure 8.4(*e*) is commonly employed in this kind of application.

8.2.1 *Precision limiters*

There are some circuit requirements in which the finite slope of the limiter characteristic beyond the break point can give rise to unacceptable errors. One such situation is when the limiter is followed by an integrator and the computation is required to proceed for an appreciable time. An input that is even a few hundred millivolts in error will then produce an integrated error of tens of volts within one or two minutes. One way of reducing this error is to use two limiters in series, with the limits set to the same values, so that the overall slope in the limiting region is the product of the individual slopes. In the example of the previous section, this would reduce the slope from 0·015 to 0·0002. However, the slope cannot be reduced to zero in this way, and a preferable method is to return to the series limiting circuit of figure 8.2(c). By adding a constant to the output, as can be seen from figure 8.2(d), a zero slope limit can be produced at any desired level, provided the diode acts as a perfect switch. A convenient way

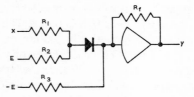

Fig. 8.5. A series limiter with an additional input provides hard limiting (assuming an ideal diode) at a non-zero level.

of adding the required constant is to connect an additional input resistor direct to the summing junction as shown in figure 8.5 so that the output is defined by

$$y = -\frac{R_f}{R_1}x - \left(\frac{R_f}{R_2} - \frac{R_f}{R_3}\right)E \qquad \text{if } x \geq -\frac{R_1}{R_2}E$$

$$y = \frac{R_f}{R_3}E \qquad\qquad\qquad \text{if } x < -\frac{R_1}{R_2}E.$$

The simple limiter of figure 8.4(a), in common with all the other

diode circuits that have been discussed so far, has a transfer characteristic that in practice departs from the ideal because the diode in the
circuit does not act as a perfect switch. In particular, silicon diodes
have an almost constant non-zero voltage drop across them when
they are conducting, with the result that the limit in figure 8.2(b) is
not at zero, but at a small but finite negative voltage. Again, this is
unimportant in many applications, but if an integrator follows the
limiter there can be large errors. A way of overcoming these difficulties
is to add another diode to give the circuit of figure 8.6(a). This circuit

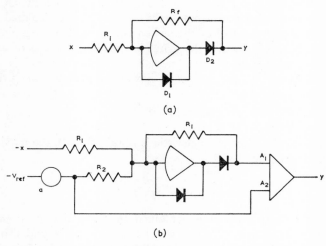

Fig. 8.6. Practical diodes have finite forward and reverse resistances.
    (a) An ideal diode circuit.
    (b) An ideal diode circuit used in a precision limiter.

acts as a normal summer if $x < 0$, when $D1$ is non-conducting and $D2$
is conducting. The forward resistance of $D2$ acts as an addition to the
output impedance of the amplifier in this case, but this will not have
a noticeable effect on the performance in any normal circuit. As x
reaches zero, $D1$ starts to conduct and this causes a sudden reduction
in the current through $D2$. The result of this is that $D2$ is cut off
abruptly as the input passes through zero, and the output limit is
held at zero. The circuit of figure 8.6(a) reproduces with physical
diodes a characteristic that closely matches that of an ideal diode, and
it is for that reason often spoken of as an ideal diode circuit. It can

be used to replace the diode in any of the circuits described in this chapter, although the sign change involved by the use of an operational amplifier needs to be taken into account. If the ideal diode circuit is used to replace the diode in figure 8.5 for example, the resulting circuit is that shown in figure 8.6(b) where

$$a = \frac{E}{V_{\text{ref}}} ; \qquad A_1 = \frac{R_f}{R_1} ; \qquad A_2 = \frac{R_f}{R_3} .$$

8.2.2 *Limiting with ring switches*

The circuit of figure 8.1(a) is most frequently used as a switch, with the output Y either connected directly to the input or isolated completely from it. Control of the switch is exercised by changing the value of E: if E is negative the switch is open for all values of X, and $Y \equiv 0$; while if E satisfies the inequality 8.5 then the switch is closed for all values of X, and $Y \equiv X$. If however E is chosen such that

$$0 \leq E \leq \left(1 + \frac{R}{R_L}\right) X_{\text{max}}$$

a symmetrical limiter characteristic is obtained, with the maximum output defined by

$$|Y|_{\text{max}} = \frac{R_L}{R + R_L} E.$$

Greater flexibility can be obtained by using the more general circuit shown in figure 8.7(a) in which the two supplies and also their associated resistors are allowed to differ in magnitude. This circuit can be analysed in much the same way as the simple circuit in section 8.1.1, but an additional complication is introduced because we are no longer able to appeal to symmetry. In the equivalent circuit of figure 8.7(b) for example, representing the effect of the source voltage acting alone when all the diodes are conducting, we cannot equate I_1 to I_3 and I_2 to I_4. We are therefore left with five unknowns, and only four nodes at which we can use Kirchhoff's current law. The necessary fifth equation is obtained by assuming that the forward resistance of each diode is equal to r and then applying Kirchhoff's voltage law around the loop formed by the four diodes. This gives

$$I_1 r + I_2 r - I_4 r - I_3 r = 0$$

or $\qquad\qquad\qquad I_1 + I_2 = I_3 + I_4. \qquad\qquad\qquad (8.11)$

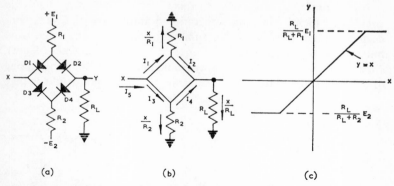

(a) (b) (c)

Fig. 8.7. A diode ring switch can be used as a limiter.
    (a) A switch with unequal supplies and resistors.
    (b) Partial equivalent circuit of (a) with all diodes conducting and supplies earthed.
    (c) The complete characteristic. Note that, since there is no amplifier in this circuit, there is no inversion.

From the node equations we obtain

$$I_2 + I_4 = \frac{X}{R_L} \qquad (8.12)$$

$$I_3 - I_4 = \frac{X}{R_2} \qquad (8.13)$$

$$I_1 - I_2 = \frac{X}{R_1} \qquad (8.14)$$

Equations 8.11 to 8.14 enable us to evaluate the current in each diode due to the signal alone, and similar methods can be used to find the current in each diode due to E_1 and $-E_2$ acting alone. By using the methods of section 8.1.1 to establish the switching points, the transfer characteristic of the circuit can then be shown to be as illustrated in figure 8.7(c). It should be particularly noted that the slope of the characteristic in the limiting regions is zero.

8.3 Comparators

A second type of unit that is required in the production of composite characteristics is one whose output does not change in response to changes in the input except at one particular point, at which a very small change in the input produces an abrupt change in the output.

A simple example of a unit with this characteristic is the *high gain amplifier*, which is simply an operational amplifier with inputs connected through resistors to the summing junction in the usual way, but with no feedback resistor connected, as shown in figure 8.8(a). An amplifier connected in this way would always in practice be in one of only two stable states; with a single input, the output would change

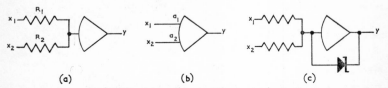

(a)   (b)   (c)

Fig. 8.8. An operational amplifier used without feedback switches from
one saturation level to the other as the input changes sign.
(a) High gain amplifier with two inputs.
(b) Symbol for (a). The 'gains' shown are inversely proportional
to the input resistors.
(c) A zener diode used to obtain binary output without overloading.

abruptly from negative to positive saturation as the input changed from positive to negative. With more than one input, as in figure 8.8(a), the switching of the amplifier takes place as the summing junction voltage passes through zero, which is when

$$x_1 R_2 + x_2 R_1 = 0. \tag{8.15}$$

With R_1 and R_2 equal, the output changes state when the sum of the inputs changes sign; this is essentially the requirement for a comparator (see section 5.8). With unequal resistors, equation 8.15 may be rewritten as

$$\frac{R_f}{R_1} x_1 + \frac{R_f}{R_2} x_2 = 0$$

or $$a_1 x_1 + a_2 x_2 = 0 \tag{8.16}$$

where R_f is any arbitrary value. The factors a_1, a_2 in equation 8.16 may be recognized as the gains that would apply if a feedback resistor R_f were connected; these values would be the ones marked on the patchboard of a general purpose computer, so that they are convenient values to use. The circuit of figure 8.8(a) can be represented by the symbol of figure 8.8(b).

In practice, of course, amplifiers are not deliberately driven into saturation; apart from anything else the overload recovery time (see section 6.6.4) would make the response very sluggish. Limiting is therefore required, and any of the circuits of figures 8.4(b), 8.4(e), or 8.5 can be used with the feedback resistor removed to provide a satisfactory comparator action.

If a comparator is required to work in an iterative or hybrid system, the output levels would need to be defined to be compatible with the logic elements of the system. If, as is often the case, one of the logic levels is zero volts, the two comparator levels can be obtained with a single Zener diode, as in figure 8.8(c), although it should perhaps be emphasized that patching an amplifier in any of these ways to act as a comparator is neither normal nor ideal. Comparators based on Schmitt trigger circuits are cheaper, and also better since the logical complement of the comparator output is also available. The amplifier circuits, however, can be useful when there are no special purpose comparators available, or sometimes for particular applications. One kind of application for which amplifier comparators can sometimes be conveniently used is where the comparator output is required not to feed a logic system but simply to operate a switch that re-routes an analogue signal. In this case, provided the switching delays inevitable with electromechanical devices can be tolerated, a relay can be connected directly to the output of an amplifier comparator so that the whole operation is then carried out at once. Here the amplifier is being used not only to make the decision but also to provide the power to operate the relay; the circuit is particularly useful in that a number of different circuits can be switched by separate relay contacts, and also because changeover contacts are readily available.

In applications in which relay switching delays cannot be tolerated, the comparator has to be used to drive an electronic switch. These are essentially on-off switches, but a changeover action can be

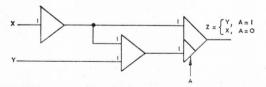

Fig. 8.9. A changeover switching action can be obtained from a single logic signal by the use of additional amplifiers.

obtained (at the cost of additional equipment) by using the circuit of figure 8.9, in which the simple logic signal A causes the output to switch between the two independent analogue inputs X and Y.

8.4 Composite characteristics

Limiters and comparators represent two particular non-linear characteristics that find widespread use in analogue simulations, but to be able to produce a characteristic of arbitrary shape, it is necessary to add a number of elements each of which produces one segment of the characteristic having the appropriate slope and break point. Examples of the ways in which this can be done will be given in the remainder of this chapter.

8.4.1 *Variable function generators*

A very versatile circuit that can be used to give a fully adjustable segment is the series limiter of figure 8.2(c), which can give four different kinds of characteristic. The non-zero part of the characteristic, starting at the break point, can extend into any one of the four quadrants, depending on which way round the diode is connected, and on whether the applied signal is $+x$ or $-x$. A general purpose

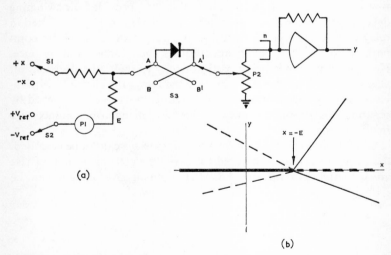

Fig. 8.10. The general purpose variable function generator.
    (a) The basic circuit, giving two linear segments.
    (b) The four possible elementary functions that can be obtained from (a).

unit, which can be switched to give any one of the characteristics, is shown in figure 8.10(a); the characteristics themselves are shown in figure 8.10(b). The quadrant is chosen by switches $S1$ and $S3$, the break point is positioned by switch $S2$ and potentiometer $P1$, and the slope is adjusted by potentiometer $P2$. A number of these units all connected to the summing junction of the output amplifier, as indicated in figure 8.10(a), can be adjusted to give a piecewise linear approximation to almost any single valued function of x. Variable function generators in general purpose computers are almost invariably built using this principle, although the detailed construction varies slightly from one manufacturer to another. The same methods are also very commonly used in fixed function generators (to form $\sin x$, x^2, $\log x$ and so on) that are provided both in computers and in some instrumentation applications. It is common, for example, for low frequency waveform generators for servo system testing to be based on a diode sine wave generator with a ramp input (see section 10.2.2). Frequency variation is then achieved simply by altering the slope of the ramp; this system is very much easier to implement and control at very low frequencies than one based on an oscillatory circuit.

8.4.2 *Dead space*

The dead space characteristic is shown in figure 8.11(a). It can be formed from two straight line segments of the kind described in figure 8.10(b) by using the circuit shown in figure 8.11(b). The sign of x used as the input to this circuit depends on the required slopes S_1 and S_2 of the characteristic: if these are positive then the input must be $-x$. Positive slopes can be obtained directly without the need of an inverter by using the circuit of figure 8.11(c), which is essentially the same as figure 8.11(b) without the operational amplifier. The only limitation of this simple circuit is that the slopes S_1 and S_2 must be numerically less than unity.

Another way of obtaining a dead space characteristic is to use a ring switch as shown in figure 8.11(d). When the switch is open the amplifier is used as a normal summer, but when it is closed the feedback resistor is short circuited and the output is tied to zero.

If the break points and slopes need to be more accurately defined, a precision dead space can be constructed by replacing the diodes by ideal diode circuits in the same way as in the precision limiter (section 8.2.1).

Dead space circuits, or modifications of them, can sometimes be useful in the construction of more elaborate characteristics. The circuit of figure 8.11(d), for example, can be modified by removing the feedback resistor and connecting a normal limiting circuit. The

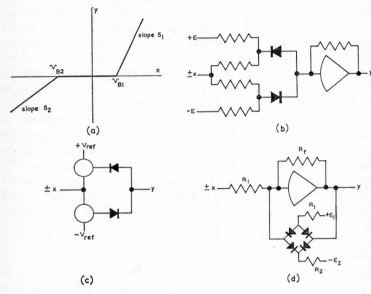

Fig. 8.11. (a) The dead space characteristic.
(b) A dead space circuit using series limiters.
(c) A dead space circuit giving slopes that are positive and less than unity.
(d) A dead space can also be produced by using a ring switch as a feedback element round an operational amplifier.

characteristic then obtained would be a comparator with a dead space in the middle: such a characteristic is useful in some control applications in which the sign of an error signal is used to determine the required sense of the correction (a bang-bang servo). A dead space about the origin can be used to avoid the jitter that would be produced by an ideal comparator due to the lack of a stable state in the region of zero-error.

Figure 8.12(a) illustrates the use of resistors in series with switches and limiting circuits to produce characteristics with non-zero slopes. The transfer characteristic of this circuit is shown in figure 8.12(b).

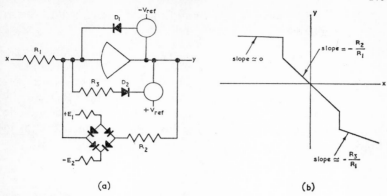

(a)   (b)

Fig. 8.12. Building a complex characteristic.
 (a) Resistors can be used with limiters and comparators to give non-zero or non-infinite slopes.
 (b) The characteristic produced by (a).

When the switch is closed, resistor R_2 acts as a normal feedback resistor; when the switch is open with x negative, comparator action coupled with normal limiting takes place; when the switch is open with x positive, comparator action coupled with limiting occurs, but with diode $D2$ conducting, resistor R_3 then acts as a feedback resistor to give a prescribed non-zero slope.

8.4.3 *Modulus*

The modulus function, shown in figure 8.13(a), can, like the dead space characteristic, be considered as consisting of two segments each

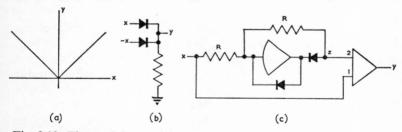

(a)   (b)   (c)

Fig. 8.13. The modulus, or absolute value, unit.
 (a) The characteristic (ideal).
 (b) A simple modulus circuit. Imperfections in the diodes cause this circuit to give inaccurate results close to the origin.
 (c) A precision modulus circuit.

N

of which can be produced by a unit of the kind described in section 8.4.1. An alternative is to use the relation

$$|x| = \max(x, -x)$$

and to use the analogue circuit shown in figure 8.13(b). The imperfections of the diodes can be overcome, as with the other circuits already discussed in this chapter, by making use of the ideal diode circuit. An economical way of doing this is shown in figure 8.13(c), in which

$$z = \begin{cases} -x \text{ if } x \geq 0 \\ 0 \text{ if } x < 0 \end{cases}$$

and

$$y = -(2z + x)$$

$$= \begin{cases} +x \text{ if } x \geq 0 \\ -x \text{ if } x < 0 \end{cases}$$

8.4.4 *Squarers and quarter square multipliers*

A particular non-linear device for which a need often exists is one whose output is proportional to the square of its input. This can be achieved using a special purpose device (see chapter 9) but more commonly a diode function generator is used. A square law is particularly suited to this method, passing through the origin and increasing monotonically in each quadrant, so that it can be produced with reasonable accuracy without requiring an impossibly large number of diode segments; five diodes in each quadrant can easily give better than 1% accuracy.

Scaling is particularly important in computer programmes involving non-linear elements of all kinds; in the case of a squaring device it is clear that the output cannot be equal to the square of the input since if the maximum value of x is 100 then the maximum value of x^2 is 10,000. The difficulty is overcome by making the output $x^2/100$ (or in general x^2/V_{ref}) so that the output has the same maximum value as the input. The importance of careful scaling can be illustrated by observing that if the maximum value of x is 30 V (which, though not ideal, would be acceptable in a summer or an integrator) the maximum value of $x^2/100$ is only nine volts.

The main reason for squarers being of particular interest in analogue computing is that they form the basis of the quarter square multiplier. This derives its name from the fact that it is based on the identity

$$xy = \frac{1}{4}[(x+y)^2 - (x-y)^2] \tag{8.17}$$

This equation can be implemented with summers and squarers: scaling requirements demand not only the factor of 100 in the squaring operation but also a factor of two in the additions, since if x and y each has a maximum value of 100, the maximum values of $x \pm y$ could be 200. Equation 8.17 is therefore re-written

$$\frac{xy}{100} = \frac{1}{100}\left(\frac{x+y}{2}\right)^2 - \frac{1}{100}\left(\frac{x-y}{2}\right)^2.$$

Several variations on this theme have been developed using slightly different algebraic relationships that are a little easier to implement. They all depend ultimately, however, on the appearance of a product term when the sum of the inputs is squared, and they are all therefore usually described as quarter square multipliers. Such multipliers, using diode networks as the squaring elements, are provided in all modern computers, and are often, in fact, the only type of multiplier available.

8.4.5 Logical synthesis

The properties of analogue logic circuits can be exploited to provide piecewise approximations to functions: such approximations need not be linear although they often are. The principle of this method is illustrated in figure 8.14(a), in which two linear functions are defined by

$$y_1 = -x + 50$$
$$y_2 = x + 10$$

and a composite function is then defined by

$$y = \min(y_1, y_2).$$

A circuit to implement this is shown in figure 8.14(b); amplifiers 1 and 2 give outputs y_1 and y_2 respectively, and these are fed to the logic circuit to give y. The scaling in this kind of circuit again needs some attention. In this example, as x varies through its permitted range of ± 100 V, y varies between -90 V and $+30$ V, which is satisfactory, but both y_1 and y_2 exceed the permitted limits. The

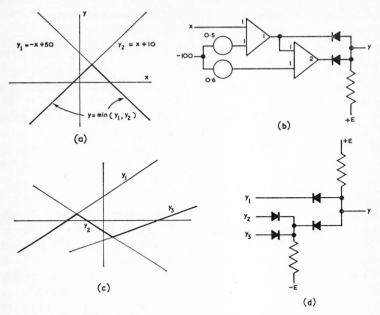

Fig. 8.14. Linear methods together with analogue logic circuits can be used to synthesise non-linear characteristics.
(a), (b) A characteristic and a circuit to give it.
(c) A more complicated characteristic requiring two levels of logic.
(d) The logic to implement (c).

overloading in this case would not affect the output, but would have the usual undesirable consequences in the overloaded amplifiers themselves (in particular, the long overload recovery time). This is one of the cases in which limiting needs to be applied to both amplifiers, but in which the precise value of the limiting output is of no consequence, as long as it is above $+30$ V, which is the largest output actually used.

This technique can be extended to give additional segments in the characteristic by making use of a double selection method. The characteristic shown in figure 8.14(c) for example, can be described by

$$y = \min [y_1, \max (y_2, y_3)]$$

and implemented by the circuit shown in figure 8.14(d). When the number of segments is increased further, however, the straightforward method of implementation can become cumbersome. It is worthwhile in these cases to use algebraic methods of simplifying the defining expression, which contains a mixture of normal algebraic operations and logical operations. Techniques of manipulating and simplifying such expressions have been developed: they amount (as in all other algebras) to the application of a set of rules defining identities between analogue logic expressions.

One particular merit of the logical synthesis technique is that it can be just as easily applied to problems of forming functions of two or more variables. The equation of a plane for example may be expressed as

$$ax_1 + bx_2 + c = 0$$

which can be generated simply by adding a further input to a summer that was forming a straight line in a two-dimensional problem. The selection amongst the various planes is then achieved using exactly the same logic circuits as in the simpler case. Multipliers, as well as more general non-linear circuits, can be designed in this way.

8.4.6 *Comparator controlled function generators*

The problem of forming an arbitrary function of two variables is one to which no entirely satisfactory solution has yet been found. Many of the devices used rely on special purpose equipment, which tends to be inflexible and expensive (see chapter 9). The logical synthesis methods mentioned in section 8.4.5 lead to relatively cheap devices, but the design has to be repeated from the start if a different function is wanted. One way of simplifying the problem is to implement the method often used to depict a function of two variables on a two-dimensional surface. The dependent variable y is plotted as a function of one of the independent variables, x_1, while the other independent variable, x_2, is held constant at various values E_0, E_1, $E_2 \ldots, E_n$. The resulting family of curves defines the output continuously with respect to x_1 and in a discrete way with respect to x_2. A typical family of curves is shown in figure 8.15(a): each curve is a straightforward function of one variable, and can be produced by a simple diode function generator. Alternatively, one of the curves, F_0, can be formed in this way, and the others by adding modification functions to F_0. This method can be implemented by the system shown in figure 8.15(b), in which x_1 is used to form a number of functions

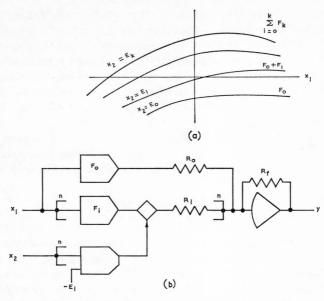

(a)

(b)

Fig. 8.15. Comparator controlled function generators can be used to form a function of two variables.
(a) A family of curves.
(b) A method of implementing (a).

$F_i(x_1)$ each of which is connected to the output amplifier through a switch. These switches are operated by x_2 acting through a bank of comparators so that the output is defined by

$$y = -\sum_{i=0}^{k} \frac{R_f}{R_i} F_i(x_1)$$

where k is such that

$$E_k < x_2 < E_{k+1}.$$

All sorts of refinements are possible in this system including a method of interpolating when x_2 is intermediate between two E values.

8.5 Asymmetrical circuits

All the circuits discussed so far in this chapter have given outputs that are single-valued functions depending only on the instantaneous value of the input or inputs. In other words, they have all been instantaneous systems (see section 7.1.1). It is sometimes useful to be able to simulate with analogue equipment devices that have some form of memory: in particular there is an interest in characteristics that depend on past events not as a function of time but simply as a chronological series. Such characteristics are defined by curves that are static but asymmetrical.

8.5.1 Bistables and monostables

Although digital circuits are freely available in block form even if they do not form part of the complement of a particular computer, it is nevertheless sometimes desirable to be able to simulate the action of these circuits using analogue computing components. By this means it is possible to have precise control over the output levels and the operating times; this is needed in investigations on the effects of component modifications on system performance, and also when using the computer as an independent waveform generator (see chapter 10).

As might be expected, all analogue two-state circuits are based on a comparator which, in its simplest form, is a symmetrical two-state device. A circuit in which the two states are stable (that is, a circuit that remains in a particular state after the removal of the input signal that caused it to enter that state) requires a positive feedback connection. The circuit of figure 8.16(a) shows one way in which this feedback can be achieved: with zero input and amplifier 1 at its positive limit, amplifier 2 supplies to amplifier 1 a negative signal which keeps it at its positive limit; similarly the circuit is stable with amplifier 1 at its negative limit. A negative value of x numerically larger than the positive output from amplifier 2 will switch the output, y, from its negative to its positive state, in which it will then stay until the input becomes sufficiently positive to switch it back. The overall characteristic is shown in figure 8.16(b): it can be used as an approximation to a hysteresis characteristic, using, if necessary, the negative of the characteristic (shown dotted in figure 8.16(b)) which is available at the output of amplifier 2. The slopes of the limited portions can be made more nearly zero either by using a precision limiter or by connecting a ring switch limiter in series with the output. Zener diodes can also be used as the feedback round amplifier 1, but this would not allow the limiting levels to be precisely controlled.

The circuit of figure 8.16(a), although it has a bistable output, does not accurately simulate a digital bistable element because it

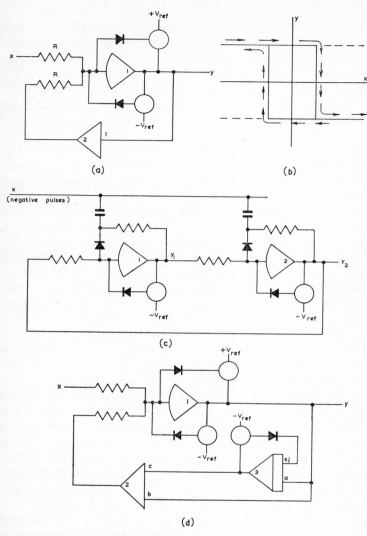

Fig. 8.16. Asymmetrical characteristics.
(a) A bistable circuit.
(b) The characteristic of (a). The dotted characteristic is obtained from amplifier 2.
(c) A bistable circuit that is switched both ways by pulses of the same sign.
(d) A monostable circuit. The gain of the integrator controls the pulse width.

needs signals of alternating sign to switch it from one state to the other. A circuit that can be switched by successive identical pulses (in this case negative) is shown in figure 8.16(c). If $D1$ is conducting with y_1 negative, $D2$ will be cut off and y_2 will be positive at a value defined by the limiting circuit. This is one stable condition: the other is with $D1$ off and $D2$ on. In either case, a negative going edge applied at x will cut off the conducting diode and so cause the circuit to change state; positive going edges produce no effect.

A monostable circuit can be produced by modifying the bistable circuit of figure 8.16(a) in such a way that in one of the two states the positive feedback is opposed by a negative feedback signal that increases with time until it is completely cancelled, at which time the circuit changes back to the other state. A way of achieving this is drawn in figure 8.16(d), in which the output from the comparator (amplifier 1) is fed back through an integrator (amplifier 3). The stable state for this circuit is with y negative: the integrator must therefore be limited in its positive excursion. This limit, together with the gains b and c in amplifier 2 must be such that the output from amplifier 2 in the stable state is positive. A negative value of x large enough to overcome the bias from amplifier 2 will then cause the circuit to change state, and to hold itself in the new state after x returns to zero because of the reversal of the sign of the bias. The integrator reduces this bias at a rate determined by the loop gain, ac, and when it has fallen to zero the circuit returns to its stable state, from which it cannot be displaced by the integrator because of the limiting circuit.

8.5.2 *Backlash*

Control systems are frequently required to supply mechanical energy by way of gearing, and in virtually all sets of gears some finite backlash is inevitably present. The simulation of this property presents new problems not met with in any of the circuits so far described, in that it is not possible to give a unique description of the characteristic. The difficulty is that the output for a given input can be any one of an infinite number of values depending on the immediate past history of the input. Whenever the input changes sign, the output remains constant until the backlash is taken up, but the change of sign of the input can occur at any point: this may be indicated by the characteristic shown in figure 8.17(a).

The method used to simulate this effect relies on using an integrator

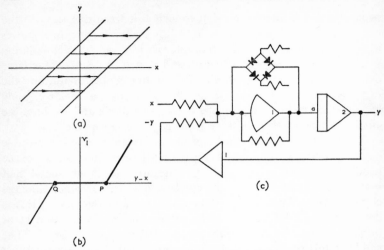

Fig. 8.17. (a) The backlash characteristic, which is another asymmetrical non-linearity.
(b) The dead space characteristic.
(c) A backlash circuit. The integrator has its input maintained at zero by the feedback action.

whose feedback is such that its output changes to maintain its input at zero. This same idea was introduced in section 5.9.2, where it was used for the error accumulator in an iterative procedure. In the circuit of figure 8.17(c), amplifier 1 is a summer with a dead space having the characteristic shown in figure 8.17(b). The output, y, remains constant as long as the input to the integrator remains zero, which it does as long as amplifier 1 remains within the dead space. If x increases so that amplifier 1 attempts to leave the dead space and produce a negative output, the integrator increases its output, which reduces the input to the amplifier 1 until it settles to point P on the characteristic. As long as x continues to increase, y will also increase to keep the operating point in the same place, but if x starts to reduce, the output remains constant while the operating point moves along the axis from P to Q. Further reduction in x would then be matched by an equal reduction in y, the operating point being kept at Q by the integrator. The gain of the integrator has no effect on the static characteristic of this circuit; it does however have an effect on the dynamic response, since a step change in x gives rise to an exponential change in y, with the time constant a.

8.6 Notes and references

Piecewise linear techniques in general, and diode switching methods in particular, are of such universal use that it would be impossible to write a book on analogue computing without reference to them, and most books have large sections devoted to them.

Slightly out of the ordinary, at least in analogue computer terms, are some of the circuits proposed by manufacturers of operational amplifiers. The applications manuals referred to in chapter 6 (see section 6.8) and also the one produced by Fenlow contain a number of such circuits, and are all worth consulting.

The analysis of diode circuits must always follow the general lines described in this chapter, but it should be appreciated that only the simplest form of this analysis was performed here. The diode ring circuit is analysed in a more comprehensive way by Millman and Taub (see page 644 of their book), and it should be particularly noticed that if we take account of the finite forward and reverse resistances of the diodes, and particularly of the fact that the forward resistances of the different diodes will not be all equal, then very different results are obtained. The use of balancing networks, essential if we are to obtain zero voltage out for zero in, can mean that the switching voltages required are an order of magnitude larger than the simple analysis would indicate.

A mathematical formalism for handling analogue logic expressions is developed by Ginsburg, who gives a number of examples of its use, including the design of a piecewise linear approximation to multiplication. Similar methods are described by Wilkinson, but the techniques (rather surprisingly) do not seem to have been taken up generally.

REFERENCES

Fenlow Electronics Ltd., *Notes on the Applications and Use of Operational Amplifiers.*

GINSBURG, S. A. (1960). Logical Method for Synthesising Function Generators. *Proc. 1st World Congress, I.F.A.C., Moscow*, Butterworth, London.

MILLMAN, J., and TAUB, H. (1965). *Pulse, Digital, and Switching Waveforms*, McGraw-Hill, New York.

WILKINSON, R. H. (1963). A Method of Generating Functions of Several Variables using Analog Diode Logic. *Trans. I.E.E.E.*, EC12, 112.

9 Special Devices for Function Generation

Piecewise linear methods of generating functions are of such widespread applicability and give rise to devices with such accuracy and frequency response that they have displaced all other methods in many general purpose analogue computers. In special purpose devices, however, and particularly in instrumentation applications, some of the older methods can sometimes be more convenient or more economical than the diode switching schemes described in chapter 8.

9.1 Servo-driven potentiometers

Potentiometers can be represented as having a transfer characteristic relating the output voltage to the angle of rotation of the wiper from one end of the track: a normal potentiometer connected as drawn in figure 9.1(a) would have the transfer characteristic shown in figure 9.1(b). The linear characteristic shown by the full line is obtained only in the ideal case in which there is no load connected; the effect of the load is shown by the dotted line. Also indicated in figure 9.1(b) is the break in the characteristic if the wiper is turned beyond the end of the track (assuming that no end stops are fitted) followed by a repetition of the characteristic if the wiper goes on turning until it reaches the beginning of the track again.

If a device is to be usable as a function generator, its output characteristic must be a function of a computer variable – that is, of a low power electrical signal. For a potentiometer to fulfil this condition requires that it should be driven by a motor through a power amplifier, and that its position should be directly controlled by a position control servomechanism. The essential features of such a system are illustrated in figure 9.1(c): the potentiometer, with its ends connected to the reference supplies, provides a feedback signal to the servo amplifier,

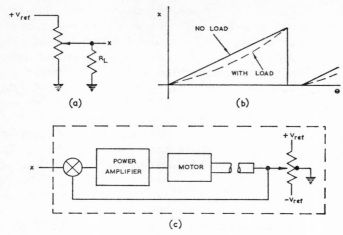

Fig. 9.1. A potentiometer forms the basis for a number of special purpose function generators.

  (a) With a fixed potential across the winding, the output is a function of wiper rotation.

  (b) The characteristic of a linear potentiometer. The dotted curve shows the effect of loading.

  (c) By using a potentiometer in a servo system, the wiper rotation can be made proportional to an input variable.

whose output causes the motor to turn until the feedback signal is equal and opposite to the input signal. By using a potentiometer with an earthed centre-tap and with positive and negative reference supplies, as shown in figure 9.1(c), the output is constrained to follow the input throughout the working range. A major limitation of servo-driven potentiometers, and the main reason for their disappearance from general purpose computers, is the inherently poor frequency response obtainable. In some special purpose applications, however, the bandwidth needed is itself small, and the special advantages of the potentiometer may then be valuable.

The system outlined above, with a single potentiometer giving an output that follows the input, would have the same function as, but poorer performance than, a straightforward summing amplifier. Such a system would have no merit for computational purposes, but is used for automatic potentiometer setting; this facility is provided in some large analogue computers, and particularly in hybrid computers where the analogue section may be used as a peripheral to the main digital computer. The potentiometer settings in the analogue programme can then be calculated within the digital part of the computer and fed into the servo setting facility by way of a digital to analogue converter. The usefulness of a servo-set potentiometer for computational purposes stems from the facility of fitting multiple-ganged potentiometers, comprising a number (up to six or eight) of track and wiper assemblies that are electrically completely separate, but are coupled mechanically by being mounted on the same shaft. One of these tracks is then used to provide the feedback signal for the servo system, leaving the others free to have any arbitrary signals applied to them, but with the common position being determined by the servo input signal.

9.1.1 *Servo multipliers*

The most widespread application for a servo driven potentiometer is as a multiplying element, using the arrangement shown in figure 9.2(a). The part enclosed in the dotted line represents the servo system of figure 9.1(c) including the feedback potentiometer: this is often described as the master potentiometer, because it defines the position

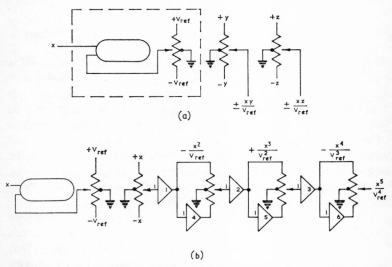

Fig. 9.2. (a) A servo-driven multi-ganged potentiometer used as a multiplier.

(b) The use of a multiplier to produce the terms of a power series.

of all the wipers, as distinct from the slave potentiometers, which follow the master. By connecting $\pm y$ to the two ends of a slave potentiometer, the wiper then gives an output of $\pm xy/V_{ref}$.

The limited frequency response of this system (a bandwidth of no more than 40 Hz or so) has already been mentioned. The device has a number of attractive features:

(a) Only one extra computing amplifier is required: y has to be supplied in both positive and negative form, but only one x signal is needed and no output amplifier is necessary provided the output is feeding a high input impedance circuit.

(b) The output can be obtained with either sign simply by interchanging the $\pm y$ connections. If, as will often be the case, a spare slave potentiometer is available, outputs of both signs can be obtained simultaneously without the need for a further inverter.

(c) By connecting further variables to other slave potentiometers, as shown in figure 9.2(a), separate products of one variable (x in this case) with several other variables can all be obtained with a single device.

(d) As a special case of (c) the output from one slave can be used as the input to the next and so on along the line of slaves as shown in figure 9.2(b), permitting the calculation of the terms of a power series. These can sometimes be used to generate an approximation to a non-linear characteristic, although the range of applicability of this method is small (see section 9.3.3).

Although some emphasis has been laid on the low bandwidth of the servo setting system, it should be observed that the same restriction does not apply to the $y, z, \ldots$ inputs to the slave potentiometers in figure 9.2(a). The whole system, in fact, is, unlike the quarter squares multiplier, asymmetrical with respect to the two inputs, not only in terms of frequency response but also in terms of input impedance. A further impedance consideration that needs to be taken into account in the use of servo driven potentiometers is the fact that the output, being taken from the wiper of a potentiometer, comes effectively from a source with a relatively high output impedance. This is simply another expression of the potentiometer loading effect (see section 5.1) and calls for some care in the use of the device. The essential point to observe is that because of the inherent feedback of the servo system, the master potentiometer is always set 'correctly'

– that is to say, the electrical setting, rather than the mechanical setting, is made to correspond with the input signal. In order to give correct multiplication, the electrical setting of the slave potentiometer must be the same as that of the master; since the mechanical settings are necessarily the same, this requirement implies that the loading of master and slave potentiometers must be made the same. It is this requirement that leads to the use of buffer amplifiers in the circuit of figure 9.2(b); amplifiers 4, 5, and 6 are needed to invert the signal, while amplifiers 1, 2, and 3 are used only to ensure that the load on each wiper is the same.

9.1.2 *Shaped track potentiometers*

The systems so far discussed have used exclusively linear potentiometers for which the output is related to the angle of rotation by the linear characteristic of figure 8.1(b). It is, however, possible to construct a potentiometer whose track, instead of being wound with uniform wire on a rectangular former, is made non-uniform either by varying the thickness of the wire or, more commonly, by varying the shape of the former. The result of either of these modifications is to produce a potentiometer whose output is no longer simply proportional to the angle of rotation, but obeys instead some prescribed non-linear relationship.

A shaped track potentiometer has limitations. It is obviously unsuitable for general purpose function generation because the function is specified by the physical construction of the device. There are also restrictions on the kinds of function that can be built in: the maximum allowable rate of change of resistance with angle of rotation is limited, for example, by the physical need to hold all the turns of the track in position. Within its limitations, however, the shaped track potentiometer has some attractive features that can make its use worthwhile. This is particularly true for potentiometers with a sinusoidal characteristic. These can take various forms, depending on how much of the cycle is presented. Perhaps the most interesting is one with a 360° track representing one complete cycle as shown in figure 9.3(a) and, in opened out form, in figure 9.3(b). By fitting taps to the winding at the maxima and minima and connecting these as shown, the voltage appearing at the wiper as it traverses the winding is proportional to x and varies sinusoidally with the angle of rotation. In practice, this type of potentiometer is commonly fitted with four wipers, each offset mechanically from its neighbours

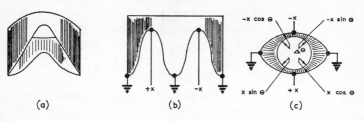

Fig. 9.3. The sine/cosine potentiometer.
   (a) The general appearance of the track used.
   (b) The track opened out.
   (c) By fitting four wipers to the track we obtain functions that
       are useful for co-ordinate transformations.

by 90° as shown in figure 9.3(c). These wipers then give simultaneous outputs of $\pm x \sin \theta$ and $\pm x \cos \theta$: this represents a considerable amount of computing for a single device and explains why it is valuable despite its limitations. Manually operated sine/cosine potentiometers find application in many special purpose devices, acting as convertors from a linear angle of rotation scale to the sine or cosine function. These functions are required most frequently to resolve vector quantities (such as force or velocity) along two mutually perpendicular axes, and hence the device is often called a resolver. The same functions are required when making transformations of a co-ordinate system, such as when rotating the axes or when converting between polar and rectangular co-ordinates.

With a continuous track occupying the full 360°, a manually operated sine/cosine potentiometer can be rotated indefinitely in either direction while maintaining the correct sinusoidal output. The use of servo driven resolvers, however, is complicated by the need for position control feedback. This must be supplied by a linear potentiometer the ends of which are connected to different fixed potentials (either positive and negative reference supplies, or one reference and earth). A continuous linear track with continuous rotation of the wiper cannot therefore be used. Some flexibility can be obtained by putting gearing between the linear master potentiometer and the slaves, or by using a multi-turn helical potentiometer; these methods allow the slaves to be turned more than the 270–300° corresponding to the track of a normal single-turn potentiometer, although this is achieved at the expense of further reduction of the bandwidth.

o

The conversion from polar to rectangular co-ordinates, as shown in figure 9.4(a), is achieved by using the relationships

$$x = R \cos \theta \qquad (9.1)$$

$$y = R \sin \theta \qquad (9.2)$$

The inverse operation is more difficult to implement directly, since the solutions are given by

$$R = \sqrt{(x^2 + y^2)} \qquad (9.3)$$

$$\theta = \tan^{-1} (y/x). \qquad (9.4)$$

It is usual, therefore, to perform rectangular to polar transformations by an implicit computation scheme in which the servo system has no direct feedback component, but is instead fed by an error signal

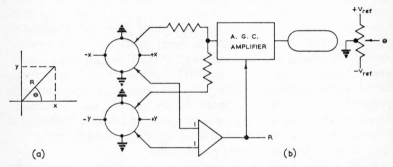

(a)

(b)

Fig. 9.4. (a) The conversion between rectangular and polar co-ordinates. (b) The use of a resolver to affect the conversion.

dependent on rotation. A suitable error signal for this purpose is derived from equation 9.4 which may be re-written

$$y \cos \theta - x \sin \theta = 0. \qquad (9.5)$$

The two terms of equation 9.5 can be obtained from a dual sine/cosine potentiometer driven by a single motor: the master potentiometer, normally required for position feedback, is not required for the operation of the system, but the output from it is available as a measure of θ.

Equation 9.3 is also awkward to implement, and use is made of equations 9.1 and 9.2.; by multiplying equation 9.1 by $\cos \theta$, and equation 9.2 by sin θ, and then adding them together we have

$$x \cos \theta + y \sin \theta = R \qquad (9.6)$$

which can again be obtained directly, provided multiple wiper potentiometers are fitted.

One complication that arises with this system is that if x and y are both small the error signal obtained from equation 9.5 is liable to be small even for large errors in the angle. To overcome this, an automatic gain control amplifier is often included in the system, as shown in figure 9.4(b), so that when R is small the gain is increased and the sensitivity to angular errors can therefore be maintained.

9.1.3 *Tapped potentiometers*

Another method of making the output voltage from the wiper of a potentiometer a non-linear function of the angle of rotation is to use a linear potentiometer with a tapped winding. The big merit of this compared with a shaped track potentiometer is that it is a general purpose device rather than being permanently committed to a specific function. The non-linear relationship can be produced in one of two ways: independent voltages can be impressed at the taps or padding resistors can be connected between taps so as to alter the effective resistance of the segment. In either case the device is set up to give prescribed outputs at the taps, and the complete characteristic is obtained by interpolation between these defined values. Ideally the interpolation is linear, but in practice it is slightly non-linear because of loading effects. As with shaped track potentiometers, very large rates of change of output with rotation cannot be obtained: with tapped potentiometers the maximum permissible rate of change is dictated by the power rating of the particular segment concerned.

A tapped potentiometer can provide a convenient solution to the problem of forming a function of two variables. It was suggested in chapter 8 (see section 8.4.6) that a function of two variables can be approximated by regarding one of the variables as a parameter and using single variable diode function generators to give an appropriate function of the second variable for each of a number of discrete values of the parameter. Thus, instead of generating the two variable function

$$z = F(x, y)$$

we form a series of functions

$$z_1 = f_1(x, y_1)$$
$$z_2 = f_2(x, y_2)$$
$$. \quad . \quad .$$
$$z_n = f_n(x, y_n)$$

where $y_1, y_2, \ldots, y_n$ are fixed values of y. The problem then becomes one of choosing which function $z_1, z_2, \ldots, z_n$ is appropriate when any particular value of y is specified. This is a problem of interpolation,

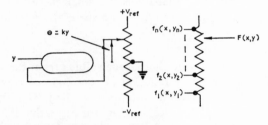

Fig. 9.5. A tapped potentiometer fed by appropriate functions gives a piecewise approximation to a function of two variables, with linear interpolation between the defined values.

and it can be solved with a tapped potentiometer as shown in figure 9.5 by feeding the functions into successive taps and making the rotation depend on y.

9.2 Other mechanical systems

For general purpose computing, as has been pointed out before, mechanical systems have disadvantages that outweigh their advantages, with the result that they are not normally used for such purposes. For particular applications they can be useful but it is becoming more and more rare to find mechanical devices incorporated into computing systems. The servomechanism, as described in the previous sections of this chapter, is the most generally useful of these devices; the rest find application only in very special circumstances.

9.2.1 X–Y plotter

The interest in the X–Y plotter as a function generation device stems from two things. The first is that it is another method of forming a function of two variables, and the second is that in most analogue computing laboratories, an $X-Y$ plotter is already available as part of the standard equipment.

Two modifications are required to the $X-Y$ plotter to accommodate this change of rôle. The pen is changed for a pick-up probe that can obtain a potential from the bed of the plotter and transmit it to the output terminal. The probe is positioned in the normal way using the X and Y driving motors, and the variation of potential over the area of the bed is determined by fitting a sheet of resistive paper on which is drawn what is to all intents and purposes a contour map showing the required lines of equal output potential. The contour lines are drawn in conducting ink, and the appropriate potentials are connected to them. As the probe moves over the area, it continuously interpolates between the contours. Different functions can be stored and refitted easily, and the instrument can also be restored to its more conventional use without difficulty. The making of the contour map, however, is laborious, and the accuracy attainable is not high.

The $X-Y$ recorder can also be used as a single variable function generator by fitting a photoelectric curve following head in place of the pen. This is a device that uses the light reflected from the paper to position itself over a line drawn in ordinary ink to represent the required function.

9.2.2 *Tape recorder*

The main use of a tape recorder in analogue simulation or computation is as a means of introducing a delay into a signal pathway. This can be needed for two purposes: for the simulation of transport lag in a system (the delay of a signal without distortion of the wave shape) and for correlation problems. A multiple head machine is needed, with the position of the heads adjustable so as to be able to simulate variable delays. Also, since normal recorders cannot deal with signals down to d.c., an f.m. recording system has to be used.

9.3 Electronic systems

The major objection to computing devices that incorporate mechanical devices is their limited speed of response. Several special purpose electronic systems have been proposed in order to overcome these difficulties, but for most applications they have few (if any) advantages compared with the diode switching methods of chapter 8 and they are, for general purpose equipment at least, now obsolete. They will be mentioned here briefly, because the techniques are interesting, and they may still find some special purpose applications.

9.3.1 *Cathode ray tube devices*

A number of special function generation devices have been based on cathode ray tubes. The earliest to be produced was the curve follower, whose operation is illustrated in figure 9.6. This depends on

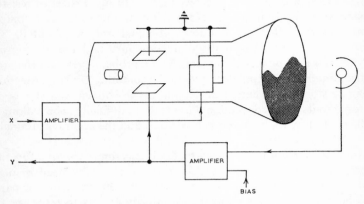

Fig. 9.6. The cathode ray tube function generator.

a mask made of opaque material covering the lower part of the face of the tube, the upper edge of the mask being shaped to correspond to the particular function required. In front of the screen is fitted a photocell that receives light produced by the spot when it appears above the mask.

The horizontal deflection of the spot is determined in the usual way by the input signal, x. The vertical deflection depends on a signal that consists of two components:

(*a*) a bias signal that tends to drive the spot to the upper boundary of the screen;

(*b*) a feedback signal, derived from the photocell, that tends to drive the spot towards the lower boundary of the screen.

The net effect of these two components is that the spot takes up a stable position at the top edge of the mask, where the photocell is able to collect enough light to produce a signal that is just sufficient to overcome the bias.

The mask, which for a cathode ray tube with linear deflection characteristics is a direct copy of the required transfer characteristic, can be made simply from a sheet of card cut manually to the appropriate shape. A number of different transfer characteristics can then be prepared and stored, the change from one to another being effected very easily. A more expensive form of mask, but one which is much easier to prepare, consists of a large number of thin metal shims held together by a clamping bar. The shims can then be adjusted to give a contour of any desired shape; in particular, this kind of mask can be adjusted empirically so that the transfer characteristic obtained experimentally matches the required one as closely as possible.

Cathode ray tubes have also been used for multiplication, the commonest type being the crossed fields multiplier, which is based on the deflection of an electron beam when it is subjected to mutually perpendicular electric and magnetic fields. The deflecting force is proportional to the product of the two field strengths, and is measured by a nulling technique: the spot is returned to the mid-position by using a feedback signal derived from a pair of photocells that detect right and left deviations. Each field strength is made proportional to one of the input variables. The signal necessary to keep the spot on the mid line is therefore a measure of the product of the two input variables.

Other variations on the cathode ray tube have also been described, but all, to a greater or lesser extent, share the same characteristics:

(a) very large computing bandwidth associated with electrostatic beam deflection systems – up to 150 kHz or more. This bandwidth, however, is not obtainable with electromagnetic beam deflection systems, which are usable only up to a few kHz. The crossed field multiplier is, therefore, like the servo multiplier (see section 9.1.1), asymmetrical with respect to its two input terminals so that some care is needed in the choice of assignment of variables to the particular inputs.

(b) not very accurate – limited by spot size to perhaps 1–2% of the reference supply.

(c) inconvenient and expensive to make.

(d) bulky and fragile.

9.3.2 Time division multipliers

The generation of functions of more than one independent variable is a problem that has excited a good deal of interest and has given rise to many different devices. A particular case of this general problem, and the one most commonly encountered in practice, is multiplication.

Several multipliers have been based on the principle of double modulation of a carrier waveform, the demodulated signal being obtained with a low pass filter. The most widely used of these schemes, and the only one that will be described here in detail, is the time division multiplier, in which the carrier is a pulse train and the two forms of modulation are amplitude and pulse width.

One form of time division multiplier is shown in figure 9.7(a). The pulse width modulation part of the system is a feedback circuit consisting of integrator 1 and the bistable circuit, whose output is

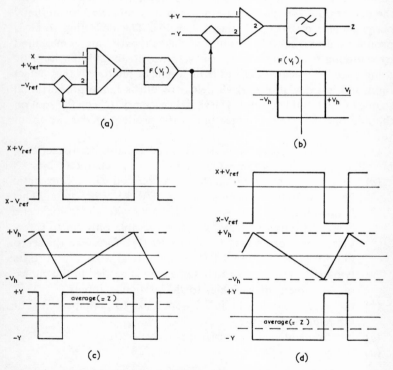

Fig. 9.7. (a) The basic circuit of the time-division multiplier.
(b) The characteristic of the bistable circuit.
(c), (d) Waveforms obtained for positive and negative values of X. The value of Y has been taken as being positive in each case.

used to drive a switch and so to alter the input to the integrator. The characteristic of the bistable is shown in figure 9.7(b); in this system a Schmitt trigger circuit can conveniently be used both to provide the balanced switching signals for the electronic switches and also to incorporate the hysteresis ($\pm V_h$). The remainder of the circuit of figure 9.7(a), consisting of amplifier 2 and the low pass filter, represents the pulse amplitude modulation and the final demodulation to give the output signal Z. The operation of the system is illustrated by the waveforms shown in figure 9.7(c) for $X > 0$ and figure 9.7(d) for $X < 0$. In each case the waveforms are drawn for $Y > 0$; for negative values of Y, the lowest waveform is inverted.

The top waveforms of figure 9.7(c) and 9.7(d) show the total input to the integrator, which is integrated to produce the triangular wave output. The periodic time, T, is assumed to be short enough for the value of X to be taken as constant, and the time for which the switches remain closed is τ. While the switch is closed, the integrator output changes from $-V_h$ to $+V_h$ in a time τ when supplied with an input $(X - V_{ref})$, so that

$$2V_h = -(X - V_{ref})\tau. \qquad (9.7)$$

While the switch is open the integrator output changes from $+V_h$ to $-V_h$ in time $(T - \tau)$ when supplied with an input $(X + V_{ref})$, giving

$$-2V_h = -(X + V_{ref})(T - \tau). \qquad (9.8)$$

The output is obtained from the bottom waveform, and (assuming perfect averaging) is given by

$$Z = \frac{Y\tau + (-Y)(T - \tau)}{T}$$

$$= \left(2\frac{\tau}{T} - 1\right)Y. \qquad (9.9)$$

Eliminating τ between equations 9.7 and 9.8 gives the periodic time as

$$T = -\frac{2V_h \cdot 2V_{ref}}{(X + V_{ref})(X - V_{ref})}. \qquad (9.10)$$

Hence, from equations 9.7 and 9.10,

$$\frac{\tau}{T} = \frac{X + V_{ref}}{2V_{ref}}. \qquad (9.11)$$

Substituting equation 9.11 into equation 9.9 gives the output

$$Z = \frac{XY}{V_{\text{ref}}}.$$ (9.12)

Several observations should be made on the operation of time division multipliers.

(a) Equation 9.12 indicates that there is no sign inversion in this system as it stands. This can easily be changed by reversing the $\pm Y$ connections in figure 9.7(a). It should, however, be noticed that in any multiplier a sign inversion may or may not be incorporated; this needs to be verified before using the device.

(b) In none of these equations is there any restriction on the sign of either X or Y; the system described here is a four quadrant multiplier.

(c) Equation 9.10 shows that T is not constant. The smallest value of T is when $X = 0$, giving $T = 4V_h/V_{\text{ref}}$. The value of T increases indefinitely as $|X| \to V_{\text{ref}}$.

(d) Since the two parts of the circuit are connected only by a switching signal, this system can be used as can a servo-multiplier (see section 9.1.1) to allow multiplication of one variable by several others simultaneously. A single bistable is used to drive a number of switched summers and output filters.

(e) The system is asymmetrical with respect to its inputs, in that the pulse width modulation part of the circuit is more frequency dependent than the amplitude modulation part.

(f) Although, being electronic in character, the main part of the circuit has a large bandwidth, the dynamic performance of the complete system is much less impressive because of the output filter.

9.3.3 Other devices

Some non-linear devices have been based on the use of semiconducting material (usually silicon carbide) which can be made into resistors having a power law relationship between the current and voltage. By the exercise of a considerable amount of ingenuity, these devices can be connected together to form various specific functions, especially those that can be expressed analytically by power series expansions. Various units have been produced commercially to give square or cube law relationships, with which general functions can be constructed, or to provide some specific functions such as sin x, but in general there appears to be little to commend this method of producing non-linear function blocks.

Many multipliers have been developed using various naturally-occurring multiplicative relationships. Among these are the Hall effect multiplier, the piezo-electric multiplier, the FET multiplier, and the heat transfer multiplier. None of these has yet shown any sign that it will displace the diode quarter squares multiplier except perhaps in special applications, and then usually only when a very approximate result is adequate for the purpose.

9.4 Notes and references

The devices described in this chapter, although sometimes useful for special purpose control and instrumentation applications, are not now of great interest in computing systems, except in the case of servo-driven potentiometers. These are used in hybrid systems, not directly as computing elements, but as a means of allowing potentiometers to be set automatically by the digital computer. The characteristics of the servo will then determine the accuracy of setting and the time needed to adjust the analogue programme. A detailed discussion of computer servomechanisms is given by Korn and Korn, who talk at length about loading, dynamic errors, and methods of compensation. There is also a fairly full treatment of the subject by Nenadal and Mirtes.

REFERENCES

KORN, G. A. and KORN, T. M. (1964). *Electronic Analog and Hybrid Computers*, McGraw-Hill, New York.
NENADAL, Z. and MIRTES, B. (1968). *Analogue and Hybrid Computers*, English Translation ed. R. J. M. GREW, Iliffe, London.

10 Generation of Forcing Functions

The final class of problems to be considered under the heading of non-linear function generation is concerned with the generation of functions of time. These are needed in computation and simulation problems to act as the disturbing forces in the system, but also find direct use in control applications where precisely defined time varying functions can sometimes be more efficiently produced using analogue computing techniques than by any other method.

Functions of time can, of course, be produced from any of the function generators described in the previous chapters simply by using a signal proportional to time (a ramp – see section 10.1) as the input signal. This chapter will be concerned only with methods of generating time varying functions directly.

10.1 Steps and ramps

A step function is often required as a stimulus when testing simulated control systems. It generally needs to be applied to the system at $t = 0$, and in this case it is achieved in a computer system by applying a constant to the input of the appropriate amplifier while the computer is in POTSET or RESET. The switching action of changing to COMPUTE (see section 5.3) then applies a step to the amplifier at the start of the computation.

If a step is required at any time other than at the start of the computation, a comparator can be used. The time at which the comparator switches can be controlled by supplying it with a constant which is compared with a ramp (see below). The comparator output can then be used to switch a constant into an amplifier (see section 5.8); alternatively, the comparator output itself can be used as an input to the amplifier. In the latter case, a high gain amplifier with limiting (see section 8.2) may be more suitable. For more precise control of the timing than is possible with a comparator, a counter driven by a digital clock can be used to supply a switching signal to a switched amplifier: this arrangement is also very suitable for producing sequences of steps or pulses (see section 10.2).

Ramp functions also present little difficulty: basically they depend on the relationship

$$\int_0^t A \, dt = At. \tag{10.1}$$

This is implemented simply by feeding an integrator with a constant as shown in figure 10.1(a). When a ramp is to be used with a compara-

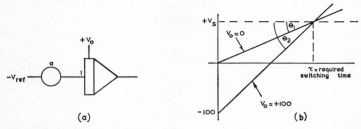

(a)   (b)

Fig. 10.1. (a) An integrator fed with a constant to give a ramp.
(b) When using a comparator with a ramp input to provide a timing signal, the ramp should be steep.

tor to give a timing signal, it should be borne in mind that the intersection of two curves will be most precisely defined if the angle between them is a right angle. If one of the curves is a horizontal straight line therefore (corresponding to a constant reference level) the ramp should be as steep as possible. Best results will be obtained by having the integrator start at one of the reference supplies rather than at zero: this is illustrated in figure 10.1(b), which shows that the angle between the lines is given by

$$\theta = \tan^{-1}\left(\frac{V_s + V_0}{\tau}\right)$$

To maximize θ, therefore, V_0 and V_s should be as large as possible. If τ is very large, however, the angle will still be small, and the cross-over time is poorly defined. Drift and noise could introduce a significant error in this case and difficulties also arise because the potentiometer setting, a, can become very small. A better method of generating a ramp with very small slope is to use a motor driven potentiometer, where the very slow speed can be accurately defined by mechanical gear ratios. The problem of loading of the potentiometer has to receive special attention: a low resistance potentiometer feeding a summer with an extra large input resistor can reduce the non-linearity due to loading to insignificant proportions.

10.2 Pulse trains

All transfer characteristics containing sharp transitions depend in one way or another on a switching action. This can take one of two forms: either a comparator (or high gain amplifier) is used to provide a component of the output of the system, or a switching circuit (which can be a comparator or a straightforward digital system) switches an (analogue) input to the output amplifier.

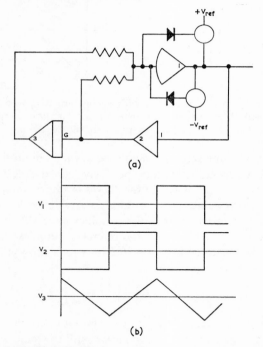

(a)

(b)

Fig. 10.2. Square and triangular waveforms are obtainable from a multivibrator circuit.

(a) The circuit, which is similar to the monostable and bistable circuits.

(b) Waveforms appearing at the outputs of each amplifier.

209

10.2.1 *Multivibrators*

The simplest form of pulse train generator is the astable multivibrator. The normal electronic circuit for this is basically the same as that for the bistable and monostable circuits; similarly, the computer astable multivibrator shown in figure 10.2(a) bears a strong resemblance to the bistable and monostable circuits described in section 8.5.1. Amplifiers 1 and 2 form a bistable circuit having the transfer characteristic (V_1/V_3) shown in figure 8.16(b). By supplying the input to the bistable with a triangular wave obtained by integrating the output of the bistable itself, the system is made self-sustaining. The waveforms obtained from each amplifier are shown in figure 10.2(b). The triangular wave obtained from amplifier 3 is often useful in its own right and also can be used to drive a function generator to give any symmetrical repetitive waveform (see section 10.3.2). The amplitude of the pulses (and also of the triangular wave) is controlled by the limiting circuits of amplifier 1 – the positive and negative limits do not have to be equal. The slope of the triangular wave is controlled directly by the gain G of amplifier 3.

10.2.2 *Impulse functions*

In the testing of control systems and the measurement of the characteristics of networks it is often desirable to find the impulse response of a simulated system. This presents some difficulties, since an ideal impulse function has infinite amplitude. The problem can however often be avoided by virtue of the fact that the integral of an impulse is a step function, which can readily be produced (see section 10.1). Many practical system simulations will contain an integrator as

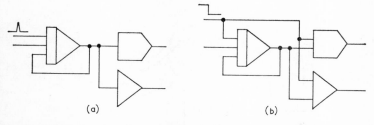

(a)   (b)

Fig. 10.3. Impulse functions cannot be accurately simulated, but the need for them can often be avoided.
    (a) A programme with an impulse as input to an integrator.
    (b) The corresponding programme with the impulse replaced by a step.

the first stage as shown in figure 10.3(a), so that instead of feeding an impulse to the input, a step can be fed to the second stage of the simulation. The sign change inherent in by-passing an amplifier must be compensated by a change in the sign of the step compared with that of the required impulse, and the step must also be supplied to each system block that is connected to the output of the by-passed integrator. This, of course, includes feedback connections, as illustrated in figure 10.3(b).

10.3 Analytical forcing functions

An important and frequently required group of forcing functions is characterized by the fact that they are analytical in form, and in particular that they are the solutions of known differential equations. These functions can therefore be generated by setting up computer programmes to solve the differential equations in the normal way. The ramp function, considered in the preceding section, is in fact a simple example of this method.

10.3.1 *Exponentials*

Exponential functions are obtained as the solutions of first order differential equations of the form

$$\dot{y} + ky + A = 0. \qquad (10.2)$$

The circuit of figure 10.4(a) can be used to implement equation 10.2 provided k is positive. The solution generated is

$$y = \frac{A}{k}(e^{-kt} - 1) - V_0. \qquad (10.3)$$

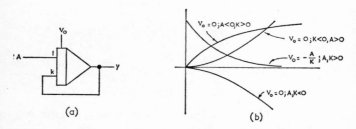

(a)

(b)

Fig. 10.4. (a) Exponential functions are obtained by solving a first order equation.
(b) Various waveforms that can be obtained.

Some of the functions represented by equation 10.3 for various values of A, k and V_0 are shown in figure 10.4(b). The curves shown for k negative require an additional inverter in the feedback path in figure 10.4(a), and represent unstable solutions that grow without limit: these can therefore be used only for a restricted solution time such that the amplifiers remain below their saturation limits.

10.3.2 *Harmonic oscillators*

Perhaps the most frequently required test function of all is the sinusoid, which conveniently obeys the simple differential equation

$$\ddot{y} + \omega^2 y = 0. \tag{10.4}$$

The solution to equation 10.4 may be written

$$y = A \sin(\omega t + \phi) \tag{10.5}$$

and can be obtained from the circuit of figure 10.5(a). The use of two potentiometers each with a setting proportional to ω rather

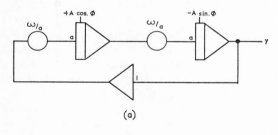

(a)

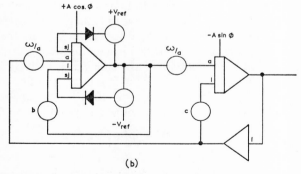

(b)

Fig. 10.5. (a) The basic circuit of the harmonic oscillator.
(b) A modified circuit with provision to remove the effects of unwanted phase shifts in the amplifiers.

than a single one with a setting proportional to ω^2 is to allow for amplitude scaling: in the circuit as shown, all three amplifiers have an output varying between $\pm A$. Moreover if a single potentiometer were used to adjust ω, then one of the initial conditions would also depend on ω.

A major difficulty with this simple form of harmonic oscillator is the effect of unwanted phase shifts in the amplifiers, which can cause the oscillation to be damped (either positively or negatively) so that the output, instead of being the pure sine wave represented by equation 10.5, is modified to

$$y_1 = Ae^{kt} \sin(\omega t + \phi). \tag{10.6}$$

This represents a sine wave whose amplitude changes progressively with time. The reasons for the response changing to that of equation 10.6 are discussed in detail in chapter 6 (section 6.7.1); the effect becomes serious if the oscillation is required to continue over many cycles, and in this case some form of correction system is necessary.

The simplest correction method for a harmonic oscillator is to supply an additional feedback connection to the basic circuit to offset the positive or negative damping due to the amplifier phase shifts. The effect is so small, however, that it is very difficult to compensate with a single potentiometer since it would have to be set to a very low value. The normal practice, therefore, is to provide two additional feedback loops, one positive and the other negative. The gains of these loops could theoretically be adjusted at any frequency to give an exact cancellation of the unwanted feedback, but this method is still not altogether satisfactory because of the difficulty of finding the equilibrium point, and of its inherently unstable nature. The usual way of overcoming these difficulties is to set the feedback gains so that the resultant value of k in equation 10.6 is just positive – that is, so that the amplitude of the sine wave is slowly increasing with time – and then to connect a limiter to the first integrator. The resulting circuit is shown in figure 10.5(b). The equation solved by this circuit (ignoring the effect of the limiting) is

$$\ddot{y} + (b-c)\dot{y} + (\omega^2 - bc)y = 0. \tag{10.7}$$

In practice, b and c are both small, so that the frequency represented by the coefficient of y in equation 10.7 is very close to ω except for very small values of ω. The effect of the limiting circuit is to flatten the peaks of the sine wave produced by the first integrator: this distortion is small if the residual damping is small, and it also tends to be smoothed in the following integrator so that the final output is acceptable for many purposes.

More accurate sinusoidal oscillators use a feedback circuit to keep the amplitude constant. This usually involves mimimizing an error signal of the form

$$V_\epsilon = X^2 + Y^2 - 1$$

where X and Y are the computed approximations to sin ωt and cos ωt. Such systems can be very accurate, but are also very expensive, requiring several multipliers for their implementation.

It is sometimes required that the frequency of oscillation of a harmonic oscillator should be controllable by an electrical signal, particularly where the frequency is to be changed during a computation. This need arises, for example, when plotting the frequency response of a system, where the input to the system needs to be a sine wave whose frequency is swept through the range of interest. This can be achieved directly with the circuit of figure 10.5(a) if the two potentiometers are ganged and servo-driven. The frequency response limitation attached to the use of servo potentiometers is not generally severe in this case, because the changes in setting are required only to follow a relatively slow ramp function. An alternative way of sweeping the frequency of the oscillator is to replace the potentiometers by multipliers as shown in figure 10.6(a). In this circuit, amplifier 4 generates a ramp that makes each of the two multipliers in the main loop act effectively as a potentiometer whose setting is increased from zero to one.

An obvious question that arises when changing the frequency of a harmonic oscillator while it remains in the COMPUTE mode concerns the amplitude of the resulting oscillation. This is normally determined by the initial conditions, so that the effect of changing the potentiometer settings without returning to the RESET mode needs to be investigated.

Consider the circuit shown in figure 10.6(b), which solves the equation

$$\ddot{y}_1 + \omega_1^2 y_1 = 0. \tag{10.8}$$

The solution to equation 10.8 with the initial conditions

$$y_1(0) = 0, \qquad \dot{y}_1(0) = A\omega_1$$

is given by

$$y_1 = |A| \sin(\omega_1 t + p\pi) \tag{10.9}$$

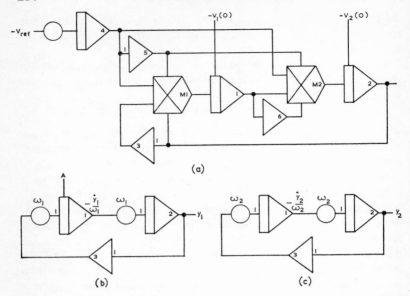

Fig. 10.6. A sine wave of varying frequency can be produced by using servo-potentiometers or multipliers.

  (a) A circuit using multipliers. The diagram shows each multiplier being supplied with each of the input variables in both normal and inverted form. This is the usual requirement in practical multipliers, so that if the inverses are not already available in the programme, two inverters have to be supplied. A third amplifier is also usually needed as an output amplifier, so that multiplication is a very expensive operation.

  (b) Equivalent circuit when the gains are set to ω_1.

  (c) Equivalent circuit after step change of gains to ω_2.

where $p = 0$ if $A > 0$ and $p = 1$ if $A < 0$.

If the potentiometers are suddenly reset at time T so that they take up new settings of ω_2 as shown in figure 10.6(c) the circuit then solves

$$\ddot{y}_2 + \omega_2^2 y_2 = 0. \qquad (10.10)$$

The solution to equation 10.10 is

$$y_2 = B \sin(\omega_2 t_1 + \phi) \qquad (10.11)$$

where $B > 0$ and t_1 is a new time scale with its origin at the switching instant. The initial conditions that determine B and ϕ are the voltages appearing at the outputs of amplifiers 1 and 2 at the time at which the potentiometers are changed, and these can be derived from equation 10.9 by putting $t = T$. This gives

$$V_2 = y_1(T) = |A| \sin (\omega_1 T + p\pi)$$
$$= |A| \sin \theta \qquad (10.12)$$

where $\theta = \omega T + p\pi$.

$$V_1 = -\frac{1}{\omega_1} \dot{y}_1(T) = -|A| \cos \theta. \qquad (10.13)$$

From equation 10.11 and figure 10.6(c) these voltages can also be related to the initial conditions of the second solution giving the relations

$$V_2 = y_2(0) = B \sin \phi \qquad (10.14)$$

$$V_1 = -\frac{1}{\omega_2} \dot{y}_2(0) = -B \cos \phi. \qquad (10.15)$$

Hence, combining equations 10.12 and 10.14, and 10.13 and 10.15, we have

$$|A| \sin \theta = B \sin \phi \qquad (10.16)$$

$$|A| \cos \theta = B \cos \phi. \qquad (10.17)$$

Squaring equations 10.16 and 10.17 and adding them together gives

$$A^2 = B^2$$

and so, since $\qquad B > 0,$

$$B = |A|$$

This demonstrates that a change of the potentiometers changes the frequency of the oscillation without changing the amplitude. It should, however, be noticed that the TIME SCALE facility cannot be used to switch between two frequencies since the capacitor used for the second computation would not have been charged to the appropriate voltage during the first part of the computation. In order to use this facility, therefore, the computer must return to RESET so that the integrators can be set with their correct initial conditions.

The methods of generating a sine wave by solution of the differential equation has serious limitations. Both very high and very low frequencies present difficulties, either by requiring large gains in the amplifiers or by requiring small settings of the potentiometers. There are also difficulties when a very wide range of variation of frequency is required. A neat way of solving all these problems is to use a diode function generator to give the sinusoidal variation, and to drive it by a triangular wave produced by a multivibrator circuit of the kind described in section 10.2. This technique is used in some commercially available low frequency waveform generators, where it has the advantage that square and triangular waveforms are available in addition to the sinusoidal waveform at no extra cost. A block diagram of this system is shown in figure 10.7: the feedback loop consisting of the

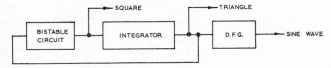

Fig. 10.7. Very low frequency sine waves are difficult to generate with a harmonic oscillator because of the low potentiometer settings required. Better results are obtained by driving a diode function generator with a triangular waveform.

bistable circuit and integrator form a multivibrator as described in section 10.2, and the triangular waveform from the integrator is used to drive a diode function generator whose transfer characteristic is described by

$$y = V_{ref} \sin \left(\frac{x}{V_{ref}} \cdot \frac{\pi}{2} \right).$$

Thus, as x varies from $-V_{ref}$ to $+V_{ref}$, y varies from $V_{ref} \sin (-\pi/2)$ to $V_{ref} \sin (\pi/2)$, and because of the symmetry of the sinusoidal function, the return of x from $+V_{ref}$ to $-V_{ref}$ correctly generates the next section of the sine wave. With this system all the waveforms have to be generated with a fixed peak to peak amplitude; variations in amplitude are obtained by the use of an attenuator on the output. As with the multivibrator circuit (section 10.2) frequency variations are obtained by adjusting the gain of the integrator.

10.4 Random signal generation

In many practical problems, and particularly when simulating control systems, a random disturbance is a common, and perhaps even the most common, of the input signals with which the system is required to operate. Most forms of regulating and controlling device, for example, from stabilized power supplies to aircraft autopilots, have as an important function the task of maintaining a specified output in the face of unpredictable variations in the environmental conditions. In other cases, random changes need to be deliberately introduced, particularly in searching and optimization schemes and in statistical evaluation programmes. The production of random signals for use either within the system or as simulations of the system forcing function is not basically difficult, since there is no shortage of electronic devices that produce noise; it is only when the characteristics of the noise are prescribed that complications emerge.

For most analogue computer applications, noise generators are required to operate at low frequencies (typically in the sub-audio range). The signal itself may be either a continuous signal having a random amplitude, or a pulse train composed of pulses with random variation in height, width, or repetition frequency. The problem of generating any kind of low frequency random signal, however, is complicated by the fact that many primary noise sources produce little or no low frequency components. This difficulty has to be overcome by using some non-linear process, such as mixing or rectification, to produce cross-modulation products at all frequencies from zero upwards, the required low frequency components being then separated by a low pass filter. With systems of this kind, it is very difficult to exercise control over the statistical properties of the output signal, and several methods have been proposed to overcome the inherent inability of all noise sources to produce statistically consistent outputs. One method is to measure the statistical properties of the noise and to use these measurements in a feedback loop to maintain constant values. Alternatively, the noise can be used to provide a random signal at relatively high frequency, and the low frequency output can be obtained by sampling. A similar method has been used to provide low frequency random step signals by the system illustrated in figure 10.8. The high frequency noise is converted into a train of constant-amplitude random-width pulses by the Schmitt Trigger circuit and these pulses are used to drive a multi-stage counter. The output from each stage of this counter is taken separately to the track-store unit, which is switched from STORE to TRACK at regular intervals under the control of the multi-vibrator. A particular merit of this method is that the exact form of the noise signal is not important, since the statistical properties of the final output are determined not by the noise source but by the

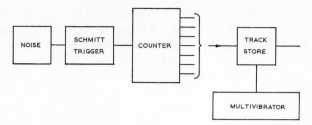

Fig. 10.8. One form of low frequency random step generator that attempts to make the statistical properties of the output independent of the characteristics of the noise source.

gains of the track/store inputs. The addition of a low pass filter at the output of this system converts the constant-width random-amplitude step waveforms into a continuous low frequency random signal.

In digital computer studies of responses to random signals, a technique that has proved to be particularly valuable is that of generating pseudo-random numbers. This has the advantage of being a true random signal as far as the simulated system is concerned (in the sense of being unpredictable – the auto-correlation function approximates closely to the ideal single spike) but yet has the additional advantage of being repeatable as far as the experimenter is concerned. Thus the performance of two systems, or for one system with and without a modification, can be compared in the knowledge that they are both fed with identical inputs, but nevertheless the two systems are responding to random perturbations. A similar device can also be used for analogue simulation. In this case the pseudo-random binary number must first be applied to a digital-analogue converter (which can be simply a summer). This produces a pseudo-random step waveform similar in form to that produced by the circuit of figure 10.8, and this again can be converted to a continuous waveform by adding a low pass filter to the output.

10.5 Notes and references

The use of the computer as a generator of various forcing functions as testing signals for other systems has been stressed by Key. It is a particularly powerful technique when the function to be generated is what might be described as 'piecewise analytic': this condition is met by cam profiles. The method of counteracting the unwanted exponential component in sinusoidal generators is described by Key and also by Korn and Korn, who also show programmes using the computer as a powerful and versatile waveform generator. The implication here is that this is a valuable technique for the construction of signal generators using ordinary commercial operational amplifiers.

The use of random signals in the study of statistical problems has been fully described by Korn, who has developed a large library of techniques using both iterative and hybrid computers. These studies depend on the provision of random signals (and pseudo-random signals) with defined characteristics.

The low frequency random step generator was described by Wilkins as a tool in biological simulation studies, and has subsequently been employed by Lewis in the study of production control.

REFERENCES

KEY, K. A. (1965). *Analogue Computing For Beginners*, Chapman and Hall, London.

KORN, G. A. (1966). *Random-Process Simulation and Measurements*, McGraw-Hill, New York.

KORN, G. A. and KORN, T. M. (1964). *Electronic Analog and Hybrid Computers*, McGraw-Hill, New York.

LEWIS, C. D. (1965). Iterative analogue computation applied to inventory policy simulation. *Computer J.* **8**, 130.

WILKINS, B. R. (1964). A low frequency random step generator. *Electron. Eng.* **36**, 386.

11 Applications of Analogue Techniques

The range of applications of the methods and devices described in the previous chapters of this book is very wide, and methods of solving many forms of mathematical problem will be found in all the standard textbooks. Rather than recapitulate these well established techniques here, a single problem has been taken and studied in depth, in an attempt to show how the specification of a particular requirement in mathematical form can be translated into a working computer programme. This could be taken further and used as the design for a hardware implementation, using available integrated circuit blocks to replace the amplifier components. This particular problem is convenient in that it draws together in a single system many of the techniques described in the earlier parts of the book.

11.1 Automatic analysis of waveforms

The problem to be considered is that of providing a system that computes the pth order moments of a function of a single variable. These quantities are of importance in statistical studies and can also be used as parameters in the identification of signal waveforms.

For any function of an independent variable x, the pth order moments form a series of quantities defined by the set of relations

$$M_p = \int_{-\infty}^{\infty} f(x) \cdot x^p dx \qquad p = 0, 1, 2, \ldots, N. \qquad (11.1)$$

In many applications of practical importance, some simplifications of equation 11.1 are possible. The most important of these is that it can usually be assumed that

$$f(x) = 0 \text{ for } x \leq 0$$

so that equation 11.1 then becomes

$$M_p = \int_0^\infty f(x) \, . \, x^p dx. \tag{11.2}$$

Since p is a numeric, the quantities M_p are simple scalars, but for computational purposes it is convenient to redefine them as

$$M_p(t) = \int_0^t f(x) \, . \, x^p dx. \tag{11.3}$$

These can then be thought of as functions of time, which approach the values of M_p as time increases indefinitely. It is not however guaranteed, and neither is it generally true, that the approach to the value of M_p is in the form of a continuously improving approximation. The usefulness of the idea lies entirely in the fact that for many functions occurring in practice

$$f(x) = 0 \text{ for } x \geq \xi$$

In this case, equation 11.2 can be rewritten

$$M_p = \int_0^\xi f(x) \, . \, x^p \, . \, dx \tag{11.4}$$

and so, from equations 11.3 and 11.4 we see that

$$M_p(t) = M_p \quad \text{if} \quad t \geq \xi.$$

The overall requirement for a moment-measuring system, therefore, is that it should have a single input, $f(x)$, (which for analogue computing purposes would need to be a function of time) and a set of time varying outputs, $M_p(t)$, $p = 0, 1, 2, \ldots, N$. The required moments would then be obtained by stopping the computation when $t \geq \xi$. Such a system is illustrated in figure 11.1.

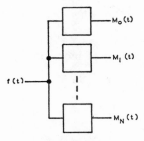

Fig. 11.1. A moment measuring system. Inputs and outputs in this case are functions of time.

The first step towards synthesizing this system is to observe that, provided the system is linear, then if its impulse response, $I(t)$, is known, the response of the system to any other input, $f(t)$, is given by the convolution integral

$$r(t) = \int_0^t I(t-\tau)f(\tau)d\tau \qquad (11.5)$$

The same relation also holds with a multiple output system, where each output can be related to the input and to its own impulse response. Equation 11.5 can then be replaced by a set of equations

$$r_p(t) = \int_0^t I_p(t-\tau)f(\tau)d\tau, \qquad p = 0, 1, 2, \ldots, N \qquad (11.6)$$

A comparison between equations 11.4 and 11.6 suggests that a set of outputs related to the moments of the input function will be obtained from a system whose outputs have impulse responses given by

$$I_p = t^p, \qquad p = 0, 1, 2, \ldots, N \qquad (11.7)$$

Substituting equation 11.7 into 11.6 gives

$$r_p(t) = \int_0^t (t-\tau)^p f(\tau)d\tau \qquad (11.8)$$

$$= \int_0^t \sum_{q=0}^p (-1)^q \frac{p!}{q!(p-q)!} t^{p-q}\tau^q f(\tau)d\tau$$

$$= \sum_{q=0}^p (-1)^q \frac{p!}{q!(p-q)!} t^{(p-q)} \int_0^t \tau^q f(\tau)d\tau$$

and substituting for the integral from equation 11.3 gives

$$r_p(t) = \sum_{q=0}^p (-1)^q \frac{p!}{q!(p-q)!} t^{(p-q)} M_q(t).$$

For a system of this kind having $(N+1)$ outputs, these outputs will therefore be related to the set of moments by the matrix equation

$$\mathbf{r} = \mathbf{\theta} \cdot \mathbf{M} \qquad (11.9)$$

where

$$\mathbf{r} = \begin{bmatrix} r_0(t) \\ r_1(t) \\ \vdots \\ r_N(t) \end{bmatrix}, \qquad \mathbf{M} = \begin{bmatrix} M_0(t) \\ M_1(t) \\ \vdots \\ M_N(t) \end{bmatrix}$$

and

$$\boldsymbol{\theta} = \begin{bmatrix} 1 & 0 & . & . & . & . & . & . \\ t & -1 & 0 & . & . & . & . & . \\ t^2 & -2t & 1 & 0 & . & . & . & . \\ \vdots & \vdots & \vdots & \vdots & & & & \\ t^N & . & . & . & . & . & . & . \end{bmatrix} \qquad (11.10)$$

The desired set of outputs, $\mathbf{M}$, can therefore be obtained from this system by applying a transformation network to the set of outputs $\mathbf{r}$: this transformation (from equation 11.9) is given by

$$\mathbf{M} = \boldsymbol{\theta}^{-1} . \mathbf{r}. \qquad (11.11)$$

From equation 11.10 the inverse of $\boldsymbol{\theta}$ can be obtained: it turns out that

$$\boldsymbol{\theta} = \boldsymbol{\theta}^{-1}$$

so that equation 11.11 can be rewritten

$$\mathbf{M} = \boldsymbol{\theta} . \mathbf{r}. \qquad (11.12)$$

Equation 11.12 is of the same form as equation 7.10, if we interpret the vector $\mathbf{M}$ as the system output and the vector $\mathbf{r}$ as the state vector. The system as it stands, however, cannot be implemented because of the impulse response requirement expressed in equation 11.7: this represents an unstable system. One way of overcoming this difficulty is to modify the impulse response by an exponential weighting factor, giving

$$I'_p = t^p e^{-t} \qquad (11.13)$$

In order to remove the additional term this would introduce into the overall response it then becomes necessary to multiply the input function by e^{-t} also, so that the new system response becomes

$$R_p(t) = \int_0^t (t-\tau)^p e^{-(t-\tau)} e^{-\tau} f(\tau) d\tau$$
$$= e^{-t} \int_0^t (t-\tau)^p f(\tau) d\tau$$
$$\mathbf{R} = e^{-t} . \mathbf{r}. \qquad (11.14)$$

Hence, from equation 11.12 and 11.14 we have

$$\mathbf{M} = e^t . \boldsymbol{\theta} . \mathbf{R} \qquad (11.15)$$

where $\mathbf{R}$ represents the state vector for this modified (and realizable) system. The system equations may be expressed in normal form (see section 7.1.2) as

$$\dot{\mathbf{R}} = \mathbf{A}\mathbf{R} + \mathbf{B}\mathbf{u} \tag{11.16}$$

where $\mathbf{u}$ is the forcing function vector. In this case there is a single input so that equation 11.16 is modified to

$$\dot{\mathbf{R}} = \mathbf{A}\mathbf{R} + \mathbf{B}e^{-t}f(t). \tag{11.17}$$

Equation 11.17 can then be taken to specify an analogue computer programme in which each component of the $\mathbf{R}$ vector appears at the output of an integrator. It remains, therefore, to define the matrix $\mathbf{A}$ and the vector $\mathbf{B}$ so that the programme can be implemented; the moments will then be obtainable by implementing equation 11.15, giving the overall system shown in figure 11.2. The exponential function is generated in the normal way (see section 10.3.1): the factor of 100 is introduced (on the assumption that we are using a 100 V computer) for the purpose of maintaining satisfactory amplitude scaling (see section 3.4.2). The values of $\mathbf{M}$ are then taken at $t = T$ where $T \geq \xi$.

The required values of $\mathbf{A}$ and $\mathbf{B}$ are obtained from the previously specified impulse response of the system defined by equation 11.13. This form of specification makes it convenient to work in terms of the set of transfer functions from the input to each output: these are (for a linear system) simply the Laplace Transforms of the impulse responses. Thus the system can be represented by

$$\mathbf{R}(s) = \mathbf{H}(s) \cdot u$$

where

$$\mathbf{H}(s) = [H_p(s)] = \begin{bmatrix} \dfrac{1}{1+s} \\ \dfrac{1}{(1+s)^2} \\ \vdots \\ \dfrac{N!}{(1+s)^{N+1}} \end{bmatrix}. \tag{11.18}$$

Examination of equation 11.18 shows that

$$H_p(s) = \frac{p}{1+s} \cdot H_{p-1}(s)$$

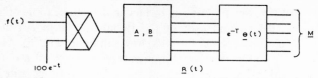

Fig. 11.2. A system consisting of two cascaded blocks. The matrix
quantities A, B, and θ characterize the blocks and are defined
in the text.

and this shows that the **R** vector can be obtained from a cascaded
set of elements each of which has a transfer function of the same
form, as shown in block diagram form in figure 11.3(a).

For implementation on an analogue computer these transfer
functions are quite convenient, except that the sign inversion associated with operational amplifiers has to be taken into account.

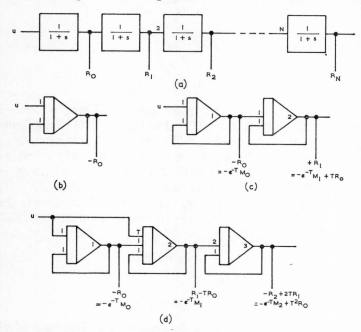

Fig. 11.3. (a) A cascaded set of identical blocks can generate the R vector.
   (b) The way of forming R_0 with a first order lag circuit.
   (c) Cascaded circuits whose outputs are related to the moments.
   (d) Modified connection to remove the unwanted component
       from the output of amplifier 2.

The required transfer function is in fact that of the exponential lag (see section 10.3.1), and also of the initial condition circuit (see section 5.2), and may be obtained as shown in figure 11.3(b). All that then remains is to form the set of moments from the set of R outputs, using the relationship given in equation 11.15, and bearing in mind that the measurements will be taken at time $t = T$ so that the factor e^T becomes a constant scaling factor. For the same reason, the matrix θ is also a constant (time-invariant) matrix, so that the moments are simply linear combinations of the components of $\mathbf{R}$, given by

$$
\left.
\begin{aligned}
e^{-T}M_0 &= R_0 \\
e^{-T}M_1 &= TR_0 - R_1 \\
e^{-T}M_2 &= T^2 R_0 - 2TR_1 + R_2 \\
&\cdot \quad \cdot \quad \cdot \quad \cdot \quad \cdot \\
e^{-T}M_N &= T^N R_0 - NT^{N-1}R_1 + \ldots
\end{aligned}
\right\}
\qquad (11.19)
$$

Thus the first moment (apart from the scaling factor e^{-T}) is generated at the output of the first of the chain of integrators, as shown in figure 11.3(c). The output of integrator 2 is then

$$
R_1 = -e^{-T}M_1 + TR_0.
$$

The unwanted term, TR_0, could be disposed of with a summer connected to the outputs of amplifiers 1 and 2, but more economically we observe that a signal $-TR_0$ will be produced at the output of amplifier 2 (or indeed any other amplifier in the chain) by supplying it with an input of T.u. This method is used in figure 11.3(d), in which amplifiers 1 and 2 are generating $-e^{-T}M_0$ and $-e^{-T}M_1$ respectively. When $-e^{-T}M_1$ is applied to the third amplifier in the chain with a gain of 2 (in accordance with the scheme of figure 11.3(a)) the output of this amplifier is

$$
V_3 = -R_2 + 2TR_1
$$

and so, from equation 11.19,

$$
V_3 = -e^{-T}M_2 + T^2 R_0.
$$

The unwanted term can again be removed by applying the original input directly to amplifier 3 with a gain of T^2. The whole programme for giving the set of moments M_0 to M_N can be obtained in the same way, and is shown in figure 11.4(a); the normal form of the equations describing its operation is

$$\dot{\mathbf{M}}(t) = - \begin{bmatrix} 1 & 0 & 0 & . & . & . & . & . & . & . & . & . \\ 1 & 1 & 0 & . & . & . & . & . & . & . & . & . \\ 0 & 2 & 1 & 0 & . & . & . & . & . & . & . \\ 0 & 0 & 3 & 1 & 0 & . & . & . & . & . \\ . & . & . & . & . & . & . & . & . & . & . \\ . & . & . & . & . & . & . & . & 1 & 0 \\ . & . & . & . & . & . & . & (N-1) & 1 \end{bmatrix} \mathbf{M}(t) + \begin{bmatrix} 1 \\ T \\ T^2 \\ . \\ . \\ . \\ T^N \end{bmatrix} e^{-t} f(t)$$

The choice of a value for T is arbitrary, and is made in any particular problem only on the grounds of convenience. Two values are particularly attractive. If $T = 1$, then all the terms in the **B** vector are 1 also, which makes the programme of figure 11.4(a) very easy to set up. Alternatively, we might choose $T = 2\cdot303$ so that $e^T = 10$. This

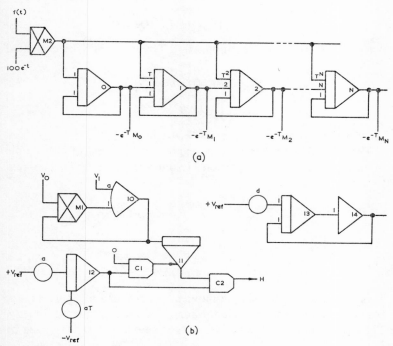

(a)

(b)

Fig. 11.4. The complete programme for moment measurement.
    (a) The computation.
    (b) The timing and control circuits for the measurement of central moments.

Q

makes the scaling of the outputs simple, but means that the gain factors become very large in the later amplifiers. This of course is not important if only a few moments are required: M_0 to M_5 can be obtained without needing any gains greater than 100.

The output values can be obtained in one of two ways. Either a set of track-store amplifiers can be used, all switched from TRACK to STORE when $t = T$, or the whole programme can be switched to HOLD at this time. Either way, a timing signal is necessary, and since the exact time is critical to the measurements, this signal is best obtained from a digital clock rather than from a comparator (see section 10.1), although again the decision on this depends finally on the particular application.

An alternative requirement that sometimes exists is for the measurement of the central moments of a waveform, defined by

$$C_n = \int_{-\infty}^{\infty} (t - \bar{t})^n f(t) dt \qquad (11.20)$$

where $\bar{t}$ is the mean of the input, $f(t)$. The mean may be evaluated from

$$\bar{t} = \frac{\int_0^T t \cdot f(t) dt}{\int_0^T f(t) dt} = \frac{M_1}{M_0} \qquad (11.21)$$

for the simple case in which $f(t) = 0$ when $t \leq 0$ and $t \geq T$.

The central moments may be expressed in terms of the simple moments by expanding equation 11.20 using the Binomial Theorem to give

$$C_n = \sum_{p=0}^{n} \frac{n!}{p!(n-p)!} (-1)^{n-p} \bar{t}^{n-p} \int_0^T t^p f(t) dt$$

$$= \sum_{p=0}^{n} (-1)^{n-p} \frac{n!}{p!(n-p)!} \bar{t}^{n-p} M_p. \qquad (11.22)$$

This suggests that the simple moment programme of figure 11.4(a) could be modified to provide the central moment sequence directly. The equation of the nth amplifier in the chain as it stands is given by

$$-\dot{V}_n = V_n + nV_{n-1} + T^n e^{-t} f(t).$$

By taking Laplace Transforms, the system can be characterized by the recursive equation

$$V_n(s) = -\frac{n}{s+1} V_{n-1}(s) - \frac{T^n}{s+1} F(s+1)$$

where $F(s)$ is the Laplace Transform of $f(t)$. This leads, by repeated substitution, to

$$V_n(s) = -\sum_{p=0}^{n} (-1)^{n-p} \frac{n!T^p}{p!} \cdot \frac{1}{(s+1)^{n-p+1}} \cdot F(s+1)$$

$$= -\sum_{p=0}^{n} (-1)^{n-p} \frac{n!}{p!(n-p)!} T^p \frac{(n-p)!}{(s+1)^{n-p+1}} \cdot F(s+1) \quad (11.23)$$

The time function obtained at the output of amplifier n is evaluated by taking the inverse transform of equation 11.23, which leads to the convolution integral

$$V_n(t) = -\left[\sum_{p=0}^{n} (-1)^{n-p} \frac{n!}{p!(n-p)!} T^p t^{n-p} e^{-t}\right] * \left[e^{-t} f(t)\right]$$

$$= -[(T-t)^n e^{-t}] * [e^{-t} f(t)]$$

$$= -\int_0^t [T-(t-\tau)]^n e^{-(t-\tau)} e^{-\tau} f(\tau) d\tau$$

$$= -e^{-t} \sum_{p=0}^{n} (T-t)^{n-p} \cdot \frac{n!}{p!(n-p)!} M_p \quad (11.24)$$

Comparing equations 11.22 and 11.24 we see that if the computation is stopped when $t = T + \bar{t}$ (which does not affect the values of the moments M_p since $f(t) = 0$ when $t \geq T$) then

$$V_n(T+\bar{t}) = -e^{-(T+\bar{t})} \sum_{p=0}^{n} (-\bar{t})^{n-p} \frac{n!}{p!(n-p)!} M_p$$

$$= -e^{-(T+\bar{t})} C_n.$$

This shows that by continuing the integration for a further time equal to the mean, the output from each integrator becomes proportional to the corresponding central moment. A system for measuring central moments therefore consists of the basic circuit of figure 11.4(a) together with control circuitry to stop the integration at the right time. A suitable control circuit is shown in figure 11.4(b). The inputs marked V_0 and V_1 come from the outputs of amplifiers 0 and 1 of figure 11.4(a), and, at time $t = T$, they are proportional to M_0

and M_1 respectively. Amplifier 10 is a high gain amplifier (using the symbolism of section 8.3) which, together with multiplier $M1$, forms an implicit function generator (see section 7.2.2), using the multiplier in the feedback path so as to give division. The output of $M1$ will be $V_0 \cdot V_{10}/V_{ref}$, and the high gain amplifier will act so as to impose the relationship

$$\frac{V_0 \cdot V_{10}}{V_{ref}} + aV_1 = 0$$

or $\qquad V_{10} = -aV_{ref}\frac{V_1}{V_0} = -A\hat{t} \qquad$ when $t = T$.

The multiplying factor, A, would of course need to be chosen in any particular problem to provide satisfactory amplitude scaling, changes in the multiplying factor being most conveniently incorporated by changing the 'gains' of the inputs to amplifier 10.

Amplifier 11 is a track-store amplifier, which tracks the output of amplifier 10 until it is switched to STORE by comparator $C1$. The time at which this occurs is governed by amplifier 12, whose output is

$$V_{12} = aTV_{ref} - aV_{ref}t$$
$$= A(T-t)$$

so that $C1$ switches when $t = T$.

For $t \geq T$, the output of amplifier 11 is constant at $+A\hat{t}$, so that comparator $C2$ switches when

$$A(T-t) + A\hat{t} = 0$$

or $\qquad\qquad\qquad t = T + \hat{t}.$

The output from comparator $C2$ is shown as going to a terminal 'H'. This represents a facility provided on all iterative computers (and often on conventional analogue computers as well) whereby the application of an appropriate signal (in this case a logic 1) switches the computer into HOLD. Amplifiers $0, 1, \ldots, N$ will then have stored in them the central moments $C_0, C_1, \ldots, C_N$, modified by the factor $e^{T+\hat{t}}$.

The final part of the circuit in figure 11.4(b), consisting of amplifiers 13 and 14, is an additional refinement. The factor $e^{T+\bar{t}}$ cannot be chosen in advance to be a convenient number as it could be in the simple moment programme, because $\hat{t}$ is not known in advance.

Amplifiers 13 and 14 form an exponential generator (see section 10.3.1) giving

$$V_{14} = d \cdot V_{ref}e^{+t}$$

so that when the computer is switched to HOLD at $t = T + \hat{t}$ the modifying factor can be read at the output of amplifier 14. This is an example of the use of an unstable generator (a positive exponential); the value of d must be chosen so that amplifiers 13 and 14 do not reach saturation within the operating time.

11.2 Analogue methods in digital systems

The use of an analogue computer for the solution of large sets of simultaneous differential equations, or for the simulation of complex systems, where in each case the use of a large number of amplifiers would be required, brings with it a number of difficulties. Many of these have been discussed at length in previous chapters: they may be summarized as follows.

(a) As in any analogue circuit, the accuracy with which a quantity can be measured depends on the ratio between the maximum value attainable and the noise level. Even under the most favourable circumstances, this uncertainty of measurement is unlikely to be better than $0 \cdot 01 \%$, and in an overall system of any complexity the accumulated tolerance will undoubtedly reach 1% or more (see section 6.2).

(b) Because of the limited linear range of the computing elements, there is a need to engage in a more or less complicated scaling exercise, involving not only a good deal of calculation but also the assessment of maximum values often based on little more than guesswork (see chapter 3).

(c) The use of active elements in feedback circuits brings with it the risk of instability and the resulting introduction of spurious components into the solution (see chapter 6, particularly section 6.7).

(d) By the nature of the components used, integration must always be with respect to time: integration with respect to other variables can be achieved, but only indirectly and with the use of a good deal of equipment (see section 7.5).

(e) Operations involving functions of two or more variables (of which perhaps the most important is multiplication) are not easy to perform accurately, and usually require complicated and expensive devices to achieve them (see chapters 8 and 9).

Against the disadvantages may be set the particular merits of analogue computation, of which some of the most important are

(a) The way in which problems are programmed allows a high degree of interaction between the programmer and the computer model. The effects of variations in parameters can be readily and directly observed.

(b) Integration with respect to time, which forms a major part of the requirement for the solution of dynamic problems, is in the nature of the device, and is performed very quickly.

(c) The computer system can be readily interconnected with external devices on both input and output sides.

Digital systems, and in particular general purpose digital computers, are often advocated as providing the most suitable computational aid for all problems, partly because they do not suffer from most of the disadvantages of the analogue approach, and partly because the general purpose digital computer is now becoming a standard laboratory facility. However, the digital computer does have disadvantages attached to its use in the analysis of dynamic systems: these weak points correspond to the particularly strong points of analogue systems. It is natural in these circumstances that efforts should have been made to develop computational systems having the accuracy and almost unlimited functional range of a digital computer while at the same time retaining the conceptual advantages of an analogue computer programming structure. These methods fall into two classes, corresponding to software and hardware approaches.

11.2.1 *Analogue simulation procedures*

The basic difficulty in using a digital computer to solve dynamic problems is that although the machine can be programmed to do virtually anything, its usefulness depends in large measure on the ease with which the problem can be coded into machine terms. The basic machine language is rather primitive, and expressing complex interrelationship in terms of machine code is liable to be somewhat ponderous. High level languages, such as ALGOL or FORTRAN, enable much more concise programmes to be written, but these languages were designed particularly for the solution of algebraic problems and are able to express these problems in a way that retains a good deal of structural similarity to the original algebraic formulation. The use of either machine code or a general purpose high level language for the solution of differential equations is possible by suitable manipulation of the mathematics, but in the process the programmer has to sacrifice any hope of close correspondence between the programme and the system being simulated. This effect is very similar to the difference in analogue computer programming between the differential analyser approach and the simulator approach (see section 2.8). The conceptual advantage of analogue computer programming, in fact, can be seen as belonging to its programming language, which is the block diagram containing functional elements such as integrators, summers, multipliers and so on, and it is this block diagram that is used as the jumping off point for all the digital simulation languages that have appeared.

The first requirement of a language is the choice of the set of basic blocks to be allowed in the system. These have invariably been based on analogue computer elements, although the properties of the blocks have often been slightly modified for convenience. It is not, for example, necessary to incorporate a sign change with each operation, and each input can have a coefficient attached to it of any magnitude and sign. With some languages, there is provision for this input coefficient to be a problem variable, so that a separate multiplier unit is then unnecessary. The provision of more powerful blocks is of course subject to danger; just as the use of a single amplifier with elaborate input and feedback impedance networks can be used as a compact representation of a complete sub-system at the expense of a total loss of flexibility (see section 7.3.2), so the use of a too complex set of functional blocks in a simulation language could reduce the conceptual advantage that it set out to achieve.

Whatever range of basic blocks is provided, there is always a need for the programmer to be able to insert his own special functions depending on the particular problems in which he is interested. This facility is often provided by means of a function generator block which operates like a diode function generator, by giving a linear interpolation between defined break points. Whether or not there is any further possibility of adding arbitrary function blocks depends on the way in which the particular language is constructed. Some simulation languages, including some of the most successful and widely used ones, perform a two stage operation when reading a programme, in that they first convert the input instructions into an equivalent programme in a standard high level language, such as FORTRAN, and then re-compile the FORTRAN programme in the normal way into a machine code programme. One particular merit of this apparently rather roundabout procedure is that it is then easy to incorporate into the original language a facility allowing blocks containing standard FORTRAN statements to be inserted directly into the programme. More important, perhaps, than this facility is the fact that modifications to the programme can readily be made in the FORTRAN version directly, which makes system adjustment and parameter manipulation rather easier than if the original system specification had to be altered. It is also possible to use the FORTRAN programme as a sub-routine within a normal FORTRAN programme, so that a complete hybrid computer system can then be simulated.

The most difficult functional block to simulate in a digital programme is of course the integrator. There is no way in which a digital computer can actually integrate: every digital integration procedure relies on some kind of approximation formula and this necessarily involves a compromise between complexity of computation and accuracy of result. Most of the languages developed so far have used an integration procedure based on the Runge-Kutta method in which the integral is evaluated at successive instants separated in time by an integration step. The error in this evaluation can then be expressed as an infinite series in terms of the integration step size; the number of terms in this series that are eliminated in the computation is specified as the order of the method, so that a third order process, for example, gives an error that depends on the fourth and higher powers of the integration step size. The resultant error, therefore, depends not only on the order of the process, which is an arbitrary decision built into the structure of the language, but also on the integration step size, which is for this reason made variable in some languages so as to allow the amount of computation to be continuously minimized depending on the characteristics of the function being integrated.

Not all simulation languages have employed such elaborate integration rules: some have deliberately chosen simplified methods and have accepted the possibility of larger errors in return for the reduced computation time. It is in fact this consideration of computing time that is at the root of a major difficulty with simulation languages; not that an individual integration is in itself a time consuming business, but, since general purpose digital computers operate serially, the time taken to advance the computation for the whole system by one integration step can easily become so large that real time operation becomes impossible. With continuing technical improvements in digital computer components this problem is becoming easier, but as long as digital computers continue to use serial processing, so the speed of operation (or effectively the bandwidth of the system) must be limited and must get worse as the size of the simulation increases. This is in contrast to the use of analogue computers, where the speed of operation is independent of the size of the system being simulated, because all the computation is carried out in parallel. The demand for real-time operation is not simply a matter of convenience in interpreting results, but has an important practical implication, because without it interconnection between the simulated system and a hardware system is impossible.

The other main problem remaining in the use of simulation languages is that of the man-machine interface. Even in the most advanced computer systems with all the modern display techniques such as computer graphics, it is still difficult at present for the operator to get the feel of the system he is simulating in the way that he can with an analogue simulation. Still worse is the position of the engineer who is simulating a system by using a general computing facility with which he can communicate only by means of tape or card input, receiving the response some hours later. Other interfacing difficulties also arise in connecting hardware systems to a digital computer even when real-time operation is possible, and this again is in contrast to the position with an analogue computer simulation. It may well be that the next few years will see the development of a fully interactive real-time system with comprehensive input/output connection facilities in which the engineer can sit at a console with complete freedom to modify the structure of the system being simulated, and to change parameters at will while receiving an immediate graphical display of the effect of the changes on performance, but this position has not yet been reached.

11.2.2 *Digital differential analyser*

A hardware method aimed at combining the merits of analogue operation with the accuracy and reliability of digital techniques was provided by the incremental computer or digital differential analyser (D.D.A.). This device was introduced in the early fifties and showed some impressive results in special purpose computation applications such as airborne navigation and machine tool control.

The basic element in the DDA is the integrator. The basic philosophy

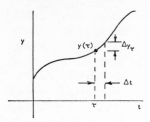

Fig. 11.5. The principle by which the D.D.A. operates. Provided the time interval is small the strip is approximately a rectangle.

of the digital integrator is that if the value of the integral at any one time is stored, then the value of a short time later can be obtained by adding a suitable increment to the stored quantity. It is assumed that in a physical system all variables will change by only a small amount during a small time interval; this permits the use of approximation formulae neglecting second and higher order terms, resulting in major simplifications in the computation procedures. Thus, if the total integral (that is, a definite integral between defined integration limits) is denoted by

$$z = \int_0^t y(t)dt$$

this may be calculated as shown in figure 11.5 by splitting the range into small elements each contributing to the integral an increment of the form

$$\Delta z = \int_\tau^{\tau+\Delta t} y(t)dt$$

and this may be approximated, if Δt is small, by

$$\Delta z \simeq y(\tau)\Delta t. \tag{11.25}$$

The value of y in this expression can also be obtained in a similar manner so that if between $t = 0$ and $t = \tau$ there are n increments denoted by Δy_r, $(r = 1, 2, \ldots, n)$ then

$$y(\tau) = y(0) + \sum_{r=1}^n \Delta y_r.$$

Integration can now be expressed in principle as a sequence of instructions which are obeyed for each integration interval:

(a) Calculate Δy and add it into the y register.

(b) Multiply y by Δt and add the result to the z register.

Some further simplification of this procedure is possible, because Δt is chosen by the operator, and may be regarded as the unit of time: in this case the multiplication in step (b) above disappears, and we are left with simple addition to perform. It is further convenient to arrange that the output from the element, rather than being the total integral, z, should be left as a series of increments Δz. These increments can clearly be added without difficulty to obtain z if it is required, but having the output in incremental form has advantages that will appear shortly.

In deciding the form of the incremental output from a digital integrator there are some special considerations of accuracy to be taken into account. In any digital system, the accuracy with which a quantity can be represented is determined by the word length. Another way of looking at this is to say that the smallest change in a quantity that can be detected is that represented by one bit in the least significant position in a register so that with an N bit register, amplitudes are quantized in 2^N levels. Referring now to equation 11.25, we see that each increment of the integral is obtained by multiplying $y(\tau)$, which is a quantity held in a register (and thus specified to N bits accuracy) by the integration step Δt, which must of necessity be very small, and is commonly taken to be equivalent to the smallest quantity that can be entered into a register of the same length, this quantity being known as a quantum. This means that we take

$$\Delta t = k.2^{-N}$$

where k is a scaling factor that will have to be applied when interpreting the results, but which need not be taken into account at this point. The effect of multiplying an N bit number by 2^{-N} is to move it N places to the right, so that the z register, in which the increments are accumulated, would need to be $2N$ bits long in order to accommodate them. If, however, a register of this length were to be used, it would be providing an appearance of accuracy that is entirely spurious, since if the function is specified to only N bits its integral cannot be computed to any better than N bits. The less significant half of the result, therefore, cannot justifiably be included in the computed integral, although it must be used in the calculation of the partial sum (Δz in equation 11.25) since this quantity can never reach a value equal to one quantum. However, by using an N bit register to accumulate $\sum \Delta z$, we can say that every time this register overflows (that is, moves from $111\ldots11$ to $000\ldots00$) this is equivalent to carrying a one into the least significant usable bit position. This stream of overflows is taken as the output of the integrator, each overflow representing an incremental change of one quantum in the integral. A digital integrator of this kind is illustrated in figure 11.6(a). It should be

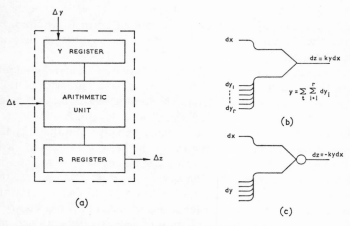

Fig. 11.6. The basic unit of the DDA is the integrator.
     (a) The incremental integrator receives as inputs increments of y and t, and gives an incremental output.
     (b) The symbol for an incremental integrator with several inputs.
     (c) Integrators are usually provided with a facility to allow a change of sign of the output. This is indicated by the use of this modified symbol.

noticed that this unit has two incremental inputs, each of which changes by one quantum at a time, and one incremental output which can also change by one quantum at a time. It is this similarity of form between inputs and outputs that leads to one of the most important properties of the device: since the only requirement for the Δt input is that it should be a stream of pulses capable of controlling the arithmetic unit, it is not essential that it be related to time. The Δt input can, in fact, be provided by the output from another integrator, and the unit will then be given an incremental form of integration with respect to any variable. The operation of the device in this case may be represented by

$$dz = kydx \qquad (11.26)$$

where k is, as before, a scaling factor. The symbol for a digital integrator is shown in figure 11.6(b), which also indicates that it is usually possible to sum several variables at once into the Y register, giving operation analogous to that of the summing integrator.

The versatility of this device is remarkable. There is little need for special components, because so many functions can be put into the form of equation 11.26. For example, multiplication can be realized by using the relationship

$$d(xy) = xdy + ydx$$

A resolver uses the relationships

$$d(\cos \theta) = -\sin \theta . d\theta; \qquad d(\sin \theta) = \cos \theta . d\theta.$$

These are essentially the relationships used in an analogue computer to generate sinusoidal time waveforms, and in fact all the function generation methods involving the solution of differential equations are available in the DDA with the added flexibility that the independent variables does not need to be time.

There are many practical points about the construction of DDA's which are beyond the scope of this chapter, but two particular details are worth mentioning. The first is that any increment must be able to take either sign. This can be provided for in one of two ways: either a binary coding is used, the two symbols representing $+1$ and -1, or a ternary coding is used, with symbols for $+1$, -1, and zero. In a binary system, a zero increment has to be represented by a string of alternate $+1$ and -1. Whichever system is used, it is usual to provide a facility at the output of each integrator for the sign of the increment to be inverted. An integrator with this facility in use is denoted by the symbol shown in figure 11.6(c).

The second practical point concerns the way in which a set of integrators is actually implemented. As it has been described so far, an integrator has been seen as a self-contained unit, each device having its own arithemetic and control units. This form is known as a simultaneous DDA, since all the integrators iterate simultaneously. The operation of this form of computer is very similar to that of the analogue computer, even to the use of a patchboard on which problems are connected up. A less expensive method of implementing the DDA is to use a general store with pairs of registers allocated to the various integrators, and to call the contents for processing in turn in a single central arithmetic unit. This form is called a sequential DDA, which is conveniently realizable in a general purpose digital computer, but which suffers from the twin faults of slowness in operation and loss of structural similarity with the problem being solved.

The final point that should be made here about the DDA or any other computing system is that freedom from scaling problems cannot be obtained except with a floating point arithmetic unit, and this means in practice that it can be obtained only with a general purpose digital computer. The simultaneous DDA, which gives much closer intercourse between the operator and his problem, requires careful scaling to ensure that quantities do not become so small that they are comparable to the quantum nor so large that the main registers overflow. The analogies here with noise level and overloading in analogue amplifiers are obvious.

The DDA, whose earlier development became overshadowed by that of the large general purpose digital computers in the early sixties, has a great deal to be said for it as a means of obtaining some of the advantages of digital working with the flexibility of an analogue system, and it may be due for a revival in the next few years under the influence of technical developments. A complete integrator in a single integrated package has already been produced, and if these become available cheaply the DDA could well become a standard simulation tool.

The future of digital systems in the field of simulation is at the moment in the balance. It seems likely that they will eventually take over, although this has been confidently forecast for several years now without ever actually happening because the digital technology (both hardware and software) has not been adequate to satisfy all the stringent demands made upon it. Certainly it seems very probable that if digital methods are to become standard it will have to be by the development of more advanced versions of one or both of the approaches discussed in this chapter, and in either case, it will require the operator to use an essentially analogue computing approach to his problems.

11.3 The operational amplifier as a building block

Whatever may be the eventual fate of the analogue computer as a general purpose design tool, it is quite certain that the use of operational amplifiers as basic building blocks will remain a very important feature of linear circuit design. This view has been advanced throughout the book, and it will bear repetition here. Technological advances again, as with the DDA, are making more and more complicated devices available to be used almost as freely as resistors and capacitors were, at prices such that complete circuits are now no more expensive than a single valve was ten or fifteen years ago. As an example, active filter circuits, as discussed in section 7.3, have proved so useful that a set of three operational amplifiers has been produced on a single chip to facilitate implementation of these circuits.

The rapid development of microelectronics has indeed been so startling that it has threatened to alter the whole academic approach to the teaching of electronics as a subject. Design with discrete components, it has been argued, is no longer a basic activity, and several University departments have based introductory courses on the hypothesis that the really fundamental component in Electronics is the linear amplifier. The effect of feedback, and the use of the amplifier in circuits, then follow naturally, leading to essentially analogue computing methods in signal processing. If these trends in Electronics are going to persist, (and they are confidently forecast by industrialists as well as by educationalists) then it may well be that analogue methods, far from being obsolescent, are in fact only now entering upon their heyday, when their evident usefulness is combined with economic feasibility.

11.4 Notes and references

The programme for the measurement of moments is based on a paper by Hiller, although the approach of the original has been slightly modified, and the suggested control circuitry has been added to it.

Other applications can be found in all books on analogue computing, and current systems are described particularly in the journal Simulation. A good selection of applications is described by Gilbert, who gives a detailed treatment of problems such as the solution of partial differential equations and algebraic equations, and the study of economic, chemical and electrical engineering systems. Fifer also gives very detailed descriptions of the formulation and solution of many problems, in his case related to the aircraft industry, including aerodynamics and structural vibrations in airframes.

Both Gilbert and Fifer were writing before iterative and hybrid methods were well established, and their accounts are of pure analogue solutions. Hybrid computer solutions are offered by Bekey and

Karplus to problems in flight simulation, optimal control, and biological modelling.

Digital simulation languages have been described in great detail in the digital computer literature. A very good critical survey of the essential features of a number of established languages was given by Brennan and Linebarger who brought out very clearly the power and the limitations of this approach to system simulation.

The digital differential analyser has not received as much attention as it perhaps deserves. A clear summary of the working of the device is given by Hersee, and a detailed discussion of the construction of a DDA and its use in practical problems is given in a book edited by Sizer. Otherwise it seems to receive no more than a paragraph or two in most books.

Two very recent events that have occurred since the main body of this book was finished seem to justify the earlier forecast of a revival of interest in the DDA. One is an article by Shum and Rae, and the other is the appearance on the market of a new machine. In each case the device described consists of a set of parallel acting elements such as integrators, summers, and multipliers, each of which operates digitally with incremental inputs and outputs. Neither device is described as a DDA, but the operating principles are clearly related to it.

The new approach to Electronics education, and the new lease of life that is thereby given to analogue methods of signal manipulation, were discussed at length at a Symposium held a few years ago. This has already been referred to (see section 1.4): the most striking feature of the Symposium was the degree of unanimity amongst industrial, University, and Technical College delegates that the systems approach was likely to be the requirement for the bulk of the next generation of Electronic Engineers. The operational amplifier must, for some time to come, certainly occupy a central position in both the teaching and the practice of Electronics.

REFERENCES

BEKEY, G. A. and KARPLUS, W. J. (1968). *Hybrid Computation*, Wiley, New York.

BRENNAN, R. D. and LINEBARGER, R. N. (1968). A survey of digital simulation: digital analog simulator programs, in 'Simulation: the Modelling of Ideas and Systems with Computers', ed. J. MCLEOD, McGraw-Hill, New York.

CETA Electronics Ltd. (1970). CETA 1600 Operational Computer Operating Notes.

FIFER, S. (1961). *Analog Computation*, 4 Volumes, McGraw-Hill, New York.

GILBERT, C. P. (1964). *The Design and Use of Electronic Analogue Computers*, Chapman and Hall, London.

HERSEE, E. H. W. (1966). *A Simple Approach to Electronic Computers*, Blackie, London.

HILLER, J. (1966). Moment-measuring filter with application to pattern recognition. *Proc. I.E.E.* **113**, 903.

SHUM, L. Y. S. and RAE, W. G. SONIC: Simultaneous Integrating Computer. *Systems Technology* No. 9 (Feb. 1970). Pub. by Plessey Co. Ltd.

SIZER, T. R. H. (1968). *The Digital Differential Analyser*, Chapman and Hall, London.

Symposium Proceedings: Education for the Microcircuit Era. University of Southampton 1967.

R

Appendix 1: Logic and Logic Elements

Digital systems almost invariably make use of binary signals, and there is therefore a need for special mathematical methods to manipulate relationships between binary signals and to describe the operation of various digital circuits. It turns out that an appropriate mathematical system is that devised originally for handling statements and arguments in propositional logic. For this reason, the manipulation of digital signals is usually referred to as *logic* and the circuits that perform the manipulations are known as *logic elements*.

A1.1 Boolean Algebra

Mathematical logic, as far as computer applications are concerned, is based on Boolean Algebra (named after its originator), the basic concepts of which will be briefly summarized here. Much of the terminology as well as the symbolism has been transferred to computer systems.

All variables in the system are binary; that is to say, at any instant each variable will have one of only two values. These two values are

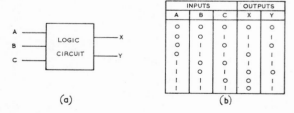

(a)

INPUTS			OUTPUTS	
A	B	C	X	Y
O	O	O	O	O
O	O	I	I	I
O	I	O	I	O
O	I	I	O	I
I	O	O	I	I
I	O	I	O	O
I	I	O	O	I
I	I	I	O	I

(b)

Fig. A1.1. A combinational logic circuit can be described by specifying the output corresponding to each input.
(a) A logic circuit.
(b) A truth table.

244

denoted by the symbols **0** and **1**. The design of all digital circuitry relies heavily on the fact that for any circuit block with n inputs there are exactly 2^n possible different sets of inputs. The operation of the block can therefore be completely defined by specifying its output for each of these different input conditions. A specification of this kind, in the form of a table setting out all the possible sets of inputs with the corresponding outputs, is called a *Truth Table*. Figure A1.1(a) shows a logic circuit with three inputs and two outputs; a truth table for this circuit is shown in figure A.1.1(b), the left hand part of which lists the $8(= 2^3)$ possible sets of inputs and the right hand part of which shows the corresponding outputs.

The simplest block that needs to be considered is the logic inverter (or complementer) shown in figure A.2(a). The operation of this

(a)   (b)

Fig. A1.2. The logic inverter.
      (a) One symbol for the inverter. There are several other symbols used by different manufacturers and authors.
      (b) Truth table for an inverter.

circuit is shown in the truth table of figure A1.2(b): the output is always the *complement* (or logic inverse) of the input. This may be expressed as

$$Y = X'.$$

There are several different symbols used to denote the complement: the commonest alternative to the prime is $\overline{X}$, other possibilities being $\sim X$, $\tilde{X}$, and X^*

It follows immediately from the basic definitions that

$$1' = 0; \qquad 0' = 1$$

A1.1.1 *Combinational logic*

There are two distinct ways in which Boolean variables can be combined, and these form the basis for combinational logic. The blocks that perform combinational operations are usually spoken of as gating circuits, the two basic types being AND gates and OR gates.

An AND gate gives an output of **1** if and only if all of its inputs are **1**.

The truth table for a two input AND gate is shown in figure A1.3(a), and the symbol for this gate is shown in figure A1.3(b). The operation of an AND gate is represented mathematically by using the multiplication symbol, so that the gate of figure A1.3(b) implements the logic equation

$$C = AB.$$

An OR gate gives an output of **1** if at least one input is **1**. The truth

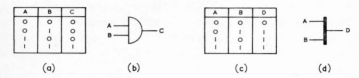

(a)   (b)   (c)   (d)

Fig. A1.3.   The two basic logic functions.
          (a), (b) Truth table and symbol for a two input AND gate.
          (c), (d) Truth table and symbol for a two input OR gate.

table and symbol for a two input OR gate are shown in figures A1.3(c) and A1.3(d). Mathematically the operation of this gate is represented by the addition symbol, so that the gate of figure A1.3(d) implements the logic equation

$$D = A + B.$$

Examination of the truth tables of figures A1.3(a) and A1.3(c) shows that

$$AB = BA$$

and that

$$A + B = B + A$$

so that the AND and OR operations are commutative. The associative and distributive laws can also be shown to apply to these operations: that is

$$A(BC) = (AB)C = ABC$$
$$A + (B + C) = (A + B) + C = A + B + C$$

and

$$A(B + C) = AB + AC$$

Other basic manipulative rules, all of which can be verified by a truth table method, are summarized by the relations below.

$$A.1 = A \qquad A.0 = 0$$
$$A+1 = 1 \qquad A+0 = A$$
$$A.A = A \qquad A+A = A$$
$$A.A' = 0 \qquad A+A' = 1$$
$$(A')' = A.$$

It follows from these identities that if

$$\sum_{i=1}^{N} A_i = 0$$

then

$$A_1 = A_2 = A_3 = \ldots = A_N = 0$$

and that if

$$\prod_{i=1}^{N} A_i = 1$$

then

$$A_1 = A_2 = A_3 = \ldots = A_N = 1$$

Other relationships that are useful for simplifying expressions are

$$A+A'B = A+B$$
$$A+AB = A$$
$$(A+B)(A+C) = A+BC.$$

Finally, De Morgan's Theorem states the rule for taking the complement of an expression. This is done by complementing each variable in the expression and by interchanging AND and OR throughout. Thus

$$[(AX'+B)(C'Y+DF)]' = (A'+X)B'+(C+Y')(D'+F')$$

A1.1.2 *Minimization*

A major reason for interest in Boolean Algebra and related techniques is the need to reduce as much as possible the cost of implementation of any given logic function. Basically this amounts to reducing the complexity of the expression that describes the function, and this in turn depends ultimately on the use of the identities presented in the previous section. In particular, terms can be eliminated by repeated use of the identity

$$AB+A'B = B.$$

This minimization can be carried out purely algebraically, and with the use of computers to design large scale digital systems algebraic methods are used exclusively, but for 'manual' design diagrammatic methods have substantial advantages. These methods depend on the fact that for a given number (N) of variables there is a finite number (2^N) of different terms that can be formed, and that any function of N variables must consist of the sum of a subset of these 2^N terms. By assigning a distinct position on a diagram to each possible term, any given function can be mapped by indicating which of the terms are included. The diagram used for this purpose is called a Veitch Diagram (or Karnaugh map); its size and shape depends on the number of variables. Figure A1.4(a) shows a four variable map with the term

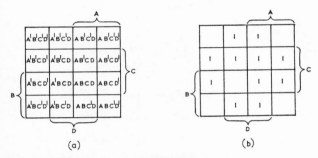

(a)   (b)

Fig. A1.4. The Veitch Diagram (or Karnaugh Map).
    (a) A Veitch diagram for four variables, showing the term represented by each cell. The extension of this method to functions with larger numbers of variables results in much more complicated diagrams; the method is not very useful if there are more than six variables.
    (b) A particular function plotted in a Veitch diagram.

represented by each cell indicated inside it. Two terms that differ by a prime on only one variable may be combined as suggested above, and it will be seen that such terms occupy adjacent cells, if the diagram is regarded as being continuous from top to bottom and also from side to side. Further simplifications are possible by combining adjacent pairs of cells, so that eventually the process of finding the simplest representation of a given function becomes the process of recognizing patterns on the diagram.

The simplified expression that is directly obtained from the Veitch diagram consists of the sum of a number of terms, each of which is a product of variables (primed or unprimed). There is another form of solution that may be required, where the function is expressed as the product of sums of variables. Consider, for example, the function mapped on to the Veitch diagram shown in figure A1.4(b). Here, a **1** is put into every cell in the diagram whose corresponding term forms part of the function. The simplest sum of products expression for this function is

$$F = AD + B'C + CD' + C'D$$

If we invert this by applying De Morgan's theorem to both sides, we obtain

$$F' = (A' + D')(B + C')(C' + D)(C + D')$$

and expanding this by removing the brackets gives

$$F' = C'D' + A'BCD. \qquad (A1.1)$$

This may be inverted again to give the answer in the required form

$$F = (C + D)(A + B' + C' + D').$$

There is however a slightly simpler way of reaching this answer, by observing that, since

$$F + F' = 1$$

F' can be obtained directly from the Veitch diagram by simply writing down the 'sum of products' expression for all the cells that do not have **1** in them. This gives equation A1.1 directly.

The Veitch diagram method of manipulating Boolean expressions is particularly valuable when the problem contains redundancies. There are terms that for some reason do not need to be specified, and can be regarded as either **1** or **0** as convenient. A redundant term is denoted on the Veitch diagram by putting an X in the appropriate cell; it can then be included in the overall expression if by so doing further combinations of terms become possible.

A1.1.3 *Sequential logic*

The Boolean operations so far described have all depended on blocks, each of which has its output value determined by the simultaneous combination of a set of values of its various inputs. The most important abilities of digital circuits, however, and the main reasons for their power and flexibility, depend on memory elements whose output at any time depends not on the values of the input at that time but on the previous history of the values of the inputs. Memory elements have two stable states, each one associated with one of the two possible output values, and the vital feature of the element is that after entering a particular state, it remains in it, giving the appropriate output indefinitely even although the inputs that caused it to enter the state may have been removed.

The use of memory elements in digital circuits means that time has to be introduced into Boolean algebra; this is not quite as straightforward as it might appear because of the fundamental incompatibility of the need for memory elements to make transitions from one state to the other and the requirement that all variables in the system should be binary. Any physical device must move from one state to the other at a finite rate, so that its output will in fact be analogue, taking all values between the two nominal logic levels. The only way round this difficulty is to ensure that the output from a memory element is never used for any subsequent processing except when it has completed its transition.

The easiest way to manage this is to operate with synchronous logic, where a master clock gives a continuous train of pulses, and the values of the variables in the system are defined and used only at the clock pulse instants. Memory elements are then designed so that a transition initiated at one clock pulse instant (known as a bit-time) does not start until that clock pulse has finished, and is completed before the next clock pulse starts. To describe the operation of a memory element of this kind, therefore, requires a method of distinguishing between values of the same variable at different bit-times. A convenient way of doing this is to denote the value of variable A at bit time k by $[A]_k$.

Memory elements, known variously as bistables or flip-flops, are of several different kinds, but all have an output denoted by Q and a number of inputs, depending on the physical construction of the device. The operation of the bistable is then represented by the transition equation

$$[Q]_{n+1} = [f(A_1, A_2, \ldots, A_r; Q)]_n \qquad (A1.2)$$

where $A_1, A_2, \ldots, A_r$ are the inputs to the bistable. This equation is called the characteristic equation of the bistable.

A complete sequential circuit is composed of a number of inputs $X_1, X_2, \ldots, X_p$, and a number of bistables giving outputs $Y_1, Y_2, \ldots, Y_q$. The operation of this circuit is then specified in terms of the transitions that take place as a result of all possible combinations of inputs – a truth table method is again a convenient way of doing this – and this gives rise to a set of equations

$$
\left.\begin{aligned}
[Y_1]_{n+1} &= [F_1(X_1, X_2, \ldots, X_p;\ Y_1, Y_2, \ldots, Y_q)]_n \\
[Y_2]_{n+1} &= [F_2(X_1, X_2, \ldots, X_p;\ Y_1, Y_2, \ldots, Y_q)]_n \\
&\quad \cdot \quad \cdot \quad \cdot \quad \cdot \quad \cdot \\
[Y_q]_{n+1} &= [F_q(X_1, X_2, \ldots, X_p;\ Y_1, Y_2, \ldots, Y_q)]_n
\end{aligned}\right\} \quad (A1.3
$$

These are the application equations for the circuit, and the final stage of the design process is to solve simultaneously the application equation and the characteristic equation for each bistable so as to derive the necessary logic connections between input and output terminals of the bistables and the circuit inputs and outputs. Direct substitution of equation A1.2 into each member of the set of equations A1.3 gives a set of implicit equations of the form

$$
f_1(A_{1s}, A_{2s}, \ldots, A_{rs};\ Y_s) = F_s(X_1, X_2, \ldots, X_p;\ Y_1, Y_2, \ldots, Y_q)
$$
(A1.4)
$$
s = 1, 2, \ldots, q
$$

where A_{vs} is the input of A_v of bistable s. These implicit equations must then be solved to obtain $A_{vs}(v = 1, 2, \ldots, r;\ s = 1, 2, \ldots, q)$ explicitly. The algebraic solution of equation A1.4 is very cumbersome, even if there is only one A variable; for two or three variables, it is very difficult indeed. The Veitch diagram can conveniently be used to avoid this difficulty, the solutions again appearing as recognizable patterns on the diagram.

A1.2 Digital circuits

The way in which operating equations need to be expressed must clearly depend on the kinds of circuit that are going to be used to implement the design. This is particularly true since the development of microelectronic devices, because the use of available circuit blocks is not only more convenient than building discrete component circuits, but it is also cheaper. Some significant features of digital circuit blocks are summarized in the remainder of this appendix.

A1.2.1 Gates and inverters

The first decision that the circuit designer has to make when building hardware implementations of Boolean functions is the circuit interpretation (in volts) of the two logic values 0 and 1. Once this is known, the function of a circuit can be interpreted in Boolean terms by using a truth table, obtaining the 'output' entries by conventional circuit analysis. Two simple diode circuits are shown in figures A1.5(a) and A1.5(b); if the two voltages representing the two logic levels are 0 and $+v$ volts, where $v < V$, the two circuits give outputs Y_1 and Y_2, as shown in the truth table of figure A1.5(c). A comparison between this truth table and the ones in figures A1.3(a) and A1.3(c) shows

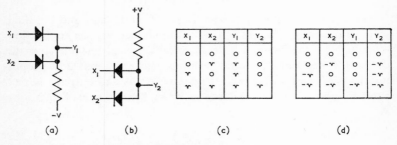

| (a) | (b) | (c) | (d) |

Fig. A1.5. (a), (b) Diode gating circuits.

    (c) Combined Truth Table showing outputs (in volts) corresponding to the use of 0 volts and $+v$ volts as the input signals.

    (d) The functions of the circuits are reversed if the input signals used are 0 volts and $-v$ volts.

that if $\mathbf{0} \equiv 0$ volts and $\mathbf{1} \equiv v$ volts then the circuits of figures A1.5(a) and A1.5(b) are an OR and an AND gate respectively. If we take these same circuits however, and apply logic levels of 0 and $-v$ volts we obtain the truth table of figure A1.15 and now if $\mathbf{0} \equiv 0$ volts and $\mathbf{1} \equiv -v$ volts then figure A1.5(a) becomes an AND gate and figure A1.5(b) becomes an OR gate. Thus the logic function of a block is not necessarily determined solely by its construction, but can depend on the signals used: this is clearly a point to be borne in mind when using commercially available blocks in special purpose equipment.

Another important practical point concerned with logic elements is that significant currents are required from the input sources to ensure that the outputs are held at the appropriate levels. This is particularly important when driving one gate from the output of another gate, and often results in a need for power amplification. This could be provided by the use of emitter followers where necessary, but in fact the solution now almost universally adopted is to incorporate into each block an individual power amplifier that also inverts the

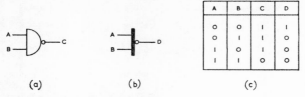

A	B	C	D
0	0	1	1
0	1	1	0
1	0	1	0
1	1	0	0

(a)   (b)   (c)

Fig. A1.6. (a) A two input NAND gate.
(b) A two input NOR gate.
(c) Truth table showing the operation of the gates.

signal. It will be apparent that logic inversion can be obtained from a single stage amplifier with the output levels suitably adjusted; by incorporating this with an AND gate a new element is derived, known as a NAND gate (derived from 'not and'). Similarly, by building an OR gate with an inverter we obtain a NOR gate. The symbols for these two gates are shown in figures A1.6(a) and A1.6(b), and a truth table describing their operation is shown in figure A1.6(c).

NAND and NOR gates have several particular advantages that have led to their adoption as standard elements. Perhaps the most important of these is the fact that all possible logic functions can be obtained by using elements of either one of these types. For the purposes of design of combinational circuits it turns out conveniently that the two-level forms of expression, as developed in section A1.1.2 for use with AND-OR logic, can also be implemented directly with NAND or NOR logic. A sum of products expression, which corresponds to a layer of AND gates followed by an OR gate, is realizable with NAND gates; a product of sums expression, which corresponds to a layer of OR gates followed by an AND gate, is realizable with NOR gates. This is illustrated in figure A1.7. In figure A1.7(a) the output is given by

$$G = AB + CD.$$

In figure A1.7(b) the outputs from the gates in the first layer are

$$E = (AB)'; \qquad F = (CD)'$$

and so the final output is given by

$$G = [(AB)'(CD)']' = AB + CD.$$

In the same way it can easily be verified that each of the circuits of figures A1.7(c) and A1.7(d) gives an output

$$H = (A + B)(C + D).$$

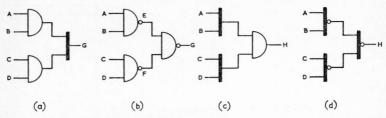

(a)   (b)   (c)   (d)

Fig. A1.7. Simple Boolean algebra often leads to a two level implementation of functions. The same structure can be used for the
same function with NAND or NOR gates.
(a), (b) NAND gates use the same structure as AND – OR
implementation.
(c), (d) NOR gates use the OR – AND structures.

A1.2.2 *Bistables*

Different kinds of bistable are distinguished by means of the names
given to the various input lines. They are all based essentially on the
same circuit: a two stage amplifier with positive feedback forming
an Eccles-Jordan type of circuit, which, being symmetrical, allows
both Q and Q' to be available as outputs. The clock pulses are
effectively fed in to additional AND gates on the inputs, and by making
the bistable respond to the trailing edge of this clock pulse the timing
conditions outlined earlier in section A1.1.3 can be fulfilled. The
inherent delay of the circuit then determines the maximum clock pulse
rate that can be used.

The main types of bistable are summarized below.

D Bistable: Delay element. The output at any bit-time is the same as
the input at the previous bit time. The characteristic equation therefore is

$$[Q]_{n+1} = [D]_n$$

T Bistable: Trigger element. A **1** on the input causes the element to
change state, while a **0** leaves it unchanged. The characteristic equation
is

$$[Q]_{n+1} = [TQ' + T'Q]_n.$$

R-S Bistable: Reset-Set element. A **1** on R causes the element to
reset to **0**, and a **1** on S causes it to be set to **1**. **0** on both leave it
unchanged, and **1** on both cause indeterminate action. For this
reason, it is specified that simultaneous **1** on R and S are not allowed:
this gives rise to a redundancy. The complete characteristic equation

must include a statement of this redundancy, which can therefore also be used to simplify the equation. The characteristic equation of the R-S bistable is

$$[Q]_{n+1} = [S + R'Q]_n$$

with $$RS = 0$$

R-S-T Bistable: This is a straightforward combination of the R-S and T elements with the proviso that only one input is allowed to be **1** at any time. The characteristic equation is

$$[Q]_{n+1} = [S + TQ' + R'T'Q]_n$$

with $$RS = ST = TR = 0.$$

J-K Bistable. This is a modified form of R-S bistable. The effect of the J and K inputs is identical to the S and R inputs respectively, except that simultaneous application of **1** is allowed, and causes the element to change state. The characteristic equation is

$$[Q]_{n+1} = [JQ' + K'Q]_n$$

All these elements are clocked bistables, for use in synchronous circuits. The design of asynchronous circuits, using elements that change state as soon as the appropriate inputs are applied, introduces new complications in that the circuit has to be protected against spurious transient effects brought about by the finite and variable transition times of the elements. The solution to these problems lies in the identification of the so-called 'hazard' conditions and the inclusion of additional terms in the input equations to ensure that hazards are avoided. This point is mentioned because asynchronous bistable elements are very easily assembled from NAND or NOR gates by applying feedback around a pair of gates as shown in figures A1.8(a) and A1.8(b). The operation of these circuits can be represented by the truth tables of figures A1.8(c) and A1.8(d), in which k is an arbitrary Boolean constant indicating that under those input conditions both P and Q can be either **0** or **1** but that either way Q is the complement of P. These circuits are combinational circuits and there is no time element involved, but it will be seen that each of the two circuits can be regarded as a kind of R-S bistable by labelling the variables appropriately: in figure A1.8(a) the necessary labelling is

$$A = R', \qquad B = S', \qquad P = Q'$$

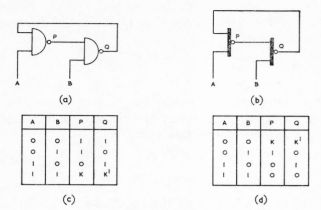

(a)   (b)

A	B	P	Q
0	0	1	1
0	1	1	0
1	0	0	1
1	1	K	K^1

(c)

A	B	P	Q
0	0	K	K^1
0	1	1	0
1	0	0	1
1	1	0	0

(d)

Fig. A1.8. Either NAND or NOR gates can be used to form bistable circuits.
(a), (b) The two circuits have the same structure, and each
has two inputs.
(c), (d) The truth tables show that the bistables are similar
in operation to $R-S$ bistables. It should be noticed,
however, that these truth tables relate to d.c. levels;
the output depends on the inputs being sustained.

and in figure A1.8(b)

$$A = S, \quad B = R, \quad P = Q'$$

Transitions, however, do not have to wait for clock pulses, but take
place as soon as the appropriate input combinations appear: the
device is a d.c. bistable. With these labellings it is interesting to
observe that although the circuit response to input $R = S = 1$ is
not consistent with the interpretation $P = Q'$, and so would in
general be best regarded as a redundant condition, it is not actually
indeterminate as it is with an amplifier type of bistable. It is therefore
possible to use this input condition, provided a new interpretation is
put on P. This may be expressed as

$$P = Q'+RS \quad \text{or} \quad P = Q'(R'+S')$$

for NAND and NOR elements respectively.
    The ability to use NAND and NOR gates to construct bistable elements
as well as to implement combinational logic is another reason for the
widespread use of these gates; it means that any logic circuit can be
built using only one kind of brick.

A1.2.3 *Monostables*

Although gates and bistables can provide all that is necessary for static or sequential switching circuits, it is convenient to be able to use some other units from time to time; some such units are made in integrated circuit form, and are also commonly provided on iterative analogue computers. Perhaps the most common is the monostable, which is essentially the same as the amplifier type of bistable except that the feedback connections are modified to make only one of the two states of the circuit stable. When the circuit moves to the other state in response to an appropriate input, it remains in that state for a fixed time before returning to its stable state. The fixed time is determined by an *R-C* combination, and is usually made adjustable by providing external controls.

A1.3 Notes and references

An excellent introduction to Boolean Algebra and its applications is given by Phister in a book which, although more than ten years old, still gives a very useful and valid introduction to the subject. The most important topics that are not mentioned by Phister are NAND-NOR implementation and asynchronous sequential circuits, both of which are well discussed by Maley and Earle. Lewin, in a more recent book, covers all aspects of switching circuit design, and also includes a large number of tutorial examples with worked solutions. All these books have many references to enable the reader to enter the subject more deeply.

REFERENCES

LEWIN, D. (1968). *Logical Design of Switching Circuits*, Nelson, London.
MALEY, G. A. and EARLE, J. (1963). *The Logic Design of Transistor Digital Computers*, Prentice-Hall, New York.
PHISTER, M. (1958). *Logical Design of Digital Computers*, Wiley, New York.

Appendix 2: Characteristics of Coupling Networks

A2.1 Transfer functions and Bode diagrams

The analysis of a linear circuit with one input and one output is conveniently carried out in terms of the complex frequency variable s, by computing a transfer function which contains in a single concise statement a complete specification of the performance of the circuit. The implications of this performance, however, can often be better understood by finding the variation of gain and phase shift with real frequency ω.

It is almost invariably the case that the transfer function of a circuit consists of the product of a number of expressions, giving

$$F(s) = \prod_{r=1}^{n} A_r(s)$$

where each $A_r(s)$ is a rational polynomial function of s. The gain and phase shift of such a circuit may then be expressed as functions of ω as

$$G(\omega) = |F(j\omega)| = \prod_{r=1}^{n} |A_r(j\omega)| \qquad (A2.1)$$

$$\phi(\omega) = \tan^{-1} \frac{Im[F(j\omega)]}{Re[F(j\omega)]}$$

$$= \sum_{r=1}^{n} \tan^{-1} \frac{Im[A_r(j\omega)]}{Re[A_r(j\omega)]} \qquad (A2.2)$$

where $Re[F]$ and $Im[F]$ are the real and imaginary parts of F.

The total phase shift of the circuit can therefore be obtained by adding the phase shift due to each term, but the total gain is the product of the individual gains. By using a logarithmic gain measure the gains can also be made additive, which makes for easier appreciation of the circuit action. The gain measure used is the decibel, defined by

$$G'(\omega) = 20 \log_{10} [G(\omega)] \text{ dB}$$

It often turns out that the gain (in dB) and phase shift of a network are proportional to powers of the real frequency, and it is therefore convenient when plotting graphs to use logarithmic frequency scales so that power law variations appear as straight lines. The slope of a straight line on such a graph indicates the particular power law being observed, and since equal linear increments on a logarithmic scale correspond to equal ratios of the original variable, rates of change of gain are expressed in dB/octave or dB/decade, where an octave is a two-fold change of frequency and a decade is a ten-fold change of frequency.

The pair of graphs, of gain in dB and phase shift against $\log \omega$, is known as a Bode Diagram, and its use will be illustrated by reference to two commonly occurring C-R coupling networks. These are of interest in their own right and also in particular because the corresponding transfer functions frequently appear as constituents of the transfer functions of computing circuits.

A2.2 High pass filter

The effect of the network shown in figure A2.1(a) can be estimated in a qualitative manner by observing that at very low frequencies the capacitor will appear to be an open circuit while at very high frequencies it will appear to be a short circuit. The network therefore allows high frequency signals to pass while attenuating low frequency signals; it is one form of high pass filter which is often represented (especially in communications literature) by the symbol shown in figure A2.1(b).

The transfer function of this network is readily obtained as

$$F_H(s) = \frac{y_H}{x_H} = \frac{RCs}{1+RCs} = \frac{Ts}{1+Ts} \tag{A2.3}$$

where $T = RC.$

The variation of gain with frequency is obtained as in equation A2.1 giving

$$G_H(\omega) = |F_H(j\omega)| = \frac{\omega T}{\sqrt{(1+(\omega T)^2)}}. \tag{A2.4}$$

s

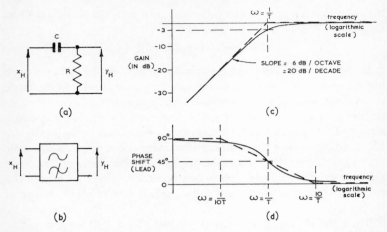

Fig. A2.1. (a) A $C-R$ coupling network, which acts as a form of high pass filter.

            (b) The symbol commonly used to denote a high-pass filter in communications systems.

            (c), (d) The gain and phase curves for a $C-R$ network. The piecewise linear approximations to these curves are shown dotted.

As in the qualitative argument above, it is convenient to consider the behaviour of the circuit at very high and very low frequencies to obtain simplified approximate expressions for the gain function. At very high frequencies it can be assumed that $\omega T \gg 1$, and so the 1 in the denominator of equation A2.4 can be neglected. This gives

$$G_H(\omega)\bigg|_{\omega T \gg 1} \simeq \frac{\omega T}{\sqrt{((\omega T)^2)}} = 1$$

or $\qquad G'_H(\omega)\bigg|_{\omega T \gg 1} \simeq 0 \text{ dB.}$

At very low frequencies, on the other hand, when $\omega T \ll 1$, the ωT term can be neglected, giving

$$G_H(\omega)\bigg|_{\omega T \gg 1} \simeq \omega T$$

or $\qquad G'_H(\omega)\bigg|_{\omega T \ll 1} \simeq 20 \log_{10} T + 20 \log_{10} \omega$

This is a straight line on the Bode diagram, and since a tenfold change in frequency produces a change of unity in the logarithm, the slope of the line is 20 dB/decade. This corresponds (since $\log_{10} 2 \simeq 0\cdot3$) to a slope of 6 dB/octave.

To a first approximation, therefore, the gain characteristic can be represented by two straight lines, as shown dotted in figure A2.1(c). They join at the point at which $\omega T = 1$; this is known as the *break point*. The true gain curve is also shown in figure A2.1(c) for comparison purposes: the discrepancy between the curves can be evaluated at the break point, where

$$G_H\left(\frac{1}{T}\right) = \frac{1}{\sqrt{(1+1^2)}} = \frac{1}{\sqrt{2}}$$

$$\therefore G'_H\left(\frac{1}{T}\right) = -20.\tfrac{1}{2}\log_{10}2 \simeq -3 \text{ dB}.$$

The variation of phase shift with frequency is obtained from equation A2.3 in the way suggested by equation A2.2 giving

$$\phi_H(\omega) = \frac{\pi}{2} - \tan^{-1}(\omega T). \tag{A2.5}$$

To find a simple approximation for this expression is less easy than it was for the gain curve. Considering very low and very high frequencies gives

$$\phi_H(\omega)\bigg|_{\omega\to0} = \frac{\pi}{2}; \qquad \phi_H(\omega)\bigg|_{\omega\to\infty} = 0$$

but it is not immediately obvious what interpretation should be placed on 'high' and 'low' frequencies. The straight line approximation usually used is that shown in figure A2.1(d): the phase shift is taken as being constant at 90° up to $\omega T = 0\cdot1$, and constant at 0° beyond $\omega T = 10$. These approximations are not in fact very good: the true phase shift at $\omega T = 0\cdot1$ is about 84° and at $\omega T = 10$ it is about 6°. Even at a distance of two decades from the break point, that is at $\omega T = 0\cdot01$ or 100, the difference between the true and approximate curves is about $\tfrac{1}{2}$°. The true curve is also shown in figure A2.1(d) for comparison: it will be seen that the approximate curve passes through the correct value of phase shift at $\omega T = 1$ (that is, $\phi = \pi/4$ or 45° – see equation A2.4).

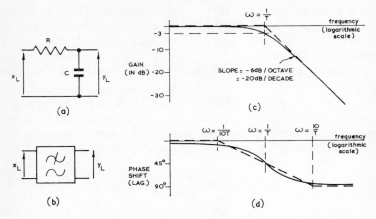

Fig. A2.2. (a) An $R-C$ network, which is a form of low-pass filter.
  (b) Symbol for a low-pass filter.
  (c), (d) Bode Diagram for $R-C$ network, with piecewise linear approximations shown dotted.

A2.3 Low pass filter

The network of figure A2.2(a), which attenuates high frequencies and transmits low frequencies, is a low pass filter, denoted by the symbol of figure A2.2(b). Its performance is mathematically similar to that of the high pass filter, and its analysis is carried out in exactly the same way.

The transfer function of the low pass filter is given by

$$F_L(s) = \frac{y_L}{x_L} = \frac{1}{1+RCs} = \frac{1}{1+Ts}$$

Hence the variation of gain with frequency is

$$G_L(\omega) = |F_L(j\omega)| = \frac{1}{\sqrt{(1+(\omega T)^2)}}.$$

Straight line approximations are obtained as before, so that

$$G_L(\omega)\bigg|_{\omega T \gg 1} \simeq \frac{1}{\omega T}$$

or
$$G'_L(\omega)\bigg|_{\omega T \gg 1} \simeq -20 \log T - 20 \log \omega$$

This is a straight line of slope -20 dB/decade ($\simeq -6$ dB octave)

$$G_L(\omega)\bigg|_{\omega T \ll 1} \simeq 1$$

$$G'_L(\omega)\bigg|_{\omega T \ll 1} \simeq 0 \text{ dB.}$$

The true gain at the break point is

$$G_L\left(\frac{1}{T}\right) = \frac{1}{\sqrt{(1+1^2)}}$$

or

$$G'_L\left(\frac{1}{T}\right) \simeq -3 \text{ dB.}$$

The true and approximate gain curves are shown in figure A2.2(c). The variation of phase shift with frequency is given by

$$\phi_L(\omega) = -\tan^{-1}(\omega T)$$

and this can again be approximated by three straight lines as shown in figure A2.2(d), which also shows the true curve. It should once again be emphasized that although the gain does not fall appreciably below 0 dB for frequencies below the break point, the phase shift is affected at a very much lower frequency, and is in fact about $\frac{1}{2}°$ when $\omega T = 0\cdot01$. There are occasions, particularly in analogue computer circuits, when phase shifts of this size can have very significant effects (see section 6.7).

A2.4 Notes and references

There are not very many descriptions of the logarithmic gain and phase plot method of analysis in books on circuit theory. This seems strange, because it is such a useful way of examining systems. There are adequate treatments by Scott (see Volume II, chapter 18), and by Nilsson.

REFERENCES

NILSSON, J. W. (1968). *Introduction to Circuits, Instruments and Electronics.* Harcourt, Brace and World Inc., New York.
SCOTT, R. E. (1960). *Linear Circuits* (2 Volumes), Addison-Wesley, New York.

Index

DATE DUE

WITHDRAWN FROM
OHIO NORTHERN
UNIVERSITY LIBRARY

GAYLORD

PRINTED IN U.S.A.

HETERICK MEMORIAL LIBRARY
621.3919 W684a
Wilkins, B   R/Analogue and iterati   onuu

3 5111 00155 1914